W9-AAZ-351

For current pricing information,
or to learn more about this or any Nextext title,
call us toll-free at **1-800-323-5435**
or visit our web site at www.nextext.com.

A NEXTEXT ANTHOLOGY

Classical and World
MYTHOLOGY

Cover: Farnese Gallery, Palazzo Farnese, Rome/SuperStock. Reproduced with permission.

Copyright © 2000 McDougal Littell, a Houghton Mifflin Company. All rights reserved.

No part of this work may be reproduced or transmitted in any form or by any means, electronic or mechanical, including photocopying and recording, or by any information storage or retrieval system without prior written permission of Nextext® unless such copying is expressly permitted by federal copyright law. With the exception of not-for-profit transcription in Braille, Nextext® is not authorized to grant permission for further uses of copy-righted selections reprinted in this text without the permission of their owners. Permission must be obtained from the individual copyright owners identified herein. Address inquiries to Manager, Rights and Permissions, McDougal Littell, P. O. Box 1667, Evanston, Illinois 60204.

Printed in the United States of America
ISBN 0-618-00375-4

3 4 5 6 7 — QKT — 06 05 04 03 02

Classical and World Mythology

PART ONE: BEGINNINGS

PART SIX: TRIUMPH AND DEFEAT

PART SEVEN: JOURNEYS

PART EIGHT: FRIEND AND FOE

PART TEN: SEARCH FOR IMMORTALITY

Vocabulary words appear in boldface type and are footnoted. Specialized or technical words and phrases appear in lightface type and are footnoted.

Beginnings

"Over the blue sea, with its streaks like purple wine, lie islands dotted away into the distance: and they too have each a tale to tell."

°

Part One

◄ *The Gods and Goddesses of Olympus*

In this painting, Zeus, the most powerful of the Greek gods, is surrounded by the other gods and goddesses of Olympus and his daughter Athena, who is pleading with her father.

Coming of the Immortals

BY ROGER LANCELYN GREEN

Roger Lancelyn Green is known for his entertaining retellings of myths, legends, and folktales from around the world. He believes that ancient people, in their "struggle against cold and hunger, or overpowering heat and drought, invented evil beings who were the things themselves, or their causes, in just the same way as [they] made the good things and instincts of life into real beings about whom stories and myths were made." The original purpose of most myths, he maintains, was to explain why things were, or how things were supposed to be.

Of course, Green says, myths were also meant to entertain. In "Coming of the Immortals," he tells why some people consider stories about the twelve gods and goddesses of Mount Olympus the most entertaining myths of them all.

If ever you are lucky enough to visit the beautiful land of Greece you will find a country haunted by more than three thousand years of history and legend.

The towering mountains slope steeply into the bluest of blue seas, and between the mountains lie valleys green and silver with the leaves of a million olive trees; golden with corn in the early summer, and then brown and white as the hot sun dries all up until the wide rivers become tinkling streams wandering in great courses of grey and yellow stones.

In winter and early spring the mountains are clothed with snow; mist hides the higher lands, and the rivers are roaring torrents racing down into the great gulfs and bays which break up Greece into little divisions as surely as the mighty mountains do.

As you wander through Greece in the late spring, you are back in those ancient days the moment you leave the towns behind. Up on the green slopes below the towering heights of the great mountains, of Parnassus or

Taygetus or Cithaeron,[1] you can sit and dream yourself back into the time when you might expect to meet an Immortal on the mountain, in the olive-groves, or in the lonely valleys.

Far away a shepherd pipes to his flock, magic notes stealing up through the warm silence: surely that is Pan, half-goat, half-human, who guarded the shepherds of old?

Among the olive leaves stand the broken columns of temples, grey, or white, or golden-yellow: everyone has a tale to tell—a legend, a story, or an actual history.

Over the blue sea, with its streaks like purple wine, lie islands dotted away into the distance: and they too have each a tale to tell. It may be Delos,[2] perhaps: no one lives on it now, but the ruins of cities and temples, harbors and theatres, cluster from the shore to the hill top on which Apollo the Shining One and his sister Artemis the Maiden Huntress were born. Or it may be rocky, rugged Ithaca, from which Odysseus sailed to the siege of Troy, and found again after ten years' wandering over strange and dragon-haunted seas.

With all the breath-taking beauty of Greece round about them, it is hardly wonderful that the ancient Greeks felt that the mountains and the valleys, the woods and streams, the very sea itself, were peopled with Immortals. There were wood-nymphs among the trees and water-nymphs in the rivers—fairies of human size who did not die and had powers which mortals do not possess. There were sea-nymphs too—mermaids, though not all of them had tails—and strange sea-beings, who might be cruel and fierce even as the sea was fierce and cruel when the storms arose. And the sea must have a King, more powerful even than the nymphs, the Immortal called Poseidon who might come up through the waters in his chariot drawn by white horses, waving his trident—the three-pronged spear which was his **scepter,**[3] or sign of power.

On land also there were Immortal powers. Apollo, shining like the sun, who was also the lord of music and poetry; Artemis the Huntress who guarded all wild things; fierce Ares the warlord, whose terrible shout might ring across the field of battle when the spears were flying and the swords of bronze or iron clanged on the shields and helmets; Athena, Immortal Lady of wisdom; the kind

---

[1] Parnassus, Taygetus, Cithaeron—mountain ranges in Greece.

[2] Delos—Greek island in the southwest Aegean; site of the oracle of Apollo.

[3] **scepter**—a rod or staff held by a king or queen as a sign of authority.

Mother Goddess, Demeter, who caused the corn to grow and the young lambs to be born, with her lovely daughter Persephone who had to spend half the year in the kingdom of the dead when dark winter was spread over the earth.

Then there was Aphrodite, Immortal Lady of Beauty and Love, with Eros her son who shot the invisible arrows that made a young man or girl fall in love; there was Hephaestus, more skilled than any mortal man in working with bronze and gold and iron, whose forge[4] was beneath the island of Lemnos, with a volcano as his furnace-chimney; there was Hermes of the winged-heels, swift messenger, more cunning than any human; there was Dionysus who gave such power to the grapes that they could be brewed into wine to be a joy and a comfort to mankind; and there was the quiet Hestia, Lady of the home and guardian of the hearth—for the hearth was the heart of the home in the days when fire was difficult to make.

All these, and more, were the Immortals, and their powers were great. But they too must surely obey laws and have a ruler set over them—and this was Zeus, the King of Heaven and of Earth, who wielded the thunderbolt, and was father of Mortals and of Immortals; and his Queen was Hera, Lady of Marriage and guardian of children. Zeus had power over all Immortals, though he seldom exercised it over his brothers, Poseidon, Lord of the Sea, and Hades, Lord of the Dead, whose kingdom of shadows was thought to be beneath the earth.

The Greeks called these Immortals the "Gods," and worshipped them, making sacrifices to them at their particular shrines: Zeus at Olympia, Apollo at Delphi, Athena at Athens, and so on. When they began to tell the stories about them they had very little idea of what gods should be, and quite naturally pictured them as very like themselves, but much more powerful, more beautiful, and more free. Nor did it seem wrong to them to imagine that gods and goddesses could be cruel, or mean, deceitful, selfish, jealous, or even wicked, according to our ideas, and as they themselves would have thought if ordinary men and women had done as the gods did.

---

[4] forge—a furnace where metals are heated or molded.

Another trouble was that the Greeks in each of the little kingdoms and cities, and in the islands, made up different stories more or less without knowing what was being told over the sea, or beyond the mountains. Then, later, when minstrels[5] traveled from place to place, and writing became more common, and people began to meet those from other parts of the Greek world, they found that many of the stories did not agree.

"Hera is the wife of Zeus," the people of Argolis would say. "Nonsense!" the Arcadians would answer. "He married Maia, and they had a son called Hermes!" "What are you talking about?" the people of Delphi or Delos would protest: "The wife of Zeus is called Leto, and they had two children called Apollo and Artemis!"

Well, there was only one thing for it: they had to agree that Zeus must have had several wives! But Hera, as the most important of the Immortals, was obviously the real Queen of Heaven.

---

[5] minstrels—medieval entertainers who traveled from place to place, especially to sing and recite poetry.

QUESTIONS TO CONSIDER

1. Who are the Immortals?

2. Why did the Greeks tell stories about them?

3. What is the tone of "Coming of the Immortals" and what does it suggest about the author's approach to mythology?

Zeus and His Family

BY INGRI AND EDGAR PARIN D'AULAIRE

The Greeks and Romans believed that Gaea, or Mother Earth, and Uranus, Lord of the Sky, were the first gods. Gaea and Uranus were parents to twelve mighty Titans, who ruled the earth for many centuries. The most powerful Titan was Cronus, who was Zeus's father. Cronus was an angry, impatient god who thought nothing of attacking his father and terrorizing his wife, Rhea. Each time Rhea gave birth to a child, Cronus took the newborn god and swallowed it. Finally, in desperation, Rhea hid her sixth child and gave Cronus a stone to swallow instead. Rhea sent her baby to the island of Crete, where he was raised by nymphs and a magic goat named Amaltheia. This little baby, who spent his entire childhood hidden in a dark cave, would grow up to be the most magnificent and powerful of all the Greek gods. He was Zeus, Lord of the Universe.

Zeus was tended by gentle nymphs and was nursed by the fairy goat Amaltheia. From the horns of the goat flowed ambrosia[1] and nectar,[2] the food and drink of the gods. Zeus grew rapidly, and it was not long before he strode out of the cave as a great new god. To thank the nymphs for tending him so well, he gave them the horns of the goat. They were horns of plenty and could never be emptied. From the hide of the goat he made for himself an **impenetrable**[3] breastplate, the Aegis, and now he was so strong that Cronus could do nothing against him.

Young Zeus chose Metis, a Titan's daughter, for his first wife. She was the goddess of **prudence**,[4] and he needed her good advice. She warned him not to try alone to overthrow his child-devouring father, for Cronus had all the other Titans and their sons on his side. First Zeus must also have strong allies.

---

[1] ambrosia—the food of the gods, thought to give immortality.

[2] nectar—a sweet liquid secreted by flowers of various plants.

[3] **impenetrable**—impossible to pierce or enter.

[4] **prudence**—caution.

Metis went to Cronus and cunningly tricked him into eating a magic herb. He thought that the herb would make him unconquerable. Instead it made him so sick that he vomited up not only the stone he had swallowed, but his five other children as well. They were the gods Hades and Poseidon and the goddesses Hestia, Demeter, and Hera, all mighty gods who right away joined forces with Zeus. When Cronus saw the six young gods rising against him, he knew that his hour had come and he surrendered his powers and fled.

Now Zeus was the Lord of the Universe. He did not want to rule alone. He shared his powers with his brothers and sisters. But the Titans and their sons revolted. They refused to let themselves be ruled by the new gods. Only Prometheus and his brother Epimetheus left the Titans to join Zeus, for Prometheus could look into the future and he knew that Zeus would win.

Zeus freed the monstrous sons of Mother Earth from Tartarus.[5] Gratefully the hundred-armed ones fought for him with all their strength, and the Cyclopes forged mighty weapons for him and his brothers.

They made a trident[6] for Poseidon. It was so forceful that when he struck the ground with it, the earth shook, and when he struck the sea, frothing waves stood mountain high.

For Hades they made a cap of invisibility so he could strike his enemies unseen, and for Zeus they forged lightning bolts. Armed with them, he was the mightiest god of them all, nothing could stand against him and his thunderbolts. The Titans fought a bitter battle, but at last they had to surrender, and Zeus locked them up in Tartarus. The hundred-armed monsters went to stand guard at the gates to see that they never escaped. Atlas, the strongest of the Titans, was sent to the end of the world to carry forever the vault of the sky on his shoulders.

Angry with Zeus for sending her sons the Titans into the dark pit of Tartarus, Mother Earth now brought forth two terrible monsters, Typhon

---

[5] the monstrous sons of Mother Earth from Tartarus— In the beginning, Mother Earth, or Gaea, had twelve children, called the Titans. These twelve gods and goddesses were huge; each was bigger than a mountain. Their father, Uranus, was proud of the Titans and carved great thrones for them. Later, Mother Earth bore more children—three Cyclopes and three monsters, each with fifty heads and one hundred arms. Uranus was disgusted with this group of children, so he flung them into Tartarus, a dark pit under the earth. To strike back, Cronus—the strongest of the Titans—attacked his father. Uranus fled, allowing Cronus to become Lord of the Universe.

[6] trident—the three-pronged spear carried by Poseidon.

and his mate, Echidna, and sent them against Zeus. They were so fearful that when the gods saw them they changed themselves into animals and fled in terror. Typhon's hundred horrible heads touched the stars, venom dripped from his evil eyes, and lava and red-hot stones poured from his gaping mouths. Hissing like a hundred snakes and roaring like a hundred lions, he tore up whole mountains and threw them at the gods.

Zeus soon regained his courage and turned, and when the other gods saw him taking his stand, they came back to help him fight the monster. A terrible battle raged, and hardly a living creature was left on earth. But Zeus was fated to win, and as Typhon tore up huge Mount Aetna to hurl at the gods, Zeus struck it with a hundred well-aimed thunderbolts and the mountain fell back, pinning Typhon underneath. There the monster lies to this very day, belching fire, lava, and smoke through the top of the mountain.

Echidna, his **hideous**[7] mate, escaped destruction. She cowered in a cave, protecting Typhon's dreadful offspring, and Zeus let them live as a challenge to future heroes.

Now at last Mother Earth gave up her struggle. There were no more **upheavals**,[8] and the wounds of the war soon healed. The mountains stood firmly anchored. The seas had their shores. The rivers had their river-beds and oxhorned river-gods watched over them, and each tree and each spring had its nymph. The earth again was green and fruitful and Zeus could begin to rule in peace.

The one-eyed Cyclopes were not only smiths but masons as well, and they built a towering palace for the gods on top of Mount Olympus, the highest mountain in Greece. The palace was hidden in clouds, and the goddesses of the seasons rolled them away whenever a god wanted to go down to earth. Nobody else could pass through the gate of clouds.

Iris, the fleet-footed messenger of the gods, had her own path down to earth. Dressed in a gown of **iridescent**[9] drops, she ran along the rainbow on her busy errands between Olympus and earth.

---

[7] **hideous**—repulsive, especially to the sight; revoltingly ugly.

[8] **upheavals**—sudden, violent disruptions or upsets.

[9] **iridescent**—brilliant.

In the gleaming hall of the palace, where light never failed, the Olympian gods sat on twelve golden thrones and reigned over heaven and earth. There were twelve great gods, for Zeus shared his powers, not only with his brothers and sisters, but with six of his children and the goddess of love as well.

Zeus himself sat on the highest throne, with a bucketful of thunderbolts beside him. On his right sat his youngest sister, Hera, whom he had chosen from all his wives as his queen. Beside her sat her son, Ares, god of war, and Hephaestus, god of fire, with Aphrodite, goddess of love, between them. Next was Zeus's son Hermes, the herald[10] of the gods, and Zeus's sister Demeter, goddess of the harvest, with her daughter, Persephone, on her lap. On the left of Zeus sat his brother Poseidon, the lord of the sea. Next to him sat the four children of Zeus: Athena, the twins Apollo and Artemis, and Dionysus, the youngest of the gods. Athena was the goddess of wisdom, Apollo, the god of light and music, Artemis, goddess of the hunt, and Dionysus, the god of wine.

Hestia, the eldest sister of Zeus, was goddess of the hearth. She had no throne, but tended the sacred fire in the hall, and every hearth on earth was her altar. She was the gentlest of all the Olympians.

Hades, the eldest brother of Zeus, was the lord of the dead. He preferred to stay in his gloomy palace in the Underworld and never went to Olympus.

The gods themselves could not die, for divine ichor[11] flowed in their veins instead of blood. Most of the time they lived happily together, feasting on sweet-smelling ambrosia and nectar, but when their wills clashed, there were violent quarrels. Then Zeus would reach for a thunderbolt and the Olympians would tremble and fall to order, for Zeus alone was stronger than all the other gods together.

---

[10] herald—a person who carries or proclaims important news; a messenger.

[11] ichor—a heavenly fluid flowing in the veins of the gods.

QUESTIONS TO CONSIDER

1. Who were Zeus's allies against Cronus?

2. Who are the twelve gods and goddesses of the Olympiad?

3. What makes Zeus so much more powerful than the other gods?

Hera

BY INGRI AND EDGAR PARIN D'AULAIRE

Zeus had many love affairs as he was growing up. He was very strong and handsome, so all the young maidens wanted to be his wife. When Zeus finally decided to choose a queen, he chose his sister Hera. Although Hera became the goddess of marriage and childbirth, she didn't have a peaceful marriage. Zeus wasn't a faithful husband, and the jealous Hera had a terrible temper. She devoted most of her time to punishing and persecuting her husband's lovers. Although their relationship was difficult, Zeus and Hera had three children together: Ares, Hebe, and Eileithyia.

Hera, the beautiful queen of Olympus, was a very jealous wife. Even Zeus, who was afraid of nothing, feared her fits of temper. She hated all his other wives, and when Zeus first asked her to be his wife, she refused. Slyly Zeus created a thunderstorm, changed himself into a little cuckoo, and, pretending to be in **distress**,[1] he flew into Hera's arms for protection. She pitied the wet little bird and hugged it close to keep it warm, but all of a sudden she found herself holding mighty Zeus in her arms instead of the bird.

Thus Zeus won Hera and all nature burst into bloom for their wedding. Mother Earth gave the bride a little apple tree that bore golden apples of immortality. Hera treasured the tree and planted it in the garden of the Hesperides, her secret garden far to the west. She put a hundred-headed dragon under the tree to guard the apples and ordered the three Nymphs of the Hesperides to water and care for the tree.

---

[1] **distress**—trouble.

Zeus loved Hera dearly, but he was also very fond of rocky Greece. He often sneaked down to earth in disguise to marry mortal girls. The more wives he had, the more children he would have, and all the better for Greece! All his children would inherit some of his greatness and become great heroes and rulers. But Hera in her jealous rage **tormented**[2] his other wives and children, and even Zeus was powerless to stop her. She knew how tricky Zeus could be and kept very close watch over him.

One day as Hera looked down on earth, she spied a small dark thundercloud where no cloud should have been. She rushed down and darted into the cloud. Zeus was there just as she had suspected, but with him was only a little snow-white cow. He had seen Hera coming and, to protect his newest bride Io from her wrath, he had changed the girl into a cow. Alas! The cow was as lovely as the girl, and Hera was not **deceived**,[3] but she pretended to suspect nothing and begged Zeus to let her have the dainty cow. Zeus could not well refuse his queen such a little wish without giving

himself away, and he had to give her the cow. Hera tied poor Io to a tree and sent her servant Argus to keep watch over her.

Argus had a hundred bright eyes placed all over his body. He was so big and strong that singlehandedly he had made an end to the monstrous Echidna, who had lived in a cave and had **devoured**[4] all who passed by. He was Hera's faithful servant and the best of watchmen, for he never closed more than half of his eyes in sleep at a time.

Argus sat down next to the cow and watched her with all his eyes, and poor Io had to walk on four legs and eat grass. She raised her mournful eyes to Olympus, but Zeus was so afraid of Hera that he did not dare to help her. At last he could no longer bear to see her distress, and he asked his son Hermes, the craftiest of the gods, to run down to earth and set Io free.

Hermes disguised himself as a shepherd and walked up to Argus

---

[2] **tormented**—tortured.

[3] **deceived**—tricked.

[4] **devoured**—ate up greedily.

playing a tune on his shepherd's pipe. Argus was bored, having nothing to do with all his eyes but watch a little cow, and he was glad to have music and company. Hermes sat down beside him, and after he had played for a while, he began to tell a long and dull story. It had no beginning and it had no end and fifty of Argus's eyes closed in sleep. Hermes droned[5] on and on and slowly the fifty other eyes fell shut, one by one. Quickly Hermes touched all the eyes with his magic wand and closed them forever in eternal sleep. Argus had been bored to death.

Hermes then untied the cow, and Io ran home to her father, the river-god Inachos. He did not recognize the cow as his daughter, and Io could not tell him what had happened, all she could say was, "Mooo!" But when she lifted up her little hoof and scratched her name, "I-O," in the river sand, her father at once understood what had happened, for he knew the ways of Zeus. Inachos rose out of his river bed and rushed off to take revenge on the mighty thunder-god. He flew at Zeus in such a rage that to save himself Zeus had to throw a thunderbolt, and ever since the bed of the river Inachos in Arcadia has been dry.

Hera was furious when she saw that Argus was dead and the cow Io had been set free. She sent a vicious gadfly[6] to sting and chase the cow. To be sure that her faithful servant Argus would never be forgotten, she took his hundred bright eyes and put them on the tail of the peacock, her favorite bird. The eyes could no longer see, but they looked gorgeous, and that went to the peacock's little head, and made it the vainest of all animals.

Pursued by the gadfly, Io ran all over Greece. Trying to escape from its tormenting sting, she jumped across the **strait**[7] that separates Europe from Asia Minor, and, ever since, it has been called the Bosporus, the "cow ford."

But still the gadfly chased her all the way to the land of Egypt. When the Egyptians saw the snow-white cow, they fell to their knees and worshiped her. She became an Egyptian goddess, and Hera now permitted Zeus to change her back to her human shape. But first he had to promise never to look at Io again.

---

[5] droned—spoke in a monotonous tone.

[6] gadfly—a fly that bites or annoys animals.

[7] **strait**—a narrow passage.

Io lived long as the goddess-queen of Egypt, and the son she bore to Zeus became king after her. Her descendants returned to Greece as great kings and beautiful queens. Poor Io's sufferings had not all been in vain.

QUESTIONS TO CONSIDER

1. How did Zeus convince Hera to marry him?

2. What was Hera's attitude toward Zeus's other wives?

3. How did Hera make sure her faithful servant, Argus, would never be forgotten?

Poseidon

BY INGRI AND EDGAR PARIN D'AULAIRE

Poseidon (called Neptune *by the Romans) was an extremely powerful god, second only to his brother, Zeus. When Zeus, Hades, and Poseidon defeated Cronus and took control of the universe, they decided to draw lots for lordship of the sea, sky, and murky underworld, leaving the earth common to all. Zeus won the sky; Hades won the Underworld; and Poseidon won the sea. At first, Poseidon was happy with his lot. He set about building a magnificent palace on a sea bed. After just a short while, however, Poseidon grew jealous of his brothers and began arguing with the other gods and goddesses. He became land-hungry and got into the habit of flooding the parts of the earth that he wanted to add to his kingdom. Soon many of the Olympians refused to have anything to do with him.*

Poseidon, lord of the sea, was a moody and violent god. His fierce blue eyes pierced the haze, and his sea-blue hair streamed out behind him. He was called the Earthshaker, for when he struck the ground with his trident, the earth trembled and split open. When he struck the sea, waves rose mountain high and the winds howled, wrecking ships and drowning those who lived on the shores. But when he was in a calm mood, he would stretch out his hand and still the sea and raise new lands out of the water.

In the days of Cronus and the Titans, the sea was ruled by Nereus, son of Mother Earth and Pontus, the seas. Nereus was an old sea god with a long gray beard and a fishtail and was the father of fifty sea nymphs, the lovely Nereids. When Poseidon, the Olympian, came to take over the kingdom of the sea, kind old Nereus gave him his daughter Amphitrite for his queen and retired to an underwater grotto. He gave the new king and queen his palace at the bottom of the sea. It was made of the palest gold and lay in a garden of corals and shimmering pearls. There Amphitrite lived contentedly surrounded by her forty-nine Nereid sisters. She had an only son, whose name was Triton. He had a fishtail instead of legs, like his grandfather Nereus, and rode about on the back of a sea monster, trumpeting on a conch shell.

Poseidon was rarely at home. He was a restless god and loved to race the waves with his team of snow-white horses. It was said that he had created the horse in the shape of breaking waves. Like his brother Zeus, Poseidon had many wives and many children, but Amphitrite was not jealous like Hera.

QUESTIONS TO CONSIDER

1. What three words would you use to describe Poseidon?

   moody, violent, restless

2. What happened when Poseidon struck the ground and the sea?

   the Earth trembled and split open

Demeter's Lost Daughter

BY ROBERT GRAVES

As god of the Underworld, Hades didn't have much contact with his brother, Zeus, or the other gods and goddesses of Olympus. A private, reclusive god, he hated visitors and kept a vicious, three-headed dog named Cerberus as a watchdog at his gate. Hades's Underworld was divided into two regions: Tartarus, where the wicked were punished, and the beautiful Elysian Fields, where the virtuous enjoyed their rewards. Not surprisingly, Hades sent more mortals to Tartarus than he did to the Elysian Fields. For this reason, he was hated and feared by those on earth.

He was also hated and feared by some of his fellow gods and goddesses. Demeter, goddess of the harvest and Hades's sister, was deeply unhappy about Hades's plans to marry her daughter, Persephone, a gentle and lovely goddess. Demeter could be just as vengeful as Hades, however, and had a temper to match. Because she had the power to stop all plants from growing, including crops and trees, Demeter had a most powerful weapon at her disposal: famine.

Hades, the gloomy God of Death, was forbidden to visit Olympus, but lived in a dark palace deep under the earth. He met his brother Zeus one day in Greece, their common ground, and confessed: "I have fallen in love with your niece Persephone, Demeter's daughter. May I have your permission to marry her?"

Zeus feared to offend Hades by saying: "No! What a horrible idea!" He also feared to offend Demeter by saying: "Why not?" So, giving Hades neither a *yes* nor a *no*, he winked at him instead.

The wink satisfied Hades. He went to Colonus near Athens, where Persephone, busily picking spring flowers, had strayed away from her friends, and carried her off in his great hearse[1] of a chariot. Persephone

---

[1] hearse—a vehicle for conveying a coffin to a church or cemetery.

screamed, but when the girls came running up she was gone, leaving no trace behind her except some crushed daisies and cornflowers. The girls told Demeter as much as they knew.

Demeter, very worried, disguised herself as an old woman and wandered through Greece searching for Persephone. Nine days she traveled, without food or drink, and nobody could give her any news. At last she headed back towards Athens. At nearby Eleusis the King and Queen treated her so kindly, offering her a position as nurse to the younger princes, that she accepted a drink of barley-water.

Presently the eldest prince, Triptolemus, who looked after the royal cows, came hurrying in: "If I am not mistaken, my lady," he said, "you are the Goddess Demeter. I fear that I bring bad news. My brother Eubuleus was feeding the pigs at Colonus, not far from here, when he heard the thunder of hooves and saw a chariot rush past. In it were a dark-faced king wearing black armor, and a frightened girl who looked like your daughter Persephone. Then the earth opened before my brother's eyes, and down the chariot rushed. All our pigs

fell in after it and were lost; for the earth closed over the hole again."

Demeter guessed that the dark-faced king must have been Hades. With her friend, the old Witch-goddess Hecate, she questioned the Sun, who sees all. The Sun refused to answer, but Hecate threatened to **eclipse**[2] him every day at noon if he would not tell them the truth. "It *was* King Hades," the Sun confessed.

"My brother Zeus must have plotted this!" said Demeter in a fury. "I will be revenged on him."

She would not return to Olympus, but wandered about Greece, forbidding her trees to bear fruit, or her grass to grow for the cattle to eat. If this went on much longer, mankind would surely die of hunger; so Zeus made Hera send her messenger Iris down the rainbow with a message to Demeter: "Please be sensible, dear Sister, and let things grow again!" When Demeter took no notice, Zeus sent Poseidon, and Hestia, and Hera herself, to offer her wonderful presents. But Demeter groaned: "Take them away. I shall do nothing for any of you, ever, until my daughter comes home to me!"

---

[2] **eclipse**—to obscure; darken.

Then Zeus sent Hermes to tell Hades: "Unless you let that girl go home, Brother, we shall all be ruined." He also gave Hermes a message for Demeter: "You may have Persephone back, so long as she has not yet tasted the Food of the Dead."

Since Persephone had refused to eat even a crust of bread, saying that she would rather starve, Hades could hardly pretend that she had gone off with him willingly. Deciding to obey Zeus, he called Persephone and said kindly: "You seem unhappy here, my dear. You have taken no nourishment at all. Perhaps you had better go home."

One of Hades's gardeners, called Ascalaphus, began to hoot with laughter. "Taken no nourishment at all, you say? This very morning I saw her pick a pomegranate[3] from your underground orchard."

Hades smiled to himself. He brought Persephone in his chariot to Eleusis, where Demeter hugged her and cried for pleasure. Hades then said: "By the way, Persephone ate seven red pomegranate seeds—this gardener of mine saw her. She must come down to Tartarus again."

"If she goes," screamed Demeter, "I shall never lift my curse from the earth, but let all men and animals die!"

In the end, Zeus sent Rhea (who was Demeter's mother as well as his own) to plead with her. The two at last agreed that Persephone should marry Hades, and spend seven months of the year in Tartarus, one month for each pomegranate seed eaten, and the rest above ground.

Demeter punished Ascalaphus by turning him into a hooting long-eared owl; but she rewarded Triptolemus by giving him a bag of barley seed and a plough. At her orders, he went all over the world in a chariot drawn by snakes, teaching mankind how to plough the fields, sow barley seed, and reap the harvest.

* * *

Tartarus, the kingdom over which King Hades and Queen Persephone reigned, lay deep below the earth. When mortals died, Hermes ordered their souls to follow through the air, and he led them to the main entrance—in a grove of black poplars[4] beside the Western Ocean—and down by a dark tunnel to an underground river, called Styx. There they paid Charon, the

---

[3] pomegranate—a type of fruit with a tough, reddish rind. A pomegranate contains many seeds, each of which is enclosed in a juicy, mildly acidic, red pulp.

[4] poplars—trees of the same family as the willow. The cottonwood and aspen are poplars.

old, bearded ferryman, to row them across, using the coins which relations had placed beneath the tongues of their corpses. They then became ghosts. Charon told ghosts who had no money that they must either shiver for ever on the riverbank, or else find their way back to Greece and take a side entrance at Taenarus, where admission would be free. Hades's enormous three-headed dog, named Cerberus, let no ghosts escape and prevented any live mortal from entering.

The nearest region of Tartarus consisted of the stony Asphodel Fields, over which ghosts endlessly wandered, but found nothing whatever to do except hunt the ghosts of deer—if that amused them. Asphodels are tall, pinkish-white flowers, with leaves like leeks,[5] and roots like sweet-potatoes. Beyond these Asphodel Fields stood Hades's towering cold palace. To the left of it grew a cypress tree, marking Lethe, the Pool of Forgetfulness, where ordinary ghosts flocked thirstily to drink. At once they forgot their past lives, which left them nothing whatever to talk about. But ghosts who had been given a secret password by Orpheus, the poet, whispered it to Hades's servants, and went instead to drink from Mnemosyne, the Pool of Memory,

marked by a white poplar. This allowed them to discuss their past lives, and they could also foretell the future. Hades let such ghosts make brief visits to the upper air, when their descendants wanted to ask them questions and would sacrifice a pig to him as a fee.

On their first arrival in Tartarus, ghosts were taken to be tried by the three Judges of the Dead: Minos, Rhadamanthys and Aeacus. Those whose lives had been neither very good nor very bad got sent to the Asphodel Fields; the very bad went to the Punishment Ground behind Hades's palace; the very good, to a gate near the Pool of Memory, which led to a land of orchards called Elysium. Elysium basked in perpetual sunshine; games, music, and fun went on there without a stop; flowers never faded; and every sort of fruit was always in season. The lucky ghosts sent to Elysium might visit the earth, unsummoned, every All Souls' Night, and whoever pleased might then creep inside a bean, hoping that some kind, healthy, rich girl would eat it; he would be later born as her baby. This explains why no decent man in those

---

[5] leeks—vegetables resembling onions.

days ate beans: fearing to swallow the ghost of one of his parents or grandparents.

Hades grew immensely rich because of all the gold and silver and jewels that lie underground; yet everyone hated him, including Persephone, who pitied the poor ghosts in his charge and had no children of her own to console her. Hades's most valuable possession was a helmet of invisibility, made by the one-eyed Cyclopes when they were sent down to Tartarus by Cronus. As soon as Cronus had been banished, Hades released the Cyclopes at Zeus's orders, and they gave him the helmet in gratitude.

QUESTIONS TO CONSIDER

1. Why do you think Demeter assumes that Zeus is behind the kidnapping?

2. Why were the mortals and gods alike afraid of Hades?

3. Do you agree that Ascalaphus deserved punishment and Triptolemus deserved a reward? Explain.

Hephaestus *and* The Birth of Hermes

The god of smithing and metal-working had a powerful mother—Hera, Zeus's wife—and a lovely bride, Aphrodite. When he was just a baby, his mother flung him off Mount Olympus, leaving the child-god lame in one leg. Sickly, shy, and unattractive, Hephaestus never quite fit in with the crowd on Mount Olympus. Still, he made many of the objects that were so important to his fellow gods and goddesses, including Poseidon's trident, Zeus's throne, and almost all of the elaborate palaces in the sky.

Like Hephaestus, Hermes (called Mercury by the Romans) was a very practical deity. He was the official messenger of the gods, as well as the inventor of the Greek alphabet, arithmetic, astronomy, and weights and measures. A friendly, likable god, he had a mischievous side: he was patron not only of travelers, but of merchants, thieves, and robbers as well. Eventually, Hermes began working for Hades, collecting and delivering the dead to the Underworld.

Hephaestus
by Bernard Evslin, Dorothy Evslin, and Ned Hoopes

No one celebrated the birth of Hephaestus. His mother, Hera, had awaited him with great eagerness, hoping for a child so beautiful, so gifted, that it would make Zeus forget his heroic swarm of children from lesser consorts.[1] But when the baby was born she was appalled to see that he was shriveled and ugly, with an irritating bleating wail. She did not wait for Zeus to see him, but snatched the infant up and hurled him off Olympus.

For a night and a day he fell, and hit the ground at the edge of the sea with such force that both of his legs were broken. He lay there on the beach mewing[2] piteously, unable to

---

[1] consorts—lovers.

[2] mewing—making the high-pitched, crying sound of a cat.

crawl, wracked with pain, but unable to die because he was immortal. Finally, the tide came up. A huge wave curled him under its arm and carried him off to sea. And there he sank like a stone, and was caught by the playful Thetis, a naiad,[3] who thought he was a tadpole.

When Thetis understood it was a baby she had caught, she made a pet of him, and kept him in her grotto. She was amazed at the way the crippled child worked shells and bright pebbles into jewelry. One day she appeared at a great festival of the gods wearing a necklace he had made. Hera noticed the ornament, and praised it, and asked her how she had come by it. Thetis told her of the strange twisted child whom someone had dropped into the ocean, and who lived now in her cave making wonderful jewels. Hera divined that it was her own son, and demanded him back.

Hephaestus returned to Olympus. There Hera presented him with a broken mountain nearby, where he could set up forges[4] and **bellows.**[5] She gave him the brawny Cyclopes to be his helpers, and promised him Aphrodite as a bride if he would labor in the mountain and make her fine things. Hephaestus agreed because he loved her, and excused her cruelty to him.

"I know that I am ugly, Mother," he said, "but the Fates would have it so. And I will make you gems so beautiful for your tapering arms and white throat and black hair that you will forget my ugliness sometimes, and rejoice that you have taken me back from the sea."

He became the smith-god, the great **artificer,**[6] lord of mechanics. And the mountain always smoked and rumbled with his toil.

The Birth of Hermes
by Robert Graves

As soon as Hermes had been born in an Arcadian cave, his mother, Maia, bustled about lighting a fire to heat some water for his first bath, while Cyllene, the nurse, took a pitcher to fill at the nearest stream. Being a god, Hermes grew within a few minutes to the size of a four-year-old boy, climbed out of his basket cradle, and tiptoed away in search of adventure. He was tempted to steal a fine herd of Apollo's own cows. To disguise their

---

[3] naiad—one of the nymphs who lived in and presided over large and small bodies of water.

[4] forges—furnaces or hearths where metals are heated or shaped.

[5] **bellows**—a device for producing a strong current of air, used to fan a fire.

[6] **artificer**—a skilled worker; a craftsperson.

tracks, he made them shoes from bark and **plaited**[7] grass, then drove the herd into a wood behind the cave, where he tied them to trees. Apollo missed the cows, and offered a reward for discovery of the thief. Silenus, Pan's son, who lived not far off with his friends the Satyrs—half goats, half men, like himself and his father—joined the search. As he came near Maia's cave, Silenus heard wonderful music coming from inside.

He stopped and, seeing Cyllene in the cave mouth, called out to her: "Who is that musician?"

Cyllene answered: "A clever little boy, born only yesterday. He's made a new sort of musical instrument by stringing cow-gut tight across the hollow shell of a tortoise."

Silenus noticed two newly **flayed**[8] white cowhides pegged down to dry. "Did the gut come from the same cows as these hides?" he asked.

"Do you accuse the innocent child of theft?"

"Certainly! Either your gifted child has stolen Apollo's white cows, or else you have."

"How dare you say such things, you nasty old man? And, please, keep your voice low, or you'll wake the child's mother."

At that moment Apollo flew down, and went straight into the cave, muttering: "I know by my magic that the thief is here." He woke Maia. "Madam, your son has stolen my cows. He must give them up at once!"

Maia yawned. "What a ridiculous charge! My son is only just born."

"These are hides from my precious white cows," said Apollo. "Come along, you bad boy!"

He caught hold of Hermes, who was pretending to be asleep, and carried him to Olympus, where he called a council of the gods and accused him of theft.

Zeus frowned, and asked: "Who are you, little boy?"

"Your son Hermes, Father," Hermes answered. "I was born yesterday."

"Then you certainly must be innocent of this crime."

"You know best, Father."

"He stole my cows," said Apollo.

"I was too young to know right from wrong yesterday," explained Hermes. "Today I do, and I beg your pardon. You may have the rest of those cows if they are yours. I killed only two, and cut them up into twelve

---

[7] **plaited**—braided.
[8] **flayed**—stripped off.

equal portions for sacrifice to the twelve gods."

"Twelve gods? Who is the twelfth?" asked Apollo.

"Myself," said Hermes, bowing politely.

They went together to the cave, where Hermes took the tortoise-shell lyre[9] from under the blankets of his cradle and played so beautifully on it that Apollo exclaimed: "Hand over that instrument. *I* am the God of Music!"

"Very well, if I may keep your cows," said Hermes.

They shook hands on the bargain, the first ever made, and returning to Olympus told Zeus that the affair had been settled.

Zeus sat Hermes on his knee. "Now, my son, be careful in the future neither to steal nor to tell lies. You seem to be a clever little boy. You arranged matters with Apollo very well."

"Then make me your **herald**,[10] Father," begged Hermes. "I promise never again to tell lies, though sometimes it may be best not to tell the whole truth."

"So be it. And you shall take charge of all treaties and all buying and selling, and protect the right of travellers to go down any public road they please, so long as they behave peaceably."

Zeus then gave Hermes his peeled wand and the white ribbons; also a golden hat against the rain; and winged golden sandals to make him fly faster than the wind.

Besides the letters of the alphabet (with which, by the way, the Three Fates helped him), Hermes also invented arithmetic, astronomy, musical scales, weights and measures, the art of boxing, and gymnastics.

---

[9] lyre—a stringed instrument of the harp family used to accompany a singer or reader of poetry, especially in ancient Greece.

[10] **herald**—a person who carries or proclaims important news; a messenger.

QUESTIONS TO CONSIDER

1. Why is it that no one celebrated the birth of Hephaestus?

2. Do you feel sorry for Hephaestus? Why or why not?

3. What is the importance of the trade between Hermes and Apollo?

4. Which of Hermes's inventions do you feel are most important? Why?

Aphrodite

BY BERNARD EVSLIN, DOROTHY EVSLIN, AND NED HOOPES

Many of the Olympic gods and goddesses were beautiful, but Aphrodite, the goddess of love, was the most beautiful of all. Known as Venus *by the Romans, she has been the subject of hundreds and hundreds of sculptures, paintings, and sketches throughout history. With the power to attract any man she desired, Aphrodite never was lonely. But she wasn't necessarily happy, either: most of the other goddesses disliked her, and her marriage to Hephaestus, god of the forge, was troubled.*

Aphrodite was the goddess of love and beauty; so there are more stories told about her than anyone else, god or mortal. Being what she is, she enters other stories; and such is the power of her magic **girdle**[1] that he who even speaks her name falls under her spell, and seems to glimpse her white shoulders and catch the perfume of her golden hair. And he loses his wits and begins to babble, and tells the same story in many ways.

But all the tales agree that she is the goddess of desire, and, unlike other Olympians, is never distracted from her duties. Her work is her pleasure, her profession, her hobby. She thinks of nothing but love, and nobody expects more of her.

She was born out of the primal murder. When Cronos butchered his father, Oranos, with the scythe[2] his mother had given him, he flung the dismembered body off Olympus into the sea, where it floated, spouting blood and foam which drifted, whitening in the sun. From the foam rose a tall beautiful maiden, naked and dripping. Waves attended her. Poseidon's white horses brought her to the island of Cythera. Wherever she stepped, the sand turned to grass and

---

[1] girdle—belt.

[2] scythe—a long, thin, slightly curved blade on a long handle.

flowers bloomed. Then she went to Cyprus. Hillsides burst into flowers, and the air was full of birds.

Zeus brought her to Olympus. She was still dripping from the sea. She wore nothing but the bright tunic of her hair which fell below her knees and was yellow as daffodils. She looked about the great throne room where the gods were assembled to meet her, arched her throat and laughed with joy.

Hera was watching Zeus narrowly. "You must marry her off," she whispered. "At once—without delay!"

"Yes," said Zeus. "Some sort of marriage would seem to be indicated."

And he said, "Brothers, sons, cousins, Aphrodite is to be married. She will choose her own husband. So make your suit."

The gods closed around her, shouting promises, pressing their claims. Earth-shaking Poseidon swung his mighty trident to clear a space about himself. "I claim you for the sea," he said. "You are sea-born, foam-born, and belong to me. I offer you **grottos,**[3] riddles, gems, fair surfaces, dark surroundings. I offer you variety. Drowned sailors, typhoons, sunsets. I offer you secrets. I offer

you riches that the earth does not know—power more **subtle,**[4] more fluid than the dull fixed land. Come with me—be queen of the sea."

He slammed his trident on the floor, and a huge green tidal wave swelled out of the sea—high, high as Olympus, curling its mighty green tongue as if to lick up the mountain— and **poised**[5] there, quivering, not breaking, as the gods gaped. Then Poseidon raised his trident, and the mighty wave **subsided**[6] like a ripple. He bowed to Aphrodite. She smiled at him, but said nothing.

Then the gods spoke in turn, offering her great gifts. Apollo offered her a throne and a crown made of hottest sun-gold, a golden chariot drawn by white swans, and the Muses for her handmaids. Hermes offered to make her queen of the crossways where all must come—where she would hear every story, see every traveler, know each deed—a rich pageant of adventure and gossip so that she would never grow bored.

She smiled at Apollo and Hermes and made no answer.

---

[3] **grottos**—caves.
[4] **subtle**—delicate or elusive, refined.
[5] **poised**—held in a state of balance or equilibrium.
[6] **subsided**—calmed down.

Then Hera, scowling, reached her long white arm and dragged Hephaestus, the lame smith-god, from where he had been hiding behind the others, ashamed to be seen. And she hissed into his ear, "Speak, fool. Say exactly what I told you to say."

He limped forward with great embarrassment, and stood before the radiant goddess, eyes cast down, not daring to look at her. He said: "I would make a good husband for a girl like you. I work late."

Aphrodite smiled. She said nothing, but put her finger under the chin of the grimy little smith, raised his face, leaned down, and kissed him on the lips.

That night they were married. And at the wedding party she finally spoke—whispering to each of her **suitors**[7]—telling each one when he might come with his gift.

---

[7] **suitors**—men who court a woman and want to marry her.

QUESTIONS TO CONSIDER

1. How was Aphrodite born?

2. Why do you think Hera insisted that Aphrodite get married right away?

3. What did each of the gods offer Aphrodite to convince her to marry him?

4. Whom did Aphrodite choose to marry, and why?

Birth of the Twins

BY BERNARD EVSLIN, DOROTHY EVSLIN, AND NED HOOPES

Zeus pursued a nymph named Leto. But Hera was watching, so he changed Leto into a quail, and then himself into a quail, and they met in a **glade.**[1] *Here the sun sifted through the trees and striped the grass with shadows, and it was difficult to see two quail whose feathers were brown and lighter brown. But the eyes of jealousy are very sharp, and Hera saw them. She flung a curse, saying, "Leto, you will grow heavy with child, but you shall not bear anywhere the sun shines."*

She sent the great serpent, Python, to enforce her curse, to hunt Leto out of any sunny place she might try to rest. Zeus sent the south wind to help the girl, and she was carried on the wings of the warm strong wind to an island called Delos. Python swam after her. Before he could reach the island, however, Zeus unmoored it and sent it floating swiftly away, pushed by the south wind, more swiftly than Python could swim. Here, on this lovely island, Leto gave birth to twins—Artemis and Apollo.

Artemis

Father Zeus was by no means an attentive parent. He had so many children in so many different circumstances he could scarcely keep them all in mind. However, he was not permitted to forget Leto's children. They were too beautiful. And beauty was the quality he found most attractive. As he looked down from Olympus, their faces seemed to blaze from among all the children on earth.

It seemed to him that they cast their own light, these twins, each one different—Apollo a ruddy light, Artemis a silver light. And he knew that they were true godlings and must be brought to Olympus.

He sent for them on their third birthday. He had Hephaestus make Apollo a golden bow and a quiver of golden arrows that could never be emptied, and a golden chariot drawn

---

[1] **glade**—an open space in a forest.

by golden ponies. But he withheld Artemis' gifts; he preferred her, and he wanted her to ask him for things. He took her on his lap, and said, "And what gifts would you fancy, little maid?"

She said, "I wish to be your maiden always, never a woman. And I want many names in case I get bored with one. I want a bow and arrow too—but silver, not gold. I want an embroidered deerskin tunic[2] short enough to run in. I need fifty ocean nymphs to sing for me, and twenty wood nymphs to hunt with me. And I want a pack of hounds, please—fierce, swift ones. I want the mountains for my special places, and one city. One will be enough; I don't like cities." She reached up and played with his beard, and smiled at him. "Yes? May I have all these things? May I?"

Zeus answered, "For a child like you it is worthwhile braving Hera's wrath once in a while. You shall have more than you ask for. You shall have the gift of eternal chastity, and also the gift of changing your mind about it at any time, which will help you not to want to. And, finally, the greatest gift of all: You shall go out and choose your own gifts so that they will have a special value."

She kissed him, and whispered her thanks into his ear, and then went running off to choose her gifts. She went to the woods and to the river and to the ocean stream and selected the most beautiful nymphs for her court. She visited Hephaestus in his smoking smithy inside the mountain, and said, "I've come for my bow. A silver one, please."

He said, "Silver is more difficult to work than gold. It needs cool light; it should be made underwater. You must go deep beneath the sea, off the island of Lipara, where my Cyclopes are making a horse **trough**[3] for Poseidon, who thinks of nothing but horses these days."

So Artemis and her nymphs swam underwater to where the Cyclopes were hammering at a great trough. The nymphs were frightened at the sight of the huge one-eyed scowling brutes, and they hated the noise of the hammering. But Artemis jumped up on the forge and said, "I come with a message from Hephaestus. He bids you put aside this horse trough and

---

[2] tunic—garment like a shirt or gown, usually reaching to the knees.

[3] **trough**—a long, narrow, generally shallow receptacle for holding water or feed for animals.

make me a silver bow and a quiver of silver arrows which will fill again as soon as it is empty. If you do this I shall give you the first game I shoot." The Cyclopes, who were very greedy and tired of working on the horse trough, agreed.

When they had finished her bow, she thanked them very prettily. But when their leader, Brontes, tried to take her on his knee, she tore a great handful of hair from his chest. He put her down quickly and went away cursing.

Holding her silver bow high, screaming with joy, she raced across field and valley and hill, followed by her nymphs who streamed after her with flashing knees and floating hair laughing and singing. She came to Arcadia where Pan was feeding his hounds.

"Oh, Pan," she cried. "Oh, little king of the wood, my favorite cousin, please give me some of your dogs— the best ones, please."

"And what will you give me in return?" he said, looking at the nymphs.

"Choose," she said. "But I should warn you, cousin, that like me they have taken an unbreakable vow of chastity."

"Never mind," said Pan. "Keep them. What dogs do you fancy?"

"That one and that one and that one," she cried. "And this one. And I must have him . . . and him."

He gave her his ten best dogs. Three of them were huge black and white hounds able to catch a live lion and drag it back to the hunter. The others were lean white deerhounds; any one of them could outrun a stag.

Artemis was wild to try out her new gifts. She sent her white hounds racing after two deer, bidding them bring back the animals unharmed. She harnessed the deer to her silver chariot and drove away. She saw a tree which had been struck by lightning; it was still smoldering. She had her nymphs break pine branches and thrust them into the cinders, for night was coming and she wanted light to shoot by. She was too impatient to wait for dawn.

Four times she shot her silver bow. First she split a pine tree, then an olive tree. Then she shot a wild boar. Lastly, she shot an arrow into a city of unjust men, and the arrow pierced all of them, never ceasing its flight till they were all dead.

And the people, seeing her ride over the mountains, wielding her silver bow, followed by the maidens and their torches, called her the Goddess of the Moon. Some called her the Maiden of the Silver Bow. Others called her Lady of the Wild Things. Some called her the Huntress. Others, simply, the Maiden. And so she had her last gift—many names.

She let no man approach her. Once a young man named Actaeon glimpsed her bathing in a stream. She was so beautiful he could not bear to go away, but hid there, watching. She saw him, and immediately changed him into a stag. Then she whistled up her hounds, who tore him to pieces.

Apollo

Apollo was the most beautiful of the gods. His hair was dark gold, his eyes stormy blue. He wore a tunic of golden panther skin, carried his golden bow, and wore a quiver of golden arrows. His chariot was beaten gold; its horses were white with golden manes and flame-colored eyes. He was god of the sun always. Later he became **patron**[4] of music, poetry, mathematics, and medicine. And, later, when he was a mature god, he preached moderation. He bade his worshippers to look first into their own hearts and find there the beginnings of wisdom, and to conduct

themselves **prudently**[5] in all things. But in his youth he did many cruel and **wanton**[6] deeds. Several times he was almost expelled from the company of the gods by Zeus whom he had angered with his wild **folly.**[7]

As soon as he was given his bow and arrows he raced down from Olympus to hunt the Python who had hunted his mother. Dryads, who were tattletales, told him he could find his enemy at Mount Parnassus. There he sped. As he stood on a hill, he saw the great serpent weaving its dusty coils far below. He notched an arrow, drew his bow, and let fly. It darted like light; he saw it strike, saw the huge coils flail in agony. Shouting with savage glee he raced down the slope, but when he got there he found the serpent gone. It had left a trail of blood which he followed to the **oracle**[8] of Mother Earth at Delphi. Python was hiding in a cave, where he could not be followed. Apollo breathed on his arrow heads and shot them into the

---

[4] **patron**—one that supports, protects, or champions someone or something, such as an institution, an event, or a cause.

[5] **prudently**—wisely; sensibly.

[6] **wanton**—immoral or unchaste; lewd.

[7] **folly**—foolishness.

[8] **oracle**—wise person who gives advice or guidance.

cave as fast as he could. They broke into flames when they hit. Smoke filled the cave, and the serpent had to crawl out. Apollo, standing on a rock, shot him so full of arrows he looked like a porcupine. He skinned the great snake and saved the hide for a gift.

Now it was a sacred place where he had done his killing; here lived the oracles of Mother Earth, whom the gods themselves consulted. They were priestesses, trained from infancy. They chewed laurel,[9] built fires of magic herbs, and sat in the smoke, which threw them into a trance[10] wherein they saw—and told in riddles—what was to come. Knowing that he had already violated a shrine, Apollo thought he might as well make his deed as large as possible, and claimed the oracles for his own—bidding them prophecy in his name.

When Mother Earth complained to Zeus about the killing of her Python, Apollo smoothly promised to make amends.[11] He instituted annual games at Delphi in celebration of his victory, and these he graciously named after his enemy, calling them the Pythian games. And he named the oracles Pythonesses.

Less excusable was Apollo's treatment of a satyr named Marsyas. This happy fellow had the misfortune to be an excellent musician—a realm Apollo considered his own—and where he would brook no rivalry. Hearing the satyr praised too often, Apollo invited him to a contest. The winner was to choose a penalty to which the loser would have to submit, and the muses were to judge. So Marsyas played his flute and Apollo played his lyre. They played exquisitely; the Muses could not choose between them. Then Apollo shouted, "Now you must turn your instrument upside down, and play and sing at the same time. That is the rule. I go first." Thereupon the god turned his lyre upside down, and played and sang a hymn praising the gods, and especially their beautiful daughters, the Muses. But you cannot play a flute upside down, and certainly cannot sing while playing it, so Marsyas was declared the loser. Apollo collected his prize. He **flayed**[12] Marsyas alive, and nailed his skin to a tree. A stream gushed from the tree's

---

[9] laurel—leaves of a small evergreen tree.

[10] trance—state of limited consciousness somewhat like sleep.

[11] amends—something given or paid to make up for a wrong.

[12] **flayed**—stripped the skin off.

roots and became a river. On the banks of that river grew reeds which sang softly when the wind blew. People called the river Marsyas, and that is still its name.

QUESTIONS TO CONSIDER

1. What kind of father was Zeus?

2. How would you describe Apollo?

3. How were Artemis and Apollo similar? How were they different?

Ares *and* Athena

There were only a few things that made Ares, the god of war, happy—battle, bloodshed, and his darling Eris, the spirit of strife and tension. Interestingly, Ares was a terrible crybaby whenever he suffered even the smallest wound. He would scream and howl in pain and drive the other gods crazy. After one difficult battle, Ares screamed so loudly that all the gods in the Pantheon covered their ears in disgust and begged Zeus to do something about his howling son.

Athena (called Minerva by the Romans) was the goddess of war, although she hated the battle and bloodshed that her brother, Ares, loved so much. If she had no choice but to go to war, however, she was a brave and clever warrior. In fact, she defeated Ares on the battlefield on two separate occasions.

Ares
by Michael Gibson

Fierce quarrels were not rare among the Greek heroes, both between gods and among the mortals, but even the immortals found the behavior of Ares and his family rather more than they could accept. When the others fought, they liked to think that they had good reason to do so, for freedom, or to right a wrong—though to be truthful this was not always borne out by the facts. However, Ares seemed to like fighting for its own sake, and would rush headlong into any battle, regardless of the rights and wrongs of the cause. Unfortunately for him he was often far from successful.

In view of his record, it is surprising that he was the Greek god of war, particularly as other gods, especially Athena, were far better at fighting than he was. Probably it was his enthusiasm and hot temper which made men seek his support for their quarrels, secure in the knowledge that he would not bother too much about the justice of the cause. His sister, Eris, was just as short-tempered as he was, and her jealous plotting often caused wars between cities or states. This was just what Ares thrived on. They would be joined in the fighting by his two sons, with the savage, man-eating horses he had given them to pull their war chariots. Altogether, they formed a formidable family.

The only one among the gods who delighted in Ares's deeds was Hades, for frequent wars meant that his underworld kingdom received a constant stream of young warriors slain on the field of battle. Amongst the goddesses, Aphrodite alone was prepared to put up with his impetuous[1] temperament but . . . the great war god gained little honor from their friendship.

In his time, the war god fought twice in battles against armies commanded by the much more skillful Athene. He lost both. During the great war of Troy, he also clashed with Athene. In this war, the gods took definite sides, often fighting to support their chosen heroes, and sometimes rescuing them if they seemed to be losing the battle. Athena supported the Greek side, Ares was for the Trojans. During a day of particularly fierce fighting, Ares was attacked by the Greek hero Diomedes. Usually, a god would have been able to win such a contest easily, but Diomedes

had immortal help himself. Athene, hidden under a helmet of darkness, took over his war chariot. When Diomedes seemed to be tiring, she charged at Ares, firing arrows from her silver bow. Badly wounded, Ares fled groaning back to Olympus.

Ares was also involved in a battle among the gods themselves. Two sons of Poseidon, Otus and Ephialtes, plotted to climb up to Mount Olympus and take the home of the gods by force. Once there, they planned to carry off Hera and Artemis.

Ephialtes and Otus were giants of men, nine fathoms tall, and of enormous strength. Their plan was in keeping with their size: it was no less than to pile two mountains, Pelion and Ossa, on top of one another so that by using them as huge stepping stones, they could reach the heights of Olympus itself.

Such a massive undertaking could scarcely go unnoticed, and Zeus soon heard of the preparations which were being made to move the rocky, pine-covered mountains. He called his armies together immediately and made ready to fight the invaders. Ares, of course, rushed to join the battle. For once he was on the right side, but

---

[1] impetuous—acting with sudden or rash energy.

though Zeus defeated the two giants utterly, before he had done so, Ares had been taken prisoner. He vanished completely.

Though a long and thorough search was made, it is hardly surprising that he was not found, for the beaten giants had hidden him in a bronze jar, from which it was impossible to escape. For thirteen months he was imprisoned there, a seemingly endless time, during which he grew weak and thin, and very cramped indeed.

The search had long been abandoned when one day Hermes happened to pass on his travels the barn where the jar was stored. It was growing dark and Hermes was weary. The barn looked inviting and warm, and he settled down to sleep on a pile of hay in one corner.

He was just drifting into sleep when he heard a faint tapping sound. At first he took no notice of it, for he imagined that it was simply the noise of rats feeding on the sacks of grain in the loft above him. But the tapping persisted and at length, unable to go to sleep again, he got up to investigate. In the gloom of one corner of the barn he found a tall jar, and the sound seemed to come from this.

"Perhaps a rat has fallen in and cannot get out," he said to himself, and he pulled the jar across the earth floor to where the moon shed its light through the open doorway. He tapped lightly on the jar, and, to his surprise, heard frantic knocking in reply. Feeling slightly foolish, he addressed the jar: "Who's in there? You are making a lot of noise for a rat!"

"It is I, Ares," came a faint reply. "Let me out of this prison and you shall have anything a mighty god can grant."

"Ares! However did you get into that humiliating position? But don't despair: I will set you free."

In a moment, Hermes had unsealed the jar and lifted its heavy lid. Stretching and groaning, a thin and dusty Ares, his armor tarnished and his beard curling around his twisted limbs, dragged himself out into the moonlight.

And so, at long last, Ares was freed to fight another day—and, knowing his nature, we can be sure he did so.

Athena
by Thomas Bulfinch

Athena, the goddess of wisdom, was the daughter of Zeus. She was said to have leaped forth from his brain, mature, and in complete armor. She presided over the useful and ornamental arts, both those of men—such as agriculture and navigation—and those of women—spinning, weaving, and needlework. She was also a warlike divinity; but it was defensive war only that she patronized,[2] and she had no sympathy with Ares's savage love of violence and bloodshed. Athens was her chosen seat, her own city, awarded to her as the prize of a contest with Poseidon, who also aspired to it. The tale ran that in the reign of Cecrops, the first king of Athens, the two deities contended for the possession of the city. The gods decreed that it should be awarded to that one who produced the gift most useful to mortals. Poseidon gave the horse; Athena produced the olive. The gods gave judgment that the olive was the more useful of the two, and awarded the city to the goddess; and it was named after her, Athens, her name in Greek being Athene.

There was another contest, in which a mortal dared to come in competition with Athena. That mortal was Arachne, a maiden who had attained such skill in the arts of weaving and embroidery[3] that the nymphs themselves would leave their groves and fountains to come and gaze upon her work. It was not only beautiful when it was done, but beautiful also in the doing. To watch her, as she took the wool in its rude state and formed it into rolls, or separated it with her fingers and carded it till it looked as light and soft as a cloud, or twirled the spindle with skillful touch, or wove the web, or, after it was woven, adorned it with her needle, one would have said that Athena herself had taught her. But this she denied, and could not bear to be thought a pupil even of a goddess.

"Let Athena try her skill with mine," said she; "if beaten, I will pay the penalty." Athena heard this and was displeased. She assumed the form of an old woman and went and gave Arachne some friendly advice.

"I have had much experience," said she, "and I hope you will not despise my counsel. Challenge your fellow mortals as you will, but do not compete with a goddess. On the contrary, I advise you to ask her forgiveness for what you have said, and as she is merciful perhaps she will pardon you."

---

[2] patronized—supported.

[3] embroidery—ornamental design sewn in cloth with a needle.

Arachne stopped her spinning and looked at the old dame with anger in her **countenance.**[4]

"Keep your counsel," said she, "for your daughters or handmaids; for my part I know what I say, and I stand to it. I am not afraid of the goddess; let her try her skill, if she dare venture."

"She comes," said Athena; and dropping her disguise stood confessed. The nymphs bent low in homage, and all the bystanders paid reverence. Arachne alone was unterrified. She blushed, indeed; a sudden color dyed her cheek, and then she grew pale. But she stood to her resolve and with a foolish conceit[5] of her own skill rushed on her fate. Athena forbore no longer nor **interposed**[6] any further advice. They proceed to the contest. Each takes her station and attaches the web to the beam. Then the slender shuttle[7] is passed in and out among the threads. The reed with its fine teeth strikes up the woof[8] into its place and compacts the web. Both work with speed; their skillful hands move rapidly, and the excitement of the contest makes the labor light. Wool of Tyrian dye is contrasted with that of other colors, shaded off into one another so **adroitly**[9] that the joining deceives the eye. Like the bow, whose long arch tinges the heavens, formed

by sunbeams reflected from the shower, in which, where the colors meet they seem as one, but at a little distance from the point of contact are wholly different.

Athena wrought on her web the scene of her contest with Neptune. Twelve of the heavenly powers are represented, Zeus, with august gravity, sitting in the midst. Poseidon, the ruler of the sea, holds his trident, and appears to have just smitten the earth from which a horse has leaped forth. Athena depicted herself with helmed head, her aegis[10] covering her breast. Such was the central circle; and in the four corners were represented incidents illustrating the displeasure of the gods at such **presumptuous**[11] mortals as had dared to contend with them. These were meant as warnings to her rival to give up the contest before it was too late.

Arachne filled her web with subjects designedly chosen to exhibit the

---

[4] **countenance**—appearance, especially the expression of the face.

[5] conceit—too high an opinion of one's ability.

[6] **interposed**—offered.

[7] shuttle—a device used in weaving to carry the woof thread back and forth between the warp threads.

[8] woof—the threads that run crosswise in a woven fabric.

[9] **adroitly**—skillfully.

[10] aegis—a shield or breastplate.

[11] **presumptuous**—going beyond what is right or proper; excessively forward.

failings and errors of the gods. One scene represented Leda caressing the swan, under which form Zeus had disguised himself; and another, Danaë, in the brazen tower in which her father had imprisoned her, but where the god effected his entrance in the form of a golden shower. Still another depicted Europa deceived by Zeus under the disguise of a bull. Encouraged by the tameness of the animal, Europa ventured to mount his back, whereupon Zeus advanced into the sea and swam with her to Crete. You would have thought it was a real bull, so naturally was it wrought, and so natural the water in which it swam. She seemed to look with longing eyes back upon the shore she was leaving, and to call to her companions for help. She appeared to shudder with terror at the sight of the heaving waves, and to draw back her feet from the water.

Arachne filled her canvas with similar subjects, wonderfully well done, but strongly marking her presumption and **impiety.**[12] Athena could not forbear to admire, yet felt indignant at the insult. She struck the web with her shuttle and rent it in pieces; she then touched the forehead of Arachne and made her feel her guilt and shame. She could not endure it and went and hanged herself. Athena pitied her as she saw her suspended by a rope. "Live," she said, "guilty woman! And that you may preserve the memory of this lesson, continue to hang, both you and your descendants, to all future times." She sprinkled her with the juices of aconite,[13] and immediately her hair came off, and her nose and ears likewise. Her form shrank up, and her head grew smaller yet; her fingers **cleaved**[14] to her side and served for legs. All the rest of her is body, out of which she spins her thread, often hanging suspended by it, in the same attitude as when Athena touched her and transformed her into a spider.

---

[12] **impiety**—lack of respect.
[13] aconite—a poisonous herb.
[14] **cleaved**—adhered to.

QUESTIONS TO CONSIDER

1. Why is it not surprising that Ares is the god of war?

2. What are some of Ares's bad qualities?

3. What was the contest between Athena and Poseidon, and how was it decided?

4. Why does Athena change Arachne into a spider?

Spider Woman

(Native American—Hopi myth)

BY G.M. MULLETT

"Spider Woman," a Hopi creation myth, is told and retold in many cultures of the world. Although the names and scenery change in each myth, the story itself remains essentially the same.

The Hopi (which means "peaceful") are a Pueblo Indian nation in the Southwestern United States. The Hopi Nation is thought to be one of the best-preserved Native American cultures in North America. This means that many of the Hopi customs and stories of today are exactly the same as the customs and stories of thousands of years ago. This is probably true for the myth of "Spider Woman," which many think of as the first Native American myth. Most scholars say "Spider Woman" is a particularly important myth because it introduces the Native American belief that the Earth is a womb from which people and animals emerge gradually. The Greeks and Romans explore this same idea in their myths about Gaea, or Mother Earth.

In the beginning there were only two: Tawa, the Sun God, and Spider Woman, the Earth Goddess. All the mysteries and power in the Above belonged to Tawa, while Spider Woman controlled the magic of the Below. In the Underworld, abode of the gods, they dwelt and they were All. There was neither man nor woman, bird nor beast, no living thing until these Two willed it to be.

In time it came to them that there should be other gods to share their labors. So Tawa divided himself and there came Muiyinwuh, God of All Life Germs; Spider Woman also divided herself so that there was Huzruiwuhti, Woman of the Hard Substances, the goddess of all hard ornaments of wealth such as coral, turquoise, silver and shell. Huzrui-wuhti became the always-bride of

Tawa. They were the First Lovers and of their union there came into being those marvelous ones the Magic Twins—Puukonhoya, the Youth, and Palunhoya, the Echo. As time unrolled there followed Hicanavaiva, Ancient of Six (the Four World Quarters, the Above and Below), Man-Eagle, the Great Plumed Serpent and many others. But Masauwuh, the Death God, did not come of these Two but was bad magic who appeared only after the making of creatures.

And then it came about that these Two had one Thought and it was a mighty Thought—that they would make the Earth to be between the Above and the Below where now lay shimmering only the Endless Waters. So they sat them side by side, swaying their beautiful bronze bodies to the pulsing music of their own great voices, making the First Magic Song, a song of rushing winds and flowing waters, a song of light and sound and life.

"I am Tawa," sang the Sun God, "I am Light. I am Life. I am Father of all that shall ever come."

"I am Kokyanwuhti," the Spider Woman crooned[1] in softer note. "I receive Light and nourish Life. I am Mother of all that shall ever come."

"Many strange thoughts are forming in my mind—beautiful forms of birds to float in the Above, of beasts to move upon the Earth and fish to swim in the Waters," intoned Tawa.

"Now let these things that move in the Thought of my lord appear," chanted Spider Woman, the while with her slender fingers she caught up clay from beside her and made the Thoughts of Tawa take form. One by one she shaped them and laid them aside—but they breathed not nor moved.

"We must do something about this," said Tawa. "It is not good that they lie thus still and quiet. Each thing that has a form must also have a spirit. So now, my beloved, we must make a mighty Magic."

They laid a white blanket over the many figures, a cunningly woven woolen blanket, fleecy as a cloud, and made a mighty **incantation**[2] over it, and soon the figures stirred and breathed.

"Now, let us make ones like unto you and me, so that they may rule over and enjoy these lesser creatures," sang Tawa, and Spider Woman

[1] **crooned**—sang softly.
[2] **incantation**—a magic spell.

shaped the Thoughts of her lord into man figures and woman figures like unto their own. But after the blanket magic had been made the figures still stayed **inert**.[3] So Spider Woman gathered them all in her arms and cradled them in her warm young bosom, while Tawa bent his glowing eyes upon them. The two now sang the magic Song of Life over them, and at last each man figure and woman figure breathed and lived.

"Now that was a good thing and a mighty thing," quoth[4] Tawa. "So now all this is finished, and there shall be no new things made by us. Those things we have made shall multiply, each one after his own kind. I will make a journey across the Above each day to shed my light upon them and return each night to Huzruiwuhti. And now I shall go to turn my blazing shield upon the Endless Waters, so that the Dry Land may appear. And this day will be the first day upon the Earth."

"Now I shall lead all these created things to the land that you shall cause to appear above the waters," said Spider Woman.

Then Tawa took down his **burnished**[5] shield from the turquoise wall of the kiva[6] and swiftly mounted his glorious way to the Above. After Spider Woman had bent her wise, all-seeing eyes upon the thronging creatures about her, she wound her way among them, separating them into groups.

"Thus and thus shall you be and thus shall you remain, each one in his own tribe forever. You are Zunis, you are Kohoninos, you are Pah-Utes—." The Hopis, all, all people were named by Kokyanwuhti then.

Placing her Magic Twins beside her, Spider Woman called all the people to follow where she led. Through all the Four Great Caverns of the Underworld she led them, until they finally came to an opening, a sipapu, which led above. This came out at the lowest depth of the Pisisbaiya (the Colorado River) and was the place where the people were to come to gather salt. So lately had the Endless Waters gone down that the Turkey, Koyona, pushing eagerly ahead, dragged his tall feathers in the black mud where the dark bands were to remain forever.

---

[3] **inert**—unable to move or act.

[4] **quoth**—said.

[5] **burnished**—polished.

[6] **kiva**—an underground or partly underground chamber in a Pueblo village, used by the men especially for ceremonies or councils.

Mourning Dove flew overhead, calling to some to follow, and those who followed where his sharp eyes had spied out springs and built beside them were called "Huwinyamu" after him. So Spider Woman chose a creature to lead each clan to a place to build their house. The Puma, the Snake, the Antelope, the Deer, and other Horn creatures, each led a clan to a place to build their house. Each clan henceforth bore the name of the creature who had led them.

Then Spider Woman spoke to them thus: "The woman of the clan shall build the house, and the family name shall descend through her. She shall be house builder and homemaker. She shall mold the jars for the storing of food and water. She shall grind the grain for food and tenderly rear the young. The man of the clan shall build kivas of stone under the ground where he shall pay homage to his gods. In these kivas the man shall make sand pictures which will be his altars. Of colored sand shall he make them and they shall be called 'ponya.' After council I shall whisper to him, he shall make Prayer sticks or paho to place upon the ponya to bear his prayers. There shall be the Wupo Paho, the Great Paho, which is mine. There shall

be four paho of blue, the Cawka Paho—one for the great Tawa, one for Muiyinwuh, one for Woman of the Hard Substances and one for the Ancient of Six. Each of these paho must be cunningly and secretly wrought with prayer and song. The man, too, shall weave the clan blankets with their proper symbols. The Snake clan shall have its symbol and the Antelope clan its symbol; thus it shall be for each clan. Many shall fashion himself weapons and furnish his family with game."

Stooping down, she gathered some sand in her hand, letting it run out in a thin, continuous stream. "See the movement of the sand. That is the life that will cause all things therein to grow. The Great Plumed Serpent, Lightning, will rear and strike the earth to fertilize it, Rain Cloud will pour down waters and Tawa will smile upon it so that green things will spring up to feed my children."

Her eyes now sought the Above where Tawa was descending toward his western kiva in all the glory of red and gold. "I go now, but have no fear, for we Two will be watching over you. Look upon me now, my children, ere I leave. Obey the words I have given you and all will be well, and if you are in need of help call upon me and I will send my sons to your aid.

The people gazed wide-eyed upon her shining beauty. Her woven upper garment of soft white wool hung tunic-wise over a blue skirt. On its left side was woven a band bearing the woman's symbols, the Butterfly and the Squash Blossom, in designs of red and yellow and green with bands of black appearing between. Her beautiful neck was hung with heavy necklaces of turquoise, shell and coral, and pendants[7] of the same hung from her ears. Her face was fair, with warm eyes and tender red lips, and her form most graceful. Upon her small feet were skin boots of gleaming white, and they now turned toward where the sand spun about in whirlpool fashion. She held up her right hand and smiled upon them, then stepped upon the whirling sand. Wonder of wonders, before their eyes the sands seemed to suck her swiftly down until she disappeared entirely from their sight.

---

[7] pendants—ornaments or pieces of jewelry that are attached to necklaces or bracelets.

QUESTIONS TO CONSIDER

1. What material does Spider Woman use to form her creatures?

2. Who is Tawa?

3. How would you describe the universe he rules?

4. What is your impression of Spider Woman? Is she an immortal worth knowing? Explain.

Izanagi and Izanami

(Japanese myth)

BY ANITA GANERI

In the Shinto religion of Japan, there is a story that tells how the world was created. In the beginning, the universe was divided into two halves. The top half was heaven. The bottom half was to become the Earth, but it had not yet been given any shape or form. A god, Izanagi, and a goddess, Izanami, were given the great task of forming the whirling water into the world that we know today.

Izanagi and Izanami stood on the Floating Bridge of Heaven, which was made of all the colors of the rainbow. They took a long, jewel-covered spear in their hands, and with it they stirred the whirling waters below. When they lifted the spear out, a drop of water fell from it and formed the island of Onokoro, the first solid land there had ever been.

Izanagi and Izanami were very pleased with their island. They decided to leave heaven and descend to Earth to live on Onokoro. They built a great palace, with a pillar that reached up to heaven to prop up the roof. Then they got married and had lots of children. The first of their children was born deformed as a punishment from the gods for their past wrong-doings. They called him the leech-child, and, placing him in a reed boat, they set him adrift on the sea to drown. But their next children were all healthy. Some became the islands of Japan. Others became the gods of the wind, the trees, and the mountains. Then tragedy struck. While she was giving birth to her last child, the god of fire, Izanami was so badly burned that she died. At first Izanagi was so upset by her death that he could do nothing but weep. From his tears sprang up more gods and goddesses. Then he fell into a terrible rage, picked up his sword, and cut off the fire god's head. More gods and goddesses were created from the fire god's blood as it dripped from the sword to the ground.

For a very long time, Izanagi was **inconsolable.**[1] Without Izanami life hardly seemed worth living. So he decided to visit Yomi, the Land of the Dead, and try to bring his wife back to life. Izanami met him at the gateway to Yomi, hidden by the shadows and shades of half-light. Izanagi begged her to come back with him to their island. She told him that she would go and ask the god of death for his advice, but she warned Izanagi not to try and look at her as she disappeared into the darkness. Izanagi meant to obey her, but she was gone for such a long time that he grew impatient. He broke off a tooth from the comb he wore in his hair and lit it to make a torch. Then he followed Izanami inside. And there in the glowing torchlight, a **hideous**[2] sight awaited him—Izanami's dead body, rotting and full of worms.

Izanagi ran away as quickly as he could. When he reached the sea, he plunged into the water to wash away the terrible memory of what he had seen. And as he washed, he produced hundreds of gods. From his left eye came Amaterasu, the goddess of the Sun and ruler of heaven; from his right eye came Tsukiyomi, the goddess of the Moon and ruler of the night. From his nose came Susanoo, the god of the sea and of storms and rain. Then Izanagi, his work completed, left the Earth and returned to heaven.

---

[1] **inconsolable**—impossible or difficult to comfort; despondent.
[2] **hideous**—repulsive; revoltingly ugly.

QUESTIONS TO CONSIDER

1. According to this myth, how are the islands of Japan formed?

2. What would you say is Izanagi's greatest fault?

3. Which deity do you feel more compassion for: Izanagi or Izanami?

Creation: The Nine Worlds

(Norse myth)

BY MARY POPE OSBORNE

From the middle of the first century B.C., *Germanic tribes lived in southern Scandinavia and northern Germany. These people were known as the ancient Norse; their stories are collectively known as Norse legends and myths. The two most important collections of Old Norse writings are known by the title of* Edda. *The Poetic Edda* (A.D. *9–12) is a collection of Icelandic poems and prose dating from the 9th to the 12th century. The second volume of the* Edda, *called the* Prose Edda (A.D. *1220?), contains stories of the creation of the world, myths about Norse gods and goddesses, and information about ancient Norse poets.*

The Norse deities are divided into two major groups, the Aesir and the Vanir. The most important of the Aesir are Odin and Thor. Odin is chief among the gods. Thor, god of the hammer, keeps order in the universe. The most important of the Vanir gods are Njord, Frey, and Freya. In many myths, the Aesir and Vanir are united in their fight against the terrible giants, who want control of the universe.

---

*Twas the earliest of times
When Ymir lived;
There was no sand nor sea
Nor cooling wave.
Earth had not been,
Nor Heaven on high,
There was a yawning void[1]
And grass no where.*

In the morning of time there was no sand, no sea, and no clouds. There was no heaven, no earth, and no grass. There was only a region of icy mist called Niflheim, a region of fire called Muspell, and a great yawning empty void between them called Ginnungagap.

---

[1] **void**—an empty space.

Over time, the flames of Muspell warmed the frozen vapors of Niflheim, and ice melted into water and began to drip. Quickened with life, the water dripped into the void and formed into two gigantic creatures.

The first was a wicked frost-giant named Ymir. The second was a huge cow named Audumla. As Ymir drank Audumla's milk, he grew bigger and stronger. One night as Ymir slept, a **troll**[2] with six heads grew from the soles of his feet, and a male and a female frost-giant sprung from Ymir's warm armpit.

The ice cow also brought about life. As she licked salty ice blocks, she slowly licked a new creature into being. The first day hair came forth; on the second day came a head—and finally, on the third day, the body of a new giant emerged. This giant was a good giant whose name was Buri. His sons and grandsons became gods instead of giants, and they stood for all that was good and honorable.

The greatest of Buri's grandsons was the god Odin. Odin led his brothers against the wicked frost-giant Ymir. They killed Ymir, and ever after that time, the gods and giants were deadly enemies.

After Odin and his brothers had slain the frost-giant, they dragged his enormous body into the void. Ymir's flesh became the earth. His blood became the sea. His bones became mountains; his hair, trees; and his teeth, stones.

Then Odin and his brothers discovered worms living in the earth that was Ymir's flesh, and they turned them into dwarves and dark elves and sent them to mine the ore beneath the mountains and hills. The world of the dwarves was called Nidavellir; and the world of the dark elves was called Svartalfheim.

The gods also discovered lovely creatures in the soil. They called them light elves and placed them in a world called Alfheim.

The blood that flowed from Ymir's veins became the sea, and it drowned all the frost-giants. Only two escaped in a boat and began a new race of giants. From this race came all **warlocks**,[3] enchanters, ogres, and witches, including a witch in the woods who gave birth to all the wolves of the world.

---

[2] **troll**—a supernatural creature of Scandinavian myth and folklore, variously portrayed as a friendly or mischievous dwarf or as a giant, who lives in caves, in the hills, or under bridges.

[3] **warlocks**—male witches, sorcerers, wizards, or demons.

Then Odin set Ymir's skull over the earth and called it the sky. He spread the giant's brains throughout the sky and called them clouds. At the four corners of the sky, he placed four dwarves named Nordri, Sudri, Austri, and Vestri—or North, South, East, and West.

Odin and his brothers caught sparks from the fires of Muspell and turned them into stars. They put a girl named Sun and a boy named Moon into two chariots of fire and placed them in the sky. From then on, Sun and Moon were continuously chased by a ferocious wolf named Moon-Hound.

Odin also gave chariots to a goddess named Night and her son Day. Night rode behind a horse called Frosty-Mane; the foam from his mouth became the dew of early morning.

Then Odin and his kin took Ymir's eyebrows and turned them into a land called Midgard. They made two humans from trees—a man from an ash and a woman from an elm. They gave the humans spirit, life, speech, hearing, sight, clothing, temples, and shrines.

Then the gods left their human friends in Midgard and crossed over a flaming rainbow bridge to a world called Asgard. There, they built golden halls—one for the gods and one for the goddesses, for the goddesses were no less important than the gods.

Odin, the greatest of the gods, was the god of War and Death. After a battle ended, warrior maidens called Valkyries picked up the dead and carried them to Odin's palace, Valhalla, Hall of the Slain.

Odin's wife, Frigg, sat on the throne next to him. She was the goddess of knowledge and knew all that happened in the worlds. Frigg could look into the future and see the fates of gods and men, but she kept all her visions a secret, never sharing them with anyone.

Odin had many sons. With Frigg, he had twin boys, Balder and Hod. Balder, their favorite, was like the sun. He was the most gentle and beautiful of all the gods. Hod was blind and ruled the black hours of night.

Odin's second favorite son was Thor. The strongest of all the gods, Thor was the god of the sky and thunder. His wife, Sif, had long hair made of gold.

The god Heimdall was also a son of Odin. Night and day, he watched the rainbow bridge, keeping out enemies. His sight was so keen, he could see in the dark; his sense of sound was so sharp, he could hear wool growing on sheep.

In the early days, there were two kinds of gods: the Aesir and the Vanir. Odin and his kin were Aesir and lived in Asgard. The Vanir, the gods of nature, lived in Vanaheim.

One day the Aesir and Vanir went to war. The fighting lasted until both grew weary and decided to become friends. Thereafter, the Vanir god Njord lived in Asgard and ruled the wind and seas. His son, Frey, ruled the rain and sunshine. And his daughter, Freya, was the goddess of love.

There was one god who was neither Aesir nor Vanir. His name was Loki, and he was the son of two giants and the foster-brother of Odin. Loki was the most dangerous of all the gods, for sometimes he was a friend and sometimes he was purely evil. No one ever knew when he could be trusted.

From the mighty halls of Asgard, the gods and goddesses ruled all the nine worlds. They were:

Niflheim, world of mist and the dead
Muspell, world of fire
Midgard, world of humans
Jotunheim, world of frost-giants
Alfheim, world of light elves
Nidavellir, world of the dwarves
Svartalfheim, world of the dark elves
Vanaheim, world of the Vanir gods
Asgard, world of the Aesir gods and goddesses

Above all these worlds was a wondrous tree called Yggdrasil, or the World Tree. A wise eagle sat on top of the tree, surveying the universe. One of the tree's roots grew into Niflheim where a dreadful serpent ceaselessly gnawed on the root. A busy squirrel named Ratatosk scurried up and down the World Tree, carrying insults back and forth between the serpent and the eagle.

Another root of the tree grew into Asgard. Under that root was Urd's Well, whose pure waters helped protect the World Tree, for it suffered terribly from deer and goats eating its leaves.

A third root coiled into Jotunheim. And under that root was Mirmir's Well, whose magic waters held all the wisdom and memory of ancient lore.

Hidden in Mimir's Well was a trumpet that belonged to Heimdall, the guardian of Asgard. All the gods knew that one day a blast on Heimdall's trumpet would announce the last bitter battle between the gods and the forces of evil. This final battle, called Ragnarok, would bring about the total destruction of the nine worlds.

QUESTIONS TO CONSIDER

1. What is the difference between the Aesir and the Vanir?

2. What is Ragnarok?

3. Which of these immortals do you think was most powerful: Odin, Thor, or Loki? Why?

4. What do you think life was like for the Norse people who believed in such gods?

5. Young children are often fascinated by Norse mythology. Why do you think this is so?

Mythic Places

▲

Apollo and the Muses on Mount Helicon
by Claude Gelée, 17th century
Mount Helicon, a fertile mountain in Greece, was the favorite haunt of the nine Muses, who were patron goddesses of poets, artists, and musicians. This painting depicts Apollo, the god of fine arts, near a sacred temple on the famous mountain.

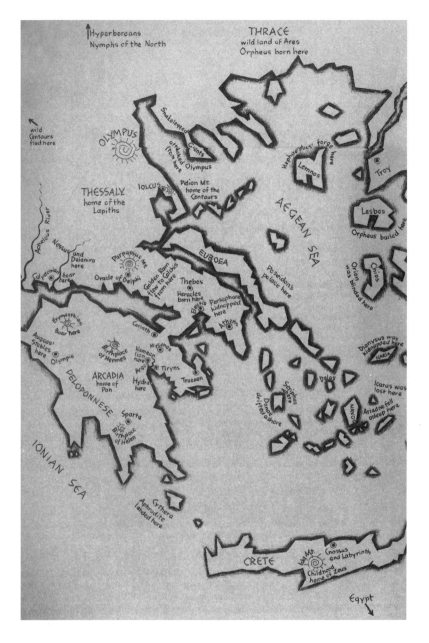

▲

The Realm of the Greek Gods and Goddesses
by Ingri and Edgar Parin D'Aulaire

This illustrated map shows Zeus's kingdom in all its splendor. Although he was technically Lord of the Sky, Zeus ruled the earth as well and kept a close watch on the many gods, goddesses, and mortals who lived in his realm.

▲

Mount Olympus
by Edward Dodell, 1820
This aquatint from Dodell's "Views of Greece" shows the highest peak in Greece. In Greek mythology, the Cyclopes built a palace atop Mount Olympus for the twelve immortal gods. Although the mountain was surrounded by clouds, the gods lived at the uppermost point and had a clear view of all the kingdom.

▲

Assembly of the Gods on Mount Olympus

In this image, Zeus and Hera assemble with the rest of the gods. As the King and Queen of Heaven, Zeus and Hera sat on the highest thrones, presiding over the feasts and gatherings of the gods. The merry group of gods frequently feasted on ambrosia and nectar.

The Siege of Troy I: The Death of Hector
by Biagio di Antonio, c. 1490-95
The name Troy refers both to a city at Hissarlik in
what is now Turkey, and to the legendary city ruled
by King Priam that was destroyed by the ancient
Greeks during the Trojan War. Hector was the
Commander of the Trojan forces and the mightiest
of the Trojan warriors. He was killed by the Greek
warrior Achilles. ▶

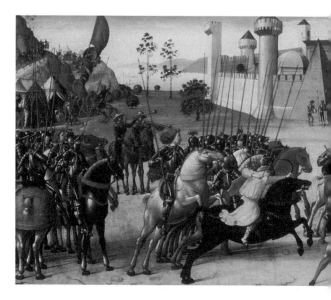

◀ ***Orpheus in Hades***
artist unknown, c. 1700
Even the most powerful
gods and goddesses wanted
nothing to do with Hades's
Underworld, the land of
the dead. Although there
were attractive parts of
Hades's kingdom, the
Underworld was generally
thought of as a place of
fire, ice, pain, and suffering.

◀ The Throne Room of the Minoan Palace
In Greek and Roman mythology, Minos was both the ruler
of Crete and, after his death, a judge of the Underworld.
(The Minoan civilization, which flourished on Crete from
about 3000 to 1450 B.C., was named for King Minos.)
This photograph shows the throne room of the palace
at Knossos, which is popularly thought to be the palace
of King Minos.

▲

The Labyrinth of Crete
artist unknown, 17th century
After Daedalus was banished from Greece for murdering his nephew, he arrived on the island of Crete, where he was asked to build a tremendous maze to house the terrible Minotaur. In this painting, Ariadne hands Theseus the thread that will help him find his way back out of the labyrinth after he slays the Minotaur.

▲

Delphi

This photograph shows an ancient sanctuary near the sacred city of Delphi, which the Greek storytellers called the *omphalos,* or center, of the Earth. Delphi was particularly important to Apollo— god of prophecy, philosophy, and the arts—who kept a temple and shrine there. Apollo's temple was home to the famed oracle of Delphi, which Oedipus and other mortals consulted for advice.

Arthurian Knight and Lady

In this undated illustration of Arthurian England, a lord and lady travel on horseback by a castle, possibly in Camelot. Camelot was the seat of King Arthur's mythical court and the home of the famous Round Table.

Arthur and His Round Table
artist unknown, c.520

This miniature shows the legendary King Arthur speaking with the knights of the Round Table. By creating this circular meeting place, Arthur encouraged the brotherhood of his knights. All were of equal importance to the group, so none could sit at the head of the table. Only the most valiant and chivalrous knights were chosen by Arthur to sit at the Round Table.

▼

The City of Cuzco

Cuzco was the capital of the Inca empire
from its beginnings in the 14th century
until the Spanish conquest in 1533. The
legendary founder of the city was Manco
Capac, the first of the Inca rulers. Cuzco
is especially known for its architecture
of enormous cut-stone blocks fitted so
perfectly that no mortar was needed.

Inca Citadel

At left is a view of the Machu Picchu
citadel, Pre-Columbian Inca, which
was probably built during the reign
of Pachacutec Yupanqui (1438-71). This
citadel is somewhat similar in appearance
and architecture to the great fortress
of Sacsahuaman, located near Cuzco.

Part Two

Heaven and Earth

"On the other side of the mountain, Quetzalcoatl found the sea. Upon seeing the great waters, he built a raft from snakes that he wove together."

◄ **Head of Quetzalcoatl from the Temple of the Feathered Serpent** *(Teotihuacan, Valley of Mexico)*

The feathered serpent god, Quetzalcoatl, is a powerful deity who was known as a creator god who could make human beings by grinding up the bones of the ancient dead and sprinkling them with his own blood.

Lost at Sea

BY MARY POPE OSBORNE

In the introduction to "Lost at Sea," Mary Pope Osborne explains that the ancient Greeks and Romans "invented stories to help explain nature and to free them from their fears of the unknown." This is certainly true for "Lost at Sea." It's possible that this myth came as an answer to a question posed by the ancient Greeks. Why—they might have asked—is one day longer or shorter than another? According to the ancient Greeks, the answer can be found in a love story between Ceyx, son of the morning star, and Alcyone, daughter of the winds.

King Ceyx, son of the morning star, walked along the shore with his wife, Alcyone, daughter of the king of the winds.

"I must leave in a few days on a long sea voyage and travel to the Oracle of Delphi," King Ceyx told his wife. "But I promise I will be gone for no more than two months."

Alcyone turned pale. She knew the rough winds in the open seas were very dangerous. "My father, Aeolus, rules the winds—I know what force he can unleash in a bad storm. I beg you, if you love me, don't go!"

King Ceyx assured Alcyone of his love for her and promised to return soon, but she would not be **consoled.**[1] A few days later, when he stood in the stern of his ship and waved good-bye, she flung herself down on the sands and wept bitterly. Then she dragged herself home and began her long wait for her husband's return.

One night, as King Ceyx's ship sailed upon the open sea, the waves began rising. "Pull in your oars! Lower the sails!" the captain shouted.

But the men could not hear him, for the winds had begun to howl, and thunder rumbled in the sky. Ocean spray leapt for the stars, as lightning

---

[1] **consoled**—comforted in time of grief.

lit the night. Then the sea turned yellow, and the heavens poured water in great torrents, as waves crashed in on the king's ship.

Ceyx's last thoughts were of Alcyone. He cried to the gods, "Wash my body to my wife over the sea!" And he called her name again and again, until a great arc of water took him down to the dark depths of the ocean. And then there was no more lightning and no more starlight; everything was pitch-black.

The morning star did not shine the next day, but hid behind the clouds, grieving for his drowned son.

Alcyone was counting the days until Ceyx returned. She wove a beautiful robe for him and a dress for herself to wear when he came home. Every day she burned incense and prayed to Juno, the goddess who protects married women, asking her to bring her husband home safely.

Hearing Alcyone's prayers, Juno felt pity. Finally she summoned her messenger, Iris, the rainbow goddess. She instructed Iris to travel to the god Sleep and ask Sleep to send Alcyone a dream, telling her that her husband had drowned at sea.

Iris took off at once, trailing her thousand colors across the sky, until she touched down upon the twilight lands of the Cimmerian country. There the god Sleep lived in the hollow of a mountain. When Iris arrived at Sleep's cave, she heard no birds singing or dogs barking or geese cackling. Only the river, Lethe, whispered sleepily in the twilight as Iris stepped past poppy beds and entered Sleep's cave.

The rainbow goddess pushed aside the empty dreams in her way, then came upon Sleep, snoring in a great ebony bed. Iris awakened the slumbering god and bid him send a dream to Alcyone. After Sleep agreed, Iris soared back to Mount Olympus, trailing her rainbow colors across the sky.

Sleep roused Morpheus, one of his thousand sons, the one who could best imitate humans. He instructed Morpheus to fly to Alcyone. Then the god returned to his bed, letting his drowsy head sink down again into the land of dreams.

On silent wings, Morpheus took off through the twilight. When he finally came to the home of Alcyone, he assumed the face and body of King Ceyx. He slipped into Alcyone's chamber and stood before her bed.

Ceyx's ghostly beard dripped with sea water, and tears ran down his face as he bent over his sleeping wife and whispered, "Oh, my love, do you see me? Have I changed in death? Cherish no hope for my return. My ship went down in a storm far out at sea, and I died, calling your name. Arise now and weep for me."

In her sleep, Alcyone wept and tried to take her husband into her arms, but it was no use. She clutched the air and cried out for him, until her own voice woke her. Alcyone realized she'd been dreaming, but fearing her dream might have been the truth, she wept until dawn.

When light crept into her bedroom chamber, Alcyone rose and slipped down to the shore, to the place where she had last seen Ceyx, standing in the stern of his boat, waving to her.

As she stared at the sea, Alcyone spotted something floating on the water. She stepped closer and saw a man's body on top of the waves. "Oh, poor sailor," she said, "and poor wife, if you're married."

When the waves washed the body closer to shore, Alcyone saw it was her husband. She cried out, "Oh, my love! Why have you come back to me this way?"

Then she rushed into the sea. And though the waves broke against her, she did not go under. Instead, she began beating the water with giant wings. Then, crying out like a bird, she rose into the air and flew over the sea to Ceyx's lifeless body. When she touched her husband's cold lips with her beak, he also became a bird, and the two of them were together again.

Since that time, every year, for seven days before the winter solstice,[2] the waves are quiet, and the water is perfectly calm. These days are called **halcyon**[3] days, for during them, the king of the winds keeps the wind at home—because his daughter, Alcyone, is **brooding**[4] on her nest upon the sea.

---

[2] solstice—Either of two times of the year when the sun is at its greatest distance from the celestial equator. The summer solstice in the Northern Hemisphere occurs about June 21, when the sun is in the zenith at the tropic of Cancer; the winter solstice occurs about December 21, when the sun is over the tropic of Capricorn. The summer solstice is the longest day of the year and the winter solstice is the shortest.

[3] **halcyon**—calm and peaceful; tranquil.

[4] **brooding**—sitting on or hatching (eggs).

QUESTIONS TO CONSIDER

1. What is the sequence of events from the time Juno hears Alcyone's prayers until Alcyone dreams of her husband?

2. According to this myth, how is the approach of the winter solstice foretold?

The Constellations

BY ALICE LOW

The ancient Greeks and Romans loved stories about the stars. How else could they explain what those little bright lights were doing way up in the sky? Among the most well-known constellation myths are the myths of Andromeda, Cassiopeia, Orion, and Castor-Pollux.

Cassiopeia

Cassiopeia, wife of King Cepheus of Ethiopia, boasted to the sea nymphs, "I and my daughter, Andromeda, are far more beautiful than you. You are plain next to us."

The lovely sea nymphs swam to Poseidon, god of the sea, to tell him about Cassiopeia's insult. "You must punish Cassiopeia," they said. "She must not get away with such boasting."

Poseidon acted quickly. He sent a huge and hungry sea monster to Ethiopia to devour scores of King Cepheus's people.

King Cepheus was distraught, and he asked an oracle, "What must I do to rid my country of this ferocious monster?"

The oracle replied, "Chain your daughter, Andromeda, to a rock by the sea. Leave her there for the sea monster to feast upon. Only in this way shall you be rid of it."

To his wife's despair, King Cepheus did as he was told, and poor Andromeda awaited her fate, chained and helpless. But as the sea monster was about to devour her, the hero Perseus flew overhead in Hermes's winged sandals. Just in time, he landed on the monster's back and thrust his sword into it repeatedly. After a raging battle, Perseus killed the monster and carried away the lovely Andromeda, who became his bride.

Perseus and Andromeda lived happily together, but the sea nymphs never forgot Cassiopeia's insult. Many years later, when Cassiopeia died, the sea nymphs again begged Poseidon to punish her.

This time Poseidon did so by setting Cassiopeia in the north sky in a most uncomfortable position. She sits in a high-backed chair that looks like a W—but during part of the year, the chair hangs upside down.

Near Cassiopeia, Athena placed the constellation Andromeda, and Andromeda's brave husband, Perseus, stands not far from her in the Milky Way. Cepheus is there, too, though dimmer, and so is Cetus, the sea monster, also called the Whale.

Castor and Pollux

Castor and Pollux were inseparable twin brothers. Their father was Zeus, and their mother was a mortal, Leda of Sparta.[1]

They were strong, athletic young men. Castor was renowned as a soldier and tamer of horses, and Pollux was an outstanding boxer. Both entered the Olympic games[2] and won many competitions. They were worshipped as gods by athletes, soldiers, and sailors.

Castor and Pollux were among the Argonauts, who aided Jason in his quest for the Golden Fleece. But after their return, they had a dispute with two young men. A terrible battle followed, and Castor, who was mortal, was killed. Pollux, who was immortal, wept over the body of his twin. He cried to his father, Zeus, "Please let me kill myself and follow my brother to the Underworld. I feel that half of myself is gone, and the half that remains is but a shadow."

Zeus took pity on Pollux and said, "Though I cannot enable you to die, for you are immortal, I shall allow you and Castor to be together always. Together you shall spend alternate days in the Underworld and on Olympus. And because of your great love for your brother, I shall raise your images into the sky. There you shall shine next to each other forever."

And Castor and Pollux became the twin stars, forming the constellation Gemini.

---

[1] Sparta—at one time the dominant city of Greece. Sparta was famous for its strict discipline and training of soldiers.

[2] Olympic games—The earliest reliable date for the first Olympics is 776 B.C., although virtually all historians say that the Games began well before then. The Olympics of 776 B.C. were held in honor of Zeus, the most powerful god in the ancient Greek pantheon. According to records, only one athletic event was held during the first games—a footrace of approximately 200 yards. A cook, Coroibus of Elis, was the first recorded winner.

Orion

Orion was a giant and a brave hunter. He could walk on water, a gift given him by his father, Poseidon, god of the sea.

One day Orion walked across the water to the island of Chios. There he fell in love with the king's daughter, Merope.

Orion said to the king, "I wish to marry your daughter, for I have fallen deeply in love with her. Tell me what I must do to gain her hand."

"Very well," said the king. "Since you are famous as a mighty hunter, you must rid my island of lions and bears and wolves. Only then will I give you my precious daughter's hand in marriage."

Orion strode through the hills and killed all the wild animals with his sword and his club. Then he brought their skins to the king and said, "Now I have finished my task. Let us set a day for the wedding."

But the king did not want to part with his daughter and kept putting off the wedding date. This angered Orion, and he tried to carry off Merope.

Her father **retaliated**.[3] He called on the god of wine, Dionysus, to put Orion into a drunken sleep. Then the king blinded Orion and flung him onto the sand by the sea.

When Orion awoke sightless, he cried out, "I am blind and helpless. How shall I ever hunt again or win Merope for my bride?"

In his despair, Orion consulted an oracle, which answered him, "O Orion, you shall regain your sight if you travel east to the place where the sun rises. The warm rays of the sun shall heal your eyes and restore their power."

But how could a blind man find his way to that distant place? Orion followed the sound of the Cyclopes's hammers to the forge of the god Hephaestus. When the god saw the blind hunter, he took pity on him and gave him a guide to lead him to the sun, just as it was rising.

Orion raised his eyes to the sun and, miraculously, he could see again. After thanking the sun, Orion set off for the island of Chios to take revenge on the king. But the king and his daughter had fled, possibly to Crete, and Orion went there to look for them. He never found them, but he met up with Artemis, goddess of the hunt, and spent his days hunting with her. They were a happy pair, roving through the woods, until Artemis's brother, Apollo, became jealous.

---

[3] **retaliated**—returned like for like, especially evil for evil.

Apollo sent a scorpion[4] to attack Orion. Orion could not pierce the scorpion's tough body with his arrows, but he dodged the poisonous insect and strode far out to sea.

Apollo was bent on destroying Orion, and he called to Artemis, "See that rock way out there in the sea? I challenge you to hit it."

Artemis loved a challenge. She drew her bow and aimed carefully. Her first arrow hit the mark, and Apollo congratulated her on her skill.

But when the waves brought Orion's body to the shore, Artemis moaned with grief. "I have killed my beloved companion. I shall never forget him. And the world shall never forget him, either."

She lifted his body up into the sky, where he remains among the stars to this day—the mighty hunter, one of the most brilliant constellations, with his sword and his club and three bright stars for his belt.

---

[4] scorpion—a poisonous spider.

QUESTIONS TO CONSIDER

1. Do the gods create constellations for Andromeda, Castor, Pollux, and Orion as punishment or reward?

2. What is Cassiopeia's greatest fault?

3. How does this fault contribute to her downfall?

4. What does Orion do to anger Apollo?

The Great Flood

BY OLIVIA E. COOLIDGE

Almost every culture of the world has its own version of the great flood story. In most of these stories, the purpose of the flood is the same—to cleanse the earth of all that is evil. Usually, all that was left after the water had gone was a single man and woman. In Sumerian mythology, for example, there is a terrible flood caused by the god Ea. The mortal Utnapishtim and his wife are the only survivors. In the biblical flood, Noah and his wife survive, along with two of every beast and bird in the universe. In this myth from Greek and Roman mythology, an old woman—Pyrrha—and her husband—Deucalion—survive a flood that is created by Zeus and the other gods of Mount Olympus.

When evil first came among mankind, people became very wicked. War, robbery, **treachery,**[1] and murder prevailed throughout the world. Even the worship of the gods, the laws of truth and honor, reverence for parents and brotherly love were neglected.

Finally, Zeus determined to destroy the race of men altogether, and the other gods agreed. All the winds were therefore shut up in a cave except the South Wind, the wet one. He raced over the earth with water streaming from his beard and long, white hair. Clouds gathered around his head, and dew dripped from his wings and the ends of his garments. With him went Iris, the rainbow goddess, while below Poseidon **smote**[2] the earth with his trident until it shook and gaped open, so that the waters of the sea rushed up over the land.

Fields and farmhouses were buried. Fish swam in the tops of the trees. Sea beasts were quietly feeding where flocks and herds had grazed before. On the surface of the water,

[1] **treachery**—betrayals and lies.
[2] **smote**—struck sharply.

boars, stags,[3] lions, and tigers struggled desperately to keep afloat. Wolves swam in the midst of flocks of sheep, but the sheep were not frightened by them, and the wolves never thought of their natural prey. Each fought for his own life and forgot the others. Over them wheeled countless birds, winging far and wide in the hope of finding something to rest upon. Eventually they too fell into the water and were drowned.

All over the water were men in small boats or makeshift[4] rafts. Some even had oars which they tried to use, but the waters were fierce and stormy, and there was nowhere to go. In time all were drowned, until at last there was no one left but an old man and his wife, Deucalion and Pyrrha. These two people had lived in truth and justice, unlike the rest of mankind. They had been warned of the coming of the flood and had built a boat and stocked it. For nine days and nights they floated until Zeus took pity on them and they came to the top of Mount Parnassus, the sacred home of the Muses.[5] There they found land and disembarked to wait while the gods recalled the water they had unloosed.

When the waters fell, Deucalion and Pyrrha looked over the land, despairing. Mud and sea slime covered the earth; all living things had been swept away. Slowly and sadly they made their way down the mountain until they came to a temple where there had been an oracle.[6] Black seaweed dripped from the pillars now, and the mud was over all. Nevertheless the two knelt down and kissed the temple steps while Deucalion prayed to the goddess to tell them what they should do. All men were dead but themselves, and they were old. It was impossible that they should have children to people the earth again. Out of the temple a great voice was heard speaking strange words.

"Depart," it said, "with veiled heads and loosened robes, and throw behind you as you go the bones of your mother."

Pyrrha was in despair when she heard this saying. "The bones of our mother!" she cried. "How can we tell now where they lie? Even if we knew, we could never do such a dreadful

---

[3] stags—male deer.

[4] makeshift—thrown together.

[5] Muses—sister goddesses who ruled over song, poetry, and the arts and sciences.

[6] oracle—a shrine where a god, through a priest or priestess, was believed to answer questions.

thing as to disturb their resting place and scatter them over the earth like an armful of stones."

"Stones!" said Deucalion quickly. "That must be what the goddess means. After all Earth is our mother, and the other thing is too horrible for us to suppose that a goddess would ever command it."

Accordingly both picked up armfuls of stones, and as they went away from the temple with faces veiled, they cast the stones behind them. From each of those Deucalion cast sprang up a man, and from Pyrrha's stones sprang women. Thus the earth was repeopled, and in the course of time it brought forth again animals from itself, and all was as before.

Only from that time men have been less sensitive and have found it easier to endure toil, and sorrow, and pain, since now they are descended from stones.

QUESTIONS TO CONSIDER

1. How did the gods create the flood?

2. Why did Deucalion and Pyrrha kneel down and kiss the temple steps when they came to the temple?

3. Why do you think the gods allowed Deucalion and Pyrrha to repeople the earth?

How Shiva Got His Blue Throat

(Hindu myth)

BY ANITA GANERI

In Hindu mythology, there is a "trimurti," or trinity, of gods responsible for all life. In the trimurti, three gods, called Brahma, Vishnu, and Shiva, work as one to create, protect, and—at times— destroy life. Lord Brahma is the creator of life on earth. Lord Vishnu is the preserver of life, and Lord Shiva is the destroyer of life. Interestingly, Shiva the destroyer is also seen as a creator, since each time he destroys something, he paves the way for new life to flourish. As you read "How Shiva Got His Blue Throat," watch for this pairing of creation and destruction.

This is the story of how Lord Shiva, the destroyer, came to have a blue throat.

While the sea of milk was being churned, the great gods—Brahma, Vishnu, and Shiva—were watching from Mount Meru. They looked on as the Devas and Asuras pulled Vasuki, the serpent king, to and fro, setting Mount Mandara spinning and the sea foaming and frothing. Of course, the aim of the churning was to extract the amrita, the elixir[1] of eternal life, from the sea. But many other wonderful and beautiful things were cast up, too.

Among them were Parijata, the tree of paradise; Varuni, the goddess of wine; and Surabhi, the cow mother. A white horse appeared for Vishnu to ride on, and an elephant for Indra. And still the Devas and Asuras churned to bring forth the amrita.

Then there appeared a beautiful goddess. She was more beautiful than any goddess ever seen before, for she was Lakshmi, the goddess of beauty

---

[1] elixir—a liquid substance thought to have the power of changing lead or iron into gold or of lengthening life indefinitely.

and fortune. Lakshmi sat smiling on an open lotus flower,[2] and she held a lotus flower in one of her four hands. The world was full of praise and love for her. Now, Lakshmi had been born to be Vishnu's wife, and the Asuras had no claim to her, much as they wanted her for themselves.

In their anger they pulled Vasuki harder and harder and set Mount Mandara spinning faster and faster. Vasuki suffered greatly. In his pain he opened his jaws, and torrents of blue poison flowed out of his mouth and poured toward the Earth. Had this river of venom reached the land, it would have destroyed the whole world—all the gods, demons, people, and animals.

The gods and people alike begged Shiva to save them from such a terrible fate. Quickly Lord Shiva leaped forward and drank the poison in one gulp before it touched the Earth. The world was safe, but ever since then, Shiva's throat has been blue where the deadly liquid burned his neck. And this is how he came to be known as Nilakantha—the blue-throated one.

_____

[2] lotus flower—a large, fragrant, pinkish flower found in southern Asia and Australia.

QUESTIONS TO CONSIDER

1. Where do Parijata, Varuni, and Surabhi come from?

2. Why does Vasuki send blue poison down to earth?

3. What inferences can you make about Lord Shiva? What was he like?

Quetzalcoatl

(Central American and Mexican legend)

BY JOAN C. VERNIERO AND ROBIN FITZSIMMONS

The feathered serpent god, Quetzalcoatl, is one of the oldest and most important deities of ancient Mesoamerica. Quetzalcoatl is a mythical being with powers that extend to the earth, water, and air. Over the centuries, many Central American rulers have taken Quetzalcoatl as their ruling name, which has caused some confusion. In some cases, scholars aren't sure what is myth and what is historical fact. In the case of the following myth, historians are certain that during the 12th century there was a ruler named King Topiltzin who was driven from the city of Tula into the mountains. Topiltzin (who called himself Quetzalcoatl after assuming the throne) vowed to return, although it's doubtful that he promised to return as a serpent god with divine powers.

Quetzalcoatl lived in Tollan in a great house constructed of gleaming silver. The house was surrounded by sweet gardens with flowers of every color of the rainbow. The fields of his land were filled with maize, or corn, that grew so tall that the stalks cast shadows on the full moon. The rooms of Quetzalcoatl's palace reflected the red of the mountain peaks, the greens and blues of turquoise stones, and the yellow of wildflowers. A thousand brightly colored birds flew among the clouds over his house and landed in the trees, where they sang songs to the people all day long.

The people of Tollan learned many useful crafts from Quetzalcoatl. He taught them about the stars and constellations of the skies. They learned how to work with silver and gems, how to build a house, how to paint and carve and sculpt. Everything they learned was taught in the spirit of peace, for Quetzalcoatl only shared the knowledge of things that were creative and beautiful. There was no war in Tollan, no fighting or jealousy or hunger.

Far away in the distant mountains, where the gray storm clouds rested from their long journey across the sky, there lived a sorcerer called Tezcatlipoca. Unlike Quetzalcoatl, he lived his life in pursuit of trouble and strife. He found pleasure in bringing heartache to others. Looking down from his dark perch, he sent a chilling, destructive wind into the valley where Quetzalcoatl's house was situated. The flowers in the garden felt the cold blast of air, closed their blooms and died.

Quetzalcoatl looked out the window of his silver house and saw what had occurred. His heart was filled with sadness. He called to one of his loyal servants and spoke to him.

"There is someone who wishes to harm me. If I am to protect this place, I must leave here today."

The servant was confused by Quetzalcoatl's words, though he packed some food for him and some warm blankets. Then he took many bags of precious jewels and gems and packed them, too. As the cold winds continued to blow, Quetzalcoatl left Tollan and went to the mountains. Several of his servants followed him.

As he traveled into the wilderness, he was tracked by a jaguar.[1] He attempted to change his path many times to avoid the animal, but it was no use. The jaguar, who was really the evil Tezcatlipoca, had Quetzalcoatl's scent and was intent on hunting him.

Quetzalcoatl grew weary. He began to age, and the muscles of his arms and legs ached with fatigue. After he had crossed a great mountain range, he found a quiet valley, where he stopped for a while to rest. From one of the sacks, he took a mirror and looked at his reflection. Looking back at him was the face of an old, tired man. Homesick and discouraged, Quetzalcoatl threw the mirror into the tall grass. He thought of his beautiful home in Tollan, and the memories of it caused him to weep. His tears fell down upon the earth and left lasting marks on the stones.

The servants who accompanied him tried to raise his spirits by playing music on their flutes. For a time he forgot the bittersweet memories of his home and the constant sound of the jaguar who stalked him.

The sacks that Quetzalcoatl and his servants carried seemed to grow heavier and heavier with each mile they

---

[1] jaguar—a large, fierce cat of Central and South America, closely related to the leopard.

traveled. Quetzalcoatl decided to dump one of the sacks in the fountain Cozcaapan. It was the bag that contained his most precious treasures.

The men climbed higher and higher into another mountain range. It snowed and sleeted and hailed for days and nights. Eventually the loyal servants who had remained with Quetzalcoatl died from the bitter cold. He was left with only his memories and the taunting wind that came from the breath of Tezcatlipoca.

On the other side of the mountain, Quetzalcoatl found the sea. Upon seeing the great waters, he built a raft from snakes that he wove together. He sailed far away from the land, out into the middle of the ocean until he arrived in the land of Tlappallan, in the country of the sun. The jaguar spirit of Tezcatlipoca finally stopped pursuing him.

In Tlappallan he drank the waters of everlasting life and threw himself into a brightly burning fire. When the fire died, only the ashes of the kind and good Quetzalcoatl remained.

Some believe that Quetzalcoatl will return one day as a young, happy man, eager to teach the people of the world the good crafts of life, like weaving

and spinning and painting and creating beautiful things. In the meantime his spirit appears as brightly colored birds, soaring and diving high above the treasure he cast in the fountain in the mountains.

QUESTIONS TO CONSIDER

1. Why does Quetzalcoatl go to the mountains?

2. Who or what is Tezcatlipoca and why was he tracking Quetzalcoatl?

3. Why do you suppose Quetzalcoatl throws himself upon the fire?

The Creation of Humans

(Native American—Zuni legend)

BY JOAN C. VERNIERO AND ROBIN FITZSIMMONS

The Zuni are a North American Indian people of western New Mexico near the Arizona border. The Zuni lived in peace until they were first contacted by Spanish explorers during the 16th century. Eventually they were forced into a pueblo where they slowly began rebuilding their lives. The Zuni society traces its ancestral descent through the maternal line. In "The Creation of Humans," one of many fascinating Zuni myths, the storyteller explains the origin of humans. In addition, this myth explains the origin of heaven, hell, and an earth filled with peaceful people who were "many wonderful shades of white and red and bronze and yellow and black."

The only living thing that existed at the beginning of time was Awonawilona, or the Maker. The universe was **shrouded**[1] in darkness. The Maker, being wise and powerful, transformed himself into the sun. As the sun he cast light and warmth, where there had only been darkness. A great mist rose from the warmth mixing with the cool darkness, and the mist gathered together to form water. Then the Maker spread seeds that he had plucked from his own flesh, upon the water, and the seeds gathered together to form land. Two great beings sprang from the creations of the Maker, and they were Awitelin Tsita, or Mother Earth, and Apoyan Ta'chu, or Father Sky. They were joined together in marriage, a perfect union.

Before long, however, Mother Earth grew larger and larger and separated herself from Father Sky. When the time came for Mother Earth to give birth, she became concerned about

---

[1] **shrouded**—covered; screened.

the destiny of her children. She kept her unborn children within her until she could consult with their father. She asked Father Sky how the children would come to know one another, and know the things of the world. The Maker heard her question and sent her a great terra-cotta bowl. Mother Earth took the bowl in her two large hands and looked inside it. It was filled with water. Mother Earth pronounced, "Each country in this world will have a rim, as this bowl has a rim, and then our children will know the boundaries of all the lands. They will know when they have left one country and entered another." And so the mountains of the world were formed.

She stirred the water within the bowl until it made foam. The foam grew bigger and bigger. Mother Earth blew gently across the foam, which drifted through the air. The foam became clouds and delivered mist and rain to the earth.

The Sky Father thus declared, "As the foam waters the earth, it will make things grow. All types of plants and vegetation will grow in the world to feed our children." Then he opened his hands wide, and from the wrinkles and **crevices**[2] in each one, he took some corn grains. He sprinkled the grains onto the surface of the water in the bowl and from the grain, tall stalks of maize, or corn, grew.

Finally the offspring of the world were born. Mother Earth gave birth to many creatures: worms, insects, flowers, toads, serpents, and humans. The living creatures all multiplied very quickly. They did not communicate in the same language, nor did they walk the same way, nor eat the same food. The earth was a place of great confusion.

One of the offspring was filled with great wisdom. His name was Poshaiyankya. When he saw that his sisters and brothers were constantly fighting and causing disruptions, he appealed to the Maker to help. The Maker looked down and saw what was occurring. He knew that he had to help creation once more. He encouraged Mother Earth and Father Sky to give birth to twins. The twins were to become the ancestors of all humans. They were to be wise and intelligent, and restore order to the earth.

At first the humans lived on the first level of the world, which was

---

[2] **crevices**—narrow cracks or openings.

cold and dark. Mother Earth and Father Sky created a straw ladder for the people to climb upon so that they would reach another level. Those who could not climb to this new level stayed behind and became monsters and demons. The second level was still dark and cold, but more **spacious**[3] than the first. Many generations of people were born here, and their skin colors were wonderful shades of white and red and bronze and yellow and black. The people continued to climb until they reached the third level. Here they found warmth from the cold. They separated into nations and tribes and wandered over the land, each claiming a place for their kind in the world.

The final level was a cave called Tepahaian tehuli. The sun rose above the crests of the mountains, and the air was filled with singing birds. This level was sacred and was entered by those who were good and kind. The people learned of their heritage from the Sky Father and Earth Mother and respected them. They obtained valuable knowledge from their parents and were good, obedient children. This was the place known as Tek'ohaian ulahnane, or the world of Light, Knowledge, and Seeing.

---

[3] **spacious**—roomy.

QUESTIONS TO CONSIDER

1. Which of these beings is most powerful: the Maker, Mother Earth, or Father Sky? Explain.

2. Why does Poshaiyankya become dissatisfied with the offspring of Mother Earth and Father Sky?

3. According to this myth, what are the four levels of the universe? Which level is most desirable and why?

The Man Who Married a Star

(Brazilian myth)

BY MARTIN ELBL AND J.T. WINIK

"The Man Who Married a Star" is a little-known myth that most likely originated in the Amazon region of Brazil. The Chamacocos were probably a tribe native to the Amazon Basin, although there is some debate about when and where they lived. Notice how similar this myth is to the constellation myths of other cultures.

On a rich, green bank of the Muddy River there once lived a young hunter. In spite of his youth, he was renowned[1] for his bravery. No man past or present could match the accuracy of his bow. Jaguar pelts[2] in plenty adorned his house, and his huntsman's necklace of teeth and claws wound more than five times around his neck. Even the rich merchants from the far-off lands near the Western Mountains traveled great distances, on foot and by river, to **barter**[3] silver and turquoise for his precious furs.

The young hunter's tribe, the brave Chamacocos, took great pride in his fame, and there was not a single girl who would not gladly have become his wife. But in vain they cooked sweet porridge for him. Their smiles were wasted on the young man who preferred to live alone, only with his dear sister, Flower. And so it was that he enjoyed well his youth, riches and glory.

One day, very suddenly, he began to sicken and wilt. His face grew pale and his eyes lifeless. More and more often he left the merry company of his

---

[1] renowned—famed.

[2] pelts—animal skins with the hair or fur still on them.

[3] **barter**—to trade goods or services without the exchange of money.

young friends and set forth on long and lonely hunting expeditions, taking only his dogs. Always he returned burdened with magnificent prey, but sadder and sulkier each time.

"Tell me, what's happened to you, oh pride of the tribe?" asked the old chief Apochangra. "You seem like a shadow from the realm of the dead! You do not eat. You are no longer joyful. Which one of the sorcerers has stolen your happiness? What sore illness weighs you down?"

"No illness, wise Apochangra" answered the young hunter. "Do not ask what ails me for there is no hope. If I told you the true cause of my grief, you would think that I've gone out of my mind."

"You should not speak so, my boy," said Apochangra. "There is no trouble so great that some **remedy**[4] cannot be found to heal it. Only tell me, what is that dark stone on your heart?"

"Look to the black sky, O **Venerable**[5] One," said the hunter. "Do you see that beautiful silver star?"

The old chief nodded, for without a doubt, one star stood out from all the rest.

"Yes," said the hunter. "It is that one and no other. Only that star spreads such great light all around. No other is so beautiful. For the sake of her my peace is gone. I love her, my chief, and there is nothing I desire more than to marry her."

"What kind of words do I hear?" **lamented**[6] Apochangra. "Who ever heard of such a thing—to have a star for a wife? Has your fame blinded you? Are not the earthly girls of our own tribe good enough for you?"

From that time on the tribe began to avoid the sad hunter. Only his sister, Flower, remained faithfully by his side, but silently, in secret, she wiped away her tears. Surely, she thought, her brother's soul would soon leave his body and soar upwards to the heavens to join his beloved star.

One night, however, the young hunter fell to rest in a woodland clearing. As he slept, a silver brilliance appeared and grew wide over the tops of the trees. From its rays the most beautiful of maidens descended. She was dressed in robes of silver with strands of starlight woven through her raven-black hair.

---

[4] **remedy**—medicine or therapy.

[5] **Venerable**—worthy of respect or reverence.

[6] **lamented**—mourned.

"Wake up from your sad dream, O hunter."

"Who are you?" he whispered, but as the words fell from his lips, he knew.

"I am Yohle, the one you so much desire and for whom you have suffered so long. I could look upon your pain no more and so I've come to your earthly region," said the Star Maiden. "I will be your wife if you wish, but there is a difficulty to it."

"I will fight with all the world to win you, if need be!" said the hunter joyously.

"No, no," smiled Yohle. "The problem is that I am a star, a child of the night sky. If I stayed with you, you would have to keep me in darkness during the daylight hours. Thus, I would be your wife only at night, only for half a life. What then will become of your huntsman's fame?"

"What is all fame to me if I have you! I can go hunting at dawn."

"Well then, but what will you do with me when your village packs up and moves to another place, as it does every year?"

"Do not worry, my fair one. I will ask my sister, Flower, to weave a great basket with a tight lid for you. In it you will rest comfortably and sheltered from the sun's rays."

But Yohle had one more request. "It must be kept a secret that I live in your hut," she said. "Only your good sister should ever know of it—no one else!"

Yohle brought only happiness into her husband's house. Flower was light of heart at seeing her brother's joy, and so peacefully flowed the time under the roof of their hut. Star told Flower many secrets and taught her wonders never known on the face of the earth. Never had anyone seen such beautiful embroideries as those that adorned the clothes of the young hunter and his sister. The good Flower, with her new knowledge, went healing illness and disease, all the while singing songs of great joy.

Alas, curiosity and jealousy spoiled the sleep of the other villagers. Their suspicions consumed them like fire.

"Who lives in your house, O Flower?" they asked. "What a strange light shines from your hut at night! Whose silvery voice sings there after the sun has set?"

"Who would live there but my brother and I?" said Flower. The villagers turned away unsoothed, whispering among themselves.

And so it was until one day a most beautiful child was seen at the young hunter's house.

"Whose is that silvery child, Flower?" said the women.

"It is mine! Whose would it be?"

"Do not try to fool us!" hissed the women. "It cannot be yours." They nagged from dawn to sunset, but still Flower told them nothing.

"We must know what secret the hunter keeps hidden in his house," said the chief's wife to the others. "Have you noticed that huge basket which Flower guards by her side every time our village is on the move? She cares for it more than for herself. The secret is most surely to be found inside." And so they made a plan.

One day when the hunter was away they wrenched the basket from Flower's keeping. Flower was powerless against the strength of the other women, but in vain did they try to open the lid. Yohle held it firmly from inside.

"Leave me in peace, women!" cried Yohle.

Yohle would not let go of the lid, and so they kindled a great fire under the basket. Suddenly the Star Maiden burst from her abode in the form of a burning thunder flash! Clasping her little son in her arms she soared high into the sky.

When the young hunter returned he was filled with great rage and sadness. When night fell, however, the Star Maiden called down to him.

"Come, my husband, to my starry land. Here, there is no evil and enough wild game for all."

The hunter gathered up his dogs and set forth instantly on his long journey. Most surely he reached the land of stars. Even today we can see him. When the sky is dark with night, look high. There, near his brilliant loved one shines the great hunter. With his bow bent and arrow at the ready, he leads his pack of hunting dogs.

QUESTIONS TO CONSIDER

1. What is the chief's reaction when he hears that the young hunter has fallen in love with a star?

2. Who or what ruins the hunter's marriage and happiness?

3. What do you think was the original purpose of this myth?

Mythical Families

The Earth and Sky give birth to the twelve Titans.

MOTHER EARTH (GAEA)
AND
FATHER SKY (URANUS)

The six male Titans married their six sisters, the Titanesses. The most famous of them were Cronus and Rhea, parents of Zeus.

MALE	FEMALE
OCEANUS	THEA
COEUS	RHEA
CRIOS	THEMIS
HYPERION	MNEMOSYNE
JAPET	PHOEBE
CRONUS	TETHYS

Metis, a Titan's daughter, helps Zeus trick Cronus into spitting up his five brothers and sisters. Then Zeus joins forces with them to make Cronus flee. Zeus becomes lord of the universe. He builds a palace on Mount Olympus and rules from there with the other gods and goddesses. Together they are known as the gods and goddesses of the Olympiad.

HERA—Zeus's queen

ARES—god of war

HEPHAESTUS—god of fire

APHRODITE—goddess of love

HERMES—messenger of the gods

DEMETER—goddess of the harvest and mother of Persephone

POSEIDON—brother of Zeus

HADES—brother of Zeus

ATHENA—daughter of Zeus

APOLLO—one of Zeus's twins

ARTEMIS—the other of Zeus's twins

DIONYSUS—youngest of the gods

Cronus and Rhea have six children, but Cronus becomes jealous of them and swallows all but one—Zeus.

HESTIA

DEMETER

HERA

ZEUS

POSEIDON

HADES

▲

Zeus

Above is one of the many hundreds of existing Greek sculptures
of Zeus. Most paintings and sculptures depict Zeus in exactly this way,
with a strong, full face and a long, flowing beard.

Hera

This sculpture of Hera is a Roman copy of an ancient
Greek original. (Quite a few pieces of art from ancient
Greece have survived the centuries, although far more have
been lost.) Notice the power conveyed by Hera's pose.
In some circles, Hera was feared as much, if not more, than
her husband Zeus. ▶

Hades

In this line engraving, the Greek god Hades is guarded by Cerberus, his three-headed, serpent-tongued watchdog. Although he ruled the Underworld, Hades was not an evil or cruel god. He was an extremely private god, however. He seldom allowed anyone who entered the Underworld to leave again. ▶

Poseidon

This is a detail of a Greek statue of Poseidon that dates from the years 460-450 B.C. This statue was created near the start of what is known as the Hellenistic period in art. During the Hellenistic period, sculpture was the most popular art form. Some of the most famous statues and sculptures in the world, including the *Venus de Milo,* were created during this period.
▼

Demeter
possibly by Leochares, c. 330 B.C.
This marble statue of Demeter, which has been partially
destroyed, was probably created by the gifted mason
Leochares. Because of its decorative appearance and
strength, marble was prized by the ancient Greeks for
its use in architecture and statuary. ▶

Hermes au Repos (Hermes in Repose)
Hermes was thought of as the rambunctious god. He was
a friendly, likable young immortal whose job was to travel
here and there delivering messages for the other gods and
goddesses. Here he is seen in a moment of rest, although
most storytellers were quick to point out that Hermes
rarely rested or even slept. ▶

▲

Aphrodite
by Thomas Matthews Rooke, 19th century
This oil painting shows the beautiful Aphrodite, goddess of love, who was perhaps the most powerful of all the Greek goddesses. Although she was married to Hephaestus, she had numerous love affairs with mortals and immortals alike.

Apollo
by Dosso Dossi, c.1530-40
Apollo, son of Zeus and Leto, was the god of prophecy,
medicine, and fine arts. This oil painting shows the god
holding a viol and a bow. ▶

◀ **Artemis**
Artemis was the sister of Apollo and the virgin goddess
of hunting and the moon. This marble statue, entitled
"Artemis the Huntress," is a replica of a Greek original
that was created during the fourth century B.C.

▲

Ares

Ares, god of war, was the powerful son of Zeus and
Hera. He was a bloodthirsty fighter who was disliked
by most of the other gods and goddesses. In this line
engraving, he is shown with a spear and shield, ready as
always for battle.

Athena

Athena, daughter of Zeus, was the goddess of
wisdom, practical arts, and war. Unlike the violent Ares,
Athena was brave, just, and peace-loving. She is
traditionally depicted wearing a helmet, as she is in this
Roman marble statue, copied from a fifth-century B.C.
Greek original. ▶

▲
Mosaic of Dionysus

This mosaic, which was created around A.D. 180, was found in the House of Masks on the
island of Delos. It shows Dionysus, god of wine and ecstasy, who is said to have enjoyed riding
in a golden chariot pulled by leopards.

Part Three

Parents and Children

"Still glimpsing the earth, the brilliant sky, the billowing, fish-filled sea and the rays of the sun, Persephone vainly hoped to see her beloved mother again."

◀ **Demeter and Persephone**

Persephone, wife of Hades, was forced to live half of each year in the Underworld with her husband. Her mother, Demeter, mourned the absence of her beloved daughter and waited eagerly to see her again. This Greek vase shows Persephone bidding farewell to her mother as she returns to her gloomy home.

Demeter and Persephone

BY PENELOPE PRODDOW

Aside from the strange bond between Oedipus and his mother, there is probably no parent-child relationship more interesting or memorable in Greek mythology than the one between Demeter and her daughter, Persephone. For the Greeks, Demeter was everything a mother was supposed to be: loving, loyal, and ferociously protective. For her part, Persephone was always the "perfect" daughter, although Hades, Charon, Cerberus, and all the other spirits who made their home in the dark Underworld would probably have disagreed.

Now I will sing
of golden-haired Demeter,
the awe-inspiring goddess,
and of her trim-ankled daughter,
Persephone,
who was **frolicking**[1] in a grassy meadow.

She was far away
from her mother.

With the deep-girdled daughters of Ocean,
the maiden was gathering flowers—
crocuses, roses and violets,
irises and lovely hyacinths
growing profusely together,

---

[1] **frolicking**—romping, joking, jesting.

with one narcissus[2] . . .

This was the snare[3]
for the innocent maiden.

She knelt in delight
to pluck the astonishing bloom
when, all of a sudden, the wide-wayed earth
split open
down the Nysian[4] meadow.

Out sprang a lord
with his deathless horses.
It was He Who Receives Many Guests,
He Who Has Many Names.

Seizing Persephone,
he caught her up in his golden chariot
despite her laments.

Her screams were shrill
as she shrieked for her father, Zeus,
but no one heard
except kind-hearted Hecate
from her cave
and Helios, the sun.

Still glimpsing the earth,
the brilliant sky,
the billowing, fish-filled sea
and the rays of the sun,
Persephone vainly hoped to see her beloved mother
again.

---

[2] narcissus—a white or yellow flower, grown from a bulb, with a trumpet-shaped center.

[3] snare—trap.

[4] Nysian—of Nysa, the mountain where Zeus sent the infant Dionysus to protect him from the anger of Hera.

The peaks of the mountains
and the ocean depths
resounded
with her immortal voice.

And her stately mother heard.
A sudden pang
went through Demeter's heart.

She set off like a bird
wildly
over the bodies of water
and the dry stretches of land,
but no one would tell her the truth—
not a god,
not a mortal,
not even a long-winged bird of **omen**.[5]

She circled the earth
for nine days
steadily,
brandishing[6] shining torches.

At the dawning
of the tenth,
Hecate approached,
holding a pine torch in her hands.

"Demeter!" she said.
"Bringer of the Seasons!
Giver of Rich Gifts!
What god in heaven,
what mortal,
has caused your heart such torment

---

[5] **omen**—a sign of what is to happen; an object or event that is thought to mean good or bad fortune.
[6] **brandishing**—waving or flourishing (a weapon, for example) menacingly.

and taken your daughter?
I heard her cries
but I did not see
who he was!"

They both hurried on
to the sun,
the watchman of gods and of men.

"Helios!" cried Demeter.
"Have pity on me—goddess that I am.
I bore a child
whose frantic voice I heard
through the barren air
as if she had been overpowered,
but I saw nothing.
Tell me,
was it a god or a mortal
who stole away my daughter
against her will—and mine?"

"Fair-tressed Demeter!" Helios replied.
"No one is guilty
among the immortals
but Zeus,
who gave her to Hades
to be his youthful bride.

"Now, Goddess,
you must stop this violent weeping!

"The Ruler of Many is not undesirable
as a son-in-law.
He wields great power,
for he is king over the dead,

with whom he lives
in the underworld."

Anguish
rent[7] the goddess's heart—
savage and terrible.

Embittered with black-clouded Zeus,
she departed broad Olympus
and the gatherings of the gods.
From that time forth,
she sought the villages and fields of mortal men
with her face disguised.

No one knew her
until she reached the palace of **prudent**[8] Celeus,
lord over fragrant Eleusis.

There by the roadside
she sank down
at the Well of the Maiden
in sorrow—
seemingly some poor old woman,
fit only for nursing a wise king's children
or keeping his shadowy halls.

The king's four daughters
saw her
when they came up with their golden pitchers
to draw the sparkling water.

"Where have you come from,
elderly mortal?"
they cried.

---

[7] **rent**—ripped.

[8] **prudent**—wise and practical.

"Lovely maidens!" Demeter replied.

"Pirates seized me
and bore me over the broad sea's back
by force—but I escaped
and came hither.

"On me, young girls, have pity!
Where can I go
to take up the tasks
allotted to elderly women—like myself—
such as nursing a newborn child in my arms?"

"Gentle woman!" said Callidice,
the fairest of Celeus' children.

"Wait,
while we go to our mother,
for she has a newborn child."

Swiftly the four
sped to their mother
and she bade them bring the woman
at once
and promise a generous reward.
Back they bounded,
holding their full skirts high,
barely touching
the shady paths,
and their hair streamed over their shoulders—
the color of yellow crocuses.[9]

Her heart aching for Persephone,
Demeter covered her head with a veil
and followed
behind the maidens.

---

[9] crocuses—small, hardy, flowering plants that bloom early in the spring.

When they came to
the palace of god-favored Celeus,
the goddess stepped on the portal[10]
and her head came up to the rafters.
The splendor of an immortal
shone
in the doorway.

Awe seized their mother, Metaneira.

"Good Lady,
your birth cannot be **lowly**,"[11]
she exclaimed.

"Here is my only son—
Damophon—
whom the gods bestowed upon me
as a companion for my old age.
If you nurse him
and he grows up handsomely,
then women throughout the land will envy you,
so great will be your reward."

"Great Lady," replied Demeter.
"May the gods grant you riches!
I will bring up your son wisely."

His mother rejoiced.

The boy then grew like a god.
He never ate food
nor drank any milk—
Demeter was feeding him ambrosia[12]

---

[10] portal—entrance.

[11] **lowly**—having or suited for a low rank or position.

[12] ambrosia—the food of the gods, in Greek and Roman myth.

by day,
as if he were the child of a goddess.

And, without the knowledge of his doting parents,
she put him to sleep
by night
in the embers of the fire.

The goddess would have made him
deathless and immortal
in this fashion,
had not Metaneira,
foolishly peeping out from her chamber,
spied her one night.

"My son!" she shrieked.
"This stranger is putting you in the fire!"

The bright goddess turned about.
Furious at the mother,
Demeter took the child
from the fire
and thrust him from her
with immortal hands.

"Senseless mortals!" she raged.
"You cannot see whether your fate
is good or bad,
even when it comes upon you!
I would have made your boy
deathless and immortal
all his days.
For I am dread Demeter!
"Now, let this land build me a temple
and a broad altar
to win back my favor."

Then the great goddess flung off her disguise
and her beauty appeared.
The light in her eyes
filled up the strong halls
like a flash of lightning.

She departed from the chamber.

Quickly, the Eleusinians
built the temple.
When they had finished,
they all returned to their homes.

But golden-haired Demeter
remained
enthroned within,
far from all of the festive gods,
wasting away with longing
for her graceful daughter.

She made that year
most shocking and frightening
for mortals
who lived on the nourishing earth.

The soil did not yield a single seed—
Demeter kept them all
underground.

In vain,
oxen hauled many curved ploughs
over the meadows.

Now, she was about to cause
the race of chattering men
to die out

altogether
from frightful hunger,
depriving those who lived on Olympus
of their lavish gifts and sacrifices.

Then Zeus noticed . . .

He sent golden-winged Iris first
to summon her.
On swift feet,
Iris spanned the distance
to Eleusis—now laden with incense—[13]
and found Demeter
within her temple,
clad in a dark gown.

"Demeter!" she announced.
"Father Zeus
in his infinite wisdom
calls you back to the family
of the undying gods."

Demeter's heart was unmoved.

Thereupon Zeus
sent forth all the gods—
the joyous beings who live forever.

Demeter scorned their speeches.
She vowed
she would not set foot on Olympus
nor let a fruit spring up on the earth
until she had seen
with her own eyes
the lovely face of her daughter.

---

[13] incense—sweet-smelling substance, burned to produce a pleasant odor.

Then Zeus dispatched Hermes
with his staff of gold.

Setting off from the Olympian seat,
Hermes dashed down
at once
into the depths of the earth.
He found Hades
in his halls
on a couch with his tender bride—
who was listless
out of longing for her mother.

"Dark-haired Hades!" said Hermes
"Zeus commands me
to bring back fair Persephone.
Her mother is planning a horrible deed—
to starve the tribes
of earth-dwelling mortals
and so, to deprive the gods
of their offerings!"

The king of the dead
raised his eyebrows,
but he did not disobey Zeus's order.

"Go, Persephone," he said,
"back to your dark-robed mother!"
Persephone smiled,
as joyfully she sprang up from the couch,
but stealthily the lord of the dead
spread out about her
delicious pomegranate seeds
to make sure she would not remain
forever
at the side of her noble mother.

Soon after, Hades
harnessed up his deathless horses
to the golden chariot.

Persephone leapt into the car.
Hermes seized the whip and the reins
in his skillful hands
and they drove off together
away from the land of the dead.

Hermes guided the horses
to Eleusis where Demeter sat
waiting,
and they drew to a halt
in front of her incense-filled temple.
Demeter,
catching sight of Persephone,
flew forward
like a maenad[14] on a mountain.

But, as she clasped her daughter,
she suspected treachery.

"My child!" she cried in fear.
"Could you have eaten anything
in the land of the dead?"

"Truthfully, Mother!"
exclaimed Persephone.
"When Hermes arrived from Zeus,
I arose with joy.
Then Hades brought out delicious pomegranate
    seeds
and urged me to eat them."

---

[14] maenad—a frenzied or raging woman.

"In that case,
you must return
to the land of the dead," said Demeter,
"for one third of the rolling seasons.

But when you come back
to me
for the other two,
the earth will burst into bloom
with flocks of sweet-smelling, spring flowers—
a great marvel to all men."

At that moment,
Wide-ruling Zeus
sent a messenger—
Rhea
with a golden band in her hair.

"Demeter, my daughter," said Rhea,
"Zeus wishes you
to return to the company of the gods.
Yield to him,
lest you carry your anger
toward dark-clouded Zeus
too far.

"And now,
bestow some nourishing fruit
on mortal men!"

Bright-garlanded Demeter
did not disobey.

Immediately, she caused the fruit
to grow in the fertile fields
and soon the wide earth
was weighed down
with buds and blossoms.

Hail to you, Demeter,
Lady of Fragrant Eleusis,
Leader of the Seasons and Giver of Shining Gifts,
you and your most beautiful daughter Persephone,
look kindly on me
and in return for my song,
grant abundant life to follow.

QUESTIONS TO CONSIDER

1. What can you infer about the speaker of this poem?

2. Why does Demeter disguise herself before she goes into the villages of the mortals?

3. Why does Demeter grow angry with Metaneira?

4. What do you think is the purpose of this myth?

Oedipus

BY INGRI AND EDGAR PARIN D'AULAIRE

The story of Oedipus has fascinated people for centuries. What kind of man would kill his father and marry his mother? What would drive him to do such a terrible thing? Scores of writers, storytellers, poets, playwrights, musicians, and artists have offered their own ideas about it. Sophocles, one of the great tragic dramatists of all time, presented his view of the myth in his play Oedipus Rex *(429–425* B.C.). *Aeschylus did the same in* Seven Against Thebes. *Voltaire, Shakespeare, Thomas Hardy, and Fyodor Dostoyevsky all wrote their own versions of the famous myth. In art, the French painter Gustave Moreau created his influential painting* Oedipus and the Sphinx; *in music, the composers Georges Enesco, Igor Stravinsky, and Jean Cocteau all offered unique versions of the same powerful myth.*

One day a blind old man came to Theseus and asked for permission to stay in his kingdom and die in peace. No one dared let him stay in their country, for he was pursued by the **avenging**[1] furies, the Erinyes. Homeless he wandered about. The old man, whose name was Oedipus, then told Theseus his sad story.

His misfortunes had started before he was born. His father, King Laius of Thebes, had been told by the oracle of Delphi that the child his queen, Jocasta, was carrying was fated to kill his father and marry his mother. This must never happen, thought the king, so when Oedipus was born he ordered a servant to take the child away and abandon him in the mountains. But destiny had willed it differently. A shepherd from the neighboring kingdom of Corinth heard the child's cries. He picked up the little boy and carried him to his king. The King and Queen of Corinth were childless and happily they adopted the handsome little boy.

---

[1] **avenging**—inflicting a punishment or penalty in return for a wrong.

They loved him dearly and he never knew that he was not their real son. Without a care in the world he grew to manhood, and one day went to Delphi to find what the future had in store for him. Great was his horror when he heard the words of the oracle! He was destined to kill his father and marry his mother.

This must never happen, thought Oedipus. He took destiny in his own hands and fled across the mountains, never to see his dear parents again.

On a narrow mountain path, he met the chariot of a **haughty**[2] lord. "Give way for our master's chariot," shouted the servants, and tried to push Oedipus off the path. Angrily Oedipus fought back and in the struggle the lord and all his servants were killed, except for one who escaped. Oedipus continued on his way and came to the city of Thebes. But its seven gates were closed. Nobody dared to enter or leave, for a monster, the Sphinx, had settled on a cliff just outside the city wall. This winged monster with a woman's head and a lion's body challenged all who passed by to solve her riddle. If they couldn't, she tore them to pieces. Nobody yet had solved the riddle of the Sphinx.

"What creature is it that walks on four feet in the morning, on two at noon, and on three in the evening," she asked with a sinister leer[3] when she saw Oedipus.

"It is man," Oedipus answered. "As a child he crawls on four. When grown, he walks upright on his two feet, and in old age he leans on a staff."

The Sphinx let out a horrible scream. Her riddle was solved and she had lost her powers. In despair she threw herself to her death. The gates of Thebes burst open and the people crowded out to thank the stranger who had freed them. Their old king had recently been killed, leaving no son to inherit the throne and when they heard that Oedipus was a prince from Corinth, they asked him to marry their widowed queen and become their king. To be sure, Queen Jocasta was much older than Oedipus, but she was still beautiful, for she wore a magic necklace that the gods had given Harmonia, the first Queen of Thebes. Those who wore that necklace stayed young and beautiful all their lives. Thus Oedipus became King of Thebes,

---

[2] **haughty**—scornful and proud.

[3] leer—evil glance.

and he ruled the city justly and wisely for many years.

One day the news reached him that the King of Corinth had died the peaceful death of old age, and while he mourned his father, he was glad that he had been spared from a terrible destiny. Shortly afterward, a **pestilence**[4] broke out in Thebes and people died in great numbers. Oedipus sent for a seer[5] and asked how he could save his people. The pestilence would last until the death of the old king had been avenged, said the seer. Oedipus swore that he would find the man who had killed the old king, and put out his eyes. He sent his men to search till they found the one surviving servant of King Laius's party. When he was brought before King Oedipus, the servant recognized him at once as the slayer of the old king! And now the whole terrible truth came out, for he was also the selfsame servant who had abandoned the infant Oedipus in the mountains, and had known all the while that the child had been found and adopted by the King of Corinth.

In despair Queen Jocasta went to her room and took her own life and Oedipus in horror put out his own eyes and left Thebes, a broken old man.

His daughter Antigone went with him, and they wandered from place to place, turned away from every city, till, at last, they came to Athens.

"Not cursed but blessed will be the place where you lie down and close your eyes," said Theseus when he had heard the story. "No man could have tried harder than you to escape his destiny."

The avenging Erinyes, who had been chasing him, now dropped their whips, and Oedipus could die in peace.

His two sons, Eteocles and Polynices, had no regard for the sufferings of their father. They stayed in Thebes and fought over the throne. At last they agreed to take turns being king, one year at a time. Eteocles ruled Thebes first, and when his year was up he refused to give up the throne.

Polynices left Thebes in a rage, taking with him the magic necklace of Harmonia, vowing to return with an army and take his rightful throne by force.

He went to his father-in-law, the King of Argos, and tried to persuade him to send an army to Thebes. The king had an aging and very vain sister

---

[4] **pestilence**—a fatal epidemic disease such as the plague.

[5] seer—one that sees the future; a clairvoyant.

who had great influence over him. Polynices promised her the magic necklace of Harmonia, which would make her young and beautiful again, if she could persuade her brother to go against Thebes. So great are the powers of a vain woman that, not only the King of Argos and his men, but seven armies of brave men set forth with Polynices to storm the seven gates of Thebes, most of them never to return.

Neither could the seven armies storm the seven gates of Thebes, nor could the Thebans drive the attackers away. So it was decided that the two brothers should fight in single combat, the winner to be king.

Eteocles gave his brother a **mortal**[6] wound, but Polynices, before he fell, dealt him a deadly blow in return.

Side by side they lay dead on the field, and all the bloodshed had been in vain.

The son of Eteocles became King of Thebes, and Harmonia's necklace, which had brought so much misfortune, was hung up in a temple in Delphi, so no woman would ever wear it again.

---

[6] **mortal**—fatal.

QUESTIONS TO CONSIDER

1. Why does Oedipus blind himself?

2. What message does this myth convey about trying to escape one's destiny?

3. How did Harmonia's magic necklace affect people?

4. Why do you think people are so fascinated by the myth of Oedipus?

The Ungrateful Daughter

BY SALLY BENSON

"The Ungrateful Daughter" tells the story of Scylla, King Minos of Crete's lovely daughter. Princess Scylla's story is not nearly as well known as that of another Scylla—Scylla, the monster with a woman's face and six snarling, ferocious dogs for a body. Interestingly, both Scyllas have a unique ability to destroy whomever or whatever gets in their way.

Minos, king of Crete, seeking to enlarge his territories, made war upon Nisus, king of Megara. The **siege**[1] had lasted six months and the city still held out, as it had been **decreed**[2] by fate that it could not be taken so long as a certain purple lock of hair remained on King Nisus's head.

Nisus had a daughter named Scylla. Every day she went to a tower on the city walls which overlooked the plain where Minos and his army were encamped. There she could look down on the tents of the invading army. The siege had lasted so long that she had learned to distinguish the leaders of the forces, and Minos, in particular, excited her admiration. In his plumed helmet with his shield in hand, he was a striking figure, and when he drew his bow, Apollo himself could not have done it more gracefully. But when he laid aside his helmet and rode his white horse, his purple robes flowing in the wind, Scylla was overcome with delight. She envied the weapon that he grasped, the reins that he held. She felt as if she could fly to him through the hostile ranks; she wished she could cast herself down from the tower into the midst of his camp, or open the gates to him—if only she could speak with him.

---

[1] **siege**—the state of being surrounded.
[2] **decreed**—ordered.

As she sat in the tower, she thought, "I know not whether to rejoice or grieve at this sad war. I grieve that Minos is our enemy, but I rejoice at any cause that brings him to my sight. Perhaps he would be willing to grant us peace and receive me as hostage. I would fly down, if I could, and alight[3] in his camp, and tell him that we yield ourselves to his mercy. Yet, that would be betraying my father! No! Rather would I never see Minos again. And still, sometimes it is the best thing for a city to be conquered when the conqueror is clement[4] and generous. Minos certainly has right on his side. I think we shall be conquered. And if that must be the end of it, why should not love unbar the gates to him instead of war? Better spare delay and slaughter if we can. What if anyone should wound or kill Minos? No one would have the heart to do it, surely. Yet someone might. I will! I will surrender myself to him with my country as a dowry,[5] and so put an end to the war. But how shall I do it? The gates are guarded and my father keeps the keys. He alone stands in my way. O, that it might please the gods to take him away. But why ask the gods to do it? Another woman, loving as I do, would remove with her own hands whatever stood in the way of her love. And can any woman dare more than I? I would encounter fire and sword for Minos. Here there is no need for fire and sword. I need only my father's purple lock. More precious than gold, it will give me all I wish."

She sat there until night came on and the whole palace slept. Silently, she crept to her father's bedchamber[6] and taking a dagger from the girdle[7] of her robe, cut off his purple lock of hair. She unfastened the keys to the city from around his neck and stole to the gates. While the sentry[8] dozed,[9] she opened them a mere crack and quietly slipped through.

Stopped at the entrance to the enemy's camp, she demanded to be led to the king. Minos was sleeping, but arose when he received her message and permitted her to appear before him. "I am Scylla," she said. "It is for love of you that I have betrayed my country. Look! Here is the purple

---

[3] alight—come down and settle gently.

[4] clement—merciful; mild.

[5] dowry—money or property brought by a bride to her husband.

[6] bedchamber—bedroom.

[7] girdle—belt around the waist.

[8] sentry—guard.

[9] dozed—slept lightly.

lock from my father's head! With this I give you my father and his kingdom."

She held out her hand. Minos shrank back and refused to take the lock. "The gods destroy thee, **infamous**[10] woman!" he cried. "You are the disgrace of our time! May neither earth nor sea give thee a resting place: Surely, my Crete, where Jupiter himself was cradled, shall not be polluted with such a monster!"

Turning from her in disgust, he gave orders that terms should be allowed to the conquered city. He bade his army to depart in friendliness, and ordered the fleet to sail home.

Scylla was **frantic**[11] when she heard these commands. "Ungrateful man," she screamed, "is it thus you leave me? I have given you victory. I have sacrificed father and country for you! I am guilty, I confess, and deserve to die. But I shall not die by your hand!"

She threw herself to the ground and lay there while the invading army made ready for their departure. As the ships started to leave the shore, she leaped into the water and seizing the rudder of the one which carried Minos, she was **borne**[12] along, an unwelcome companion on their journey.

Back in the city Nisus learned of his daughter's **treachery.**[13] He cursed her to the gods, and they changed him into a sea eagle and bade him follow her. He soared across the waters, and seeing Scylla clinging to the rudder below, he pounced down upon her, and struck her again and again with his beak and claws. In terror she let go of the ship and would have drowned if some kindly deity had not changed her into a bird. The sea eagle still cherishes his hatred and now when he sees her in his lofty flight, you may see him dart down upon her, with beak and claws, to take vengeance for the ancient crime.

---

[10] **infamous**—disgraceful.

[11] **frantic**—excited with fear.

[12] **borne**—carried.

[13] **treachery**—betrayal.

QUESTIONS TO CONSIDER

1. How does Scylla feel about Minos?

2. In what ways is Scylla an ungrateful daughter?

3. Why did Scylla seize the rudder of Minos's ship?

4. Do you feel sorry for Scylla? Why or why not?

Phaeton and the Chariot of the Sun

BY GERALDINE MCCAUGHREAN

In Greek mythology, Helios was the sun god. His radiance lit the sky day after day, month after month. The Greeks invented the myth of Helios to help explain the movement of the sun over the course of a 24-hour period. According to the storytellers of long ago, each morning Helios would harness his glowing chariot and drive his strong horses up the steep path to heaven. At high noon, he would reach the top and stop for a long rest. When he and his horses felt fresh again, they raced back down the other side of the course—toward the west—faster and faster. By the time they returned home again, dusk had covered the land. According to the Greeks, Helios failed his course only once—on the day he allowed his son to drive the chariot.

Once, the weather was always pleasant, no matter where, no matter when. Each day, as now, the sun god Helios mounted his fiery chariot and rode through the Portals of Dawn, up into the sky. Nothing deflected him from his path across the blue **cosmos,**[1] though each day the route changed a little, according to season.

It was from up there that he saw the **nymph**[2] Clymene and fell in love with her. They had three girls and a boy—Phaeton—and although the girls were content to help their father harness the horses to his sun chariot, Phaeton wanted more.

"May I drive, Father? May I? One day? May I, please?"

"No," said Helios. "You haven't the strength. You haven't the art. The task is mine, and too much depends on it."

---

[1] **cosmos**—universe.

[2] **nymph**—a young female deity who lives in nature.

But Phaeton kept on **wheedling**[3] and pleading for a chance to drive the chariot, and his foolish mother joined in on his behalf. "Let him, Helios. Let him drive it. Just once. Then perhaps he'll give us some peace."

"No," said Helios.

But Phaeton was a spoiled boy and accustomed to getting his way. At last he wore out the patience of Helios.

"Drive it, then! But for my sake and your own—take care. Drive no faster than I drive, and keep to the appointed path!"

Angry at himself for giving in, Helios withdrew to a **turret**[4] of dark cloud, away from his pestering family.

Laughing and teasing, Phaeton's sisters happily harnessed the horses. Nostrils flared, hoofs stamping, the horses sensed an unfamiliar weight on the running board, unfamiliar hands on the reins. And no sooner did Phaeton lay hold of his father's golden whip than he cracked it in their ears.

From standing, they leaped to a gallop, eyes rolling, teeth clenching the bit between their teeth. Dawn that day was a flash of orange on the horizon, and then it was noon.

This was thrilling, exhilarating! Phaeton gave a whoop of triumph and braced his knees against the chariot sides. Perhaps a little slower, he thought. But when he did draw back on the reins, the stallions simply reared up and tossed their heads, **wrenching**[5] his arms in their sockets, burning his hands as the reins pulled through his fingers. The chariot wheels left their well-trodden[6] track.

To left and right the chariot slewed,[7] evaporating cloudbanks, scorching flocks of birds. The world's soothsayers[8] looked up and foretold miracles and catastrophes as the sun zigzagged around the sky.

Phaeton tried to take control by **flogging**[9] the horses with the golden whip. "Stop, I said! Slow down! Stop!" But the stallions only panicked under the whip, ducked their heads, and plowed downward—down toward the earth.

Where the fiery blaze of the chariot passed close to the earth, its forests caught fire, and black smoke rose off waving fields of flame. Rivers turned to steam, lakes boiled, and even the

---

[3] **wheedling**—trying to get one's way using flattery.

[4] **turret**—small tower on a building.

[5] **wrenching**—sharply pulling.

[6] well-trodden—worn and familiar.

[7] slewed—slid off course, skidded.

[8] soothsayers—people who predict the future.

[9] **flogging**—whipping.

shallow fringes of the sea dried to salt pans, white and peppered with dying fish.

Phaeton pulled on the reins till his fingers bled. At the last moment, the horses lifted their heads before they would crash into the earth. But now they stampeded so high into the sky that the air was too thin to breathe.

Far below, the earth was robbed of its warmth; crops died, the sea froze. Sweat streaming from the necks of Helios's horses fell in large, fluffy flakes, and rivers slowed into glaciers of ice.

The blood vessels standing proud on their sweat-dark necks, the horses plunged up and down, to and fro in a **frenzy**[10] of panic. And beneath them the face of the earth was transformed forever—burned or frozen or flooded. The animals found their habitats[11] transformed. The bears went north, seeking coolness, the penguins went south. Monkeys fled jabbering to the jungles, and the people sought shade or warmth.

Phaeton hauled on the reins till the reins frayed through on the chariot's copper prow,[12] and snapped.

Helios emerged from his turret of cloud, his face white as the moon. "What have you done?" he howled.

Zeus emerged from the Cloudy Citadel. "What have you done, Helios, letting a child play with your chariot? My world is in ruins, and what ruin is still to come if he isn't stopped?" From his armory of thunderbolts, Zeus took the largest.

"No! No! Not my son!" screamed Clymene.

"No! No! Not Phaeton!" cried his sisters.

Zeus glared at Helios, and the sun god bowed his head. "It is the only way," he agreed.

The thunderbolt flew with perfect aim as Phaeton clung in terror to the wildly veering chariot. It struck him on the forehead, and he fell without a cry, terribly slowly, somersaulting and wheeling through clouds, past skeins[13] of geese, and into the blue of the sea. The broken reins were found still gripped in his hands when his sisters carried him ashore and buried him.

Three tall slender exclamations of grief, they stood by his grave swaying and moaning. "It was our fault,"

---

[10] **frenzy**—wildly excited state.
[11] habitats—environments.
[12] prow—projecting forward part.
[13] skeins—flocks.

they wept. "We helped to harness the horses." But it was no one's fault but Phaeton's. Too proud, too rash, too spoiled, and too stupid, he brought ruin to whole **tracts**[14] of his planet, and shame to his father.

Seeing the three sisters, Zeus took pity on them and turned them into poplar trees, tall, slender, and waving. But still they wept, tears of amber welling through their tree bark in big golden drops that caught the sun.

---

[14] **tracts**—large areas.

QUESTIONS TO CONSIDER

1. What is Helios's job and why is it important that he can let no one else do it?

2. Why do the horses panic when Phaeton drives them?

3. What happened to earth when the horses flew very high into the sky?

4. In your opinion, was Phaeton, alone, to blame for the disaster or were others responsible as well?

The Birth of Pan

BY MORDICAI GERSTEIN

*Even those who have never read a Greek myth know about Pan, the playful god of nature. Pan,
who was actually a lonely and moody god, had a goat's legs, an elf's face, and was covered
all over with shaggy black hair. Some myths say that when Pan was born, his mother, a nymph,
ran screaming and crying from the room. In all accounts of his birth, however, Pan's father—
Hermes, messenger to the gods—greeted his son with great joy.*

*As a child, Pan was quick to laugh and quick to anger. When he was in a happy mood, he
would dance his way through the meadows and forests of earth, all the while playing sweet
melodies on his pipe. When he was in a foul temper, however, he would hide in a cave, howling
and screaming for all to hear.*

It was not on Mount Olympus but in a beautiful gardenlike valley in Arcadia that Pan was born. While his father Hermes, the quick messenger of the gods, was rushing around the world delivering the mail, Pan was getting ready to make his appearance. The midwife listened at his mother Dryope's belly for the baby's heart.

"I don't believe it!" she yelped, falling off her chair. "I hear giggles and **snickering!**"[1]

Pan was born a minute later. He came out laughing, shouting, and kicking his little legs in all directions. When the nurse saw that they were goat legs, she screamed. She ran out the door smack into Hermes, who was just getting home.

"Is it a boy or a girl?" Hermes asked her.

The nurse screamed again. Then she ran down the road and out of sight. Hermes rushed in and his happy wife showed him their new son.

---

[1] **snickering**—laughing in a sly or hidden manner.

His heart filled with joy when he saw that along with the goat legs, the baby had two curly little horns growing out of his forehead, and a curly little beard on his chin.

"This is the son I've always wanted!" cried Hermes, kissing his wife. He took the baby in his arms, all wrapped in mountain rabbit skins, and flew right through the roof.

Hermes flew straight to Mount Olympus to show off his son to the other gods. He put the baby right in Zeus's lap.

"What is this?" asked Zeus, unwrapping the rabbit skins.

The baby jumped up laughing and kicked Zeus in the nose. Zeus looked at him and began to laugh too. Then all the gods began to laugh. They passed the baby around and even Hera, the crabby queen, had to smile. They called him Pan because he delighted all their hearts. Pan means "all."

QUESTIONS TO CONSIDER

1. How would you describe the midwife's reaction to Pan?

2. Why did the sight of Pan delight the gods?

3. How would you describe Hermes's reaction to his son?

4. Why do you think Pan, god of nature, was born with horns, goat legs, and a laughing, happy manner?

Glooscap and the Baby

(Native American—Algonquin myth)

BY RICHARD ERDOES AND ALFONSO ORTIZ

The Algonquin tribes of North America told many stories about Glooscap, or First Man, who is both trickster and god. The story of "Glooscap and the Baby" is an interesting one because it pits Glooscap (a great warrior) against a tiny baby no bigger than the warrior's hand. Can you guess who will win this contest of wills?

Glooscap, having conquered the Kewawkqu, a race of giants and magicians, and the Medecolin, who were cunning sorcerers,[1] and Pamola, a wicked spirit of the night, besides hosts of **fiends, goblins, cannibals,**[2] and witches, felt himself great indeed, and boasted to a woman that there was nothing left for him to **subdue.**[3]

But the woman laughed and said, "Are you quite sure, master? There is still one who remains unconquered, and nothing can overcome him."

In some surprise Glooscap inquired the name of this mighty one.

"He is called Wasis," replied the woman, "but I strongly advise you to have no dealings with him."

Wasis was only a baby, who sat on the floor sucking a piece of maple sugar and crooning a little song to himself. Now Glooscap had never married and was ignorant of how children are managed, but with perfect confidence he smiled at the baby and asked it to come to him. The baby smiled back but never moved, whereupon Glooscap imitated a beautiful birdsong. Wasis, however, paid no attention and went

---

[1] sorcerers—those who have supernatural power over others.

[2] **fiends, goblins, cannibals**—evil or wicked beings; ugly, elfin creatures; eaters of human flesh.

[3] **subdue**—to conquer and tame.

on sucking his maple sugar. Unaccustomed to such treatment, Glooscap **lashed**[4] himself into a rage and in terrible threatening accents ordered Wasis to come to him at once. But Wasis burst into **dire**[5] howls, which quite drowned the god's thundering, and would not budge for any threats.

Glooscap, thoroughly **aroused**,[6] summoned all his magical resources. He recited the most terrible spells, the most dreadful **incantations.**[7] He sang the songs which raise the dead, and those which send the Devil scurrying to the nethermost depths. But Wasis merely smiled and looked a trifle[8] bored.

At last Glooscap rushed from the hut in despair, while Wasis, sitting on the floor, cried, "Goo, goo!" And to this day the Indians say that when a baby says "Goo," he remembers the time when he conquered mighty Glooscap.

---

[4] **lashed**—moved swiftly or violently; thrashed.
[5] **dire**—urgent; desperate.
[6] **aroused**—stirred up; agitated.
[7] **incantations**—magic spells.
[8] trifle—a bit.

QUESTIONS TO CONSIDER

1. What kind of personality does Glooscap have?

2. Why can't Glooscap subdue the Wasis?

3. What lesson do you think is to be learned from "Glooscap and the Baby"?

Aladdin: A Most Faithful Son

(Arabian legend)

BY JOAN C. VERNIERO AND ROBIN FITZSIMMONS

The legend of Aladdin's lamp has been translated into many languages throughout the world. It is one of the most popular stories from The Arabian Nights, *which is a large collection of Arabian, Indian, and Persian tales written in Arabic between the 14th and 16th centuries. The* Arabian Nights *is actually a frame story, which means that it is a story within a story. The outer frame is the tale of the woman-hating Persian King Schahriah, who marries a different woman each night and then murders her the next morning. The bride Scheherazade tells the king a series of stories for 1001 nights, each night withholding the ending of the story until the following night. In this way, she saves her life. The legend of Aladdin, his mother, and a powerful genie is one of the stories Scheherazade tells.*

There once was a poor Chinese tailor who had a lazy, rude son named Aladdin. Despite the tailor's efforts to try and teach his son a **trade,**[1] the boy preferred to daydream and idle the hours away playing in the streets of the city.

When Aladdin's father passed away, it became his mother's burden alone to feed and clothe Aladdin.

One day an old man appeared in Aladdin's home, identifying himself as the brother of Aladdin's dead father. He told Aladdin's mother that he had come to see her, upon learning of his brother's death, and would try to teach her son a respectable trade so that he might have a good livelihood. Aladdin's mother was overjoyed at the news.

The uncle proposed that he open a shop for Aladdin. He gave him gold

---

[1] **trade**—an occupation, especially one requiring skilled labor; a craft.

and new clothing. He took Aladdin to many different lands to do business with merchants. On one such journey the two stopped in the desert to rest from their travels. Aladdin's uncle built a fire for warmth. Then he did something quite strange. He threw a handful of dust into the fire and recited bizarre words that Aladdin could not understand.

The earth began to shake and tremble. With a mighty jolt a **crevice**[2] appeared in the sand, like a long, narrow tunnel. The uncle instructed Aladdin to crawl into the tunnel.

"In this tunnel are riches galore, Aladdin," his uncle told him. "Climb in and secure them for me. Please be careful not to touch anything else you see." Then the man added, "Take this lamp with you so that you can see what you are doing. When you have gone deep into the tunnel, empty the oil from the lamp and blow out the light. Tuck the lamp into your belt. Be certain to bring the lamp back to me."

Aladdin was confused, but did as the man asked. He crawled down into the crevice in the sand. To his amazement, he saw enormous trees bearing jewels and precious gemstones in every color of the rainbow. Some of the stones were the size of his fist.

Aladdin gathered as many as he could, blew out the light of the lamp, emptied the oil from it, and returned to the surface. He reached out his hand to his uncle for assistance in climbing out of the tunnel, but his uncle refused.

"Give me the lamp first, and then I will help you," he told Aladdin.

As his arms were full of gems, Aladdin could not give the lamp to his uncle. "I will give it to you as soon as I am out!" he told the man.

But Aladdin's uncle did not listen. He grabbed several stones from Aladdin's arms, then pronounced more strange words. The tunnel began to close around Aladdin. He fell helplessly to the bottom.

Aladdin now knew that his uncle was not his uncle at all, but really an evil magician. He rubbed the old lamp in his belt, in hopes of coaxing a bit more oil from its sides so that he could light another fire, but it was hopeless. Or nearly hopeless.

From the spout of the lamp, a stream of **unearthly**[3] gas appeared. It rose over Aladdin's head and collected itself into the shape of an odd-looking man.

---

[2] **crevice**—a narrow crack or opening; a fissure or cleft.
[3] **unearthly**—not of this earth; supernatural.

"I am the genie[4] of the lamp," the figure said to Aladdin. "Until you emptied the oil of this lamp in the presence of the treasure buried here, I was doomed to remain inside the lamp forever. Now I am free. What is it that you desire, O Master?"

Aladdin rubbed his eyes. He could not believe what he was seeing.

"Anything that I want?"

"Yes," answered the genie.

"Please, return me to my mother," Aladdin asked him. No sooner had he said the words, then the genie blinked his eyes, and Aladdin was transported to his mother's home. She was overjoyed to see her son, safe and sound.

"You must never share this lamp with your uncle, or let him know that you are alive," she told Aladdin when he related to her what had happened that day.

The genie granted Aladdin and his mother many wishes. No longer did his mother have to work hard to earn money for food. They had all they could hope for.

Years passed and Aladdin and his mother were very happy, until one day Aladdin expressed his desire to marry the sultan's[5] daughter.

"You cannot do this," his mother told him. "You are the poor son of a tailor!"

Aladdin replied, "But I am the poor son of a tailor who has a lamp. With the genie's help I can wear fine clothes and present many wondrous things to this princess."

"Even so," his mother answered him, "the princess you wish to marry is promised to the grand wezir's[6] son. They are to be married this very morning."

Aladdin panicked. Perhaps it was too late to make his dream come true. He rubbed the lamp and asked the genie for help. Together they devised a special plan. On the night that the grand wezir's son married the princess, the genie placed a spell on him. Instead of sleeping in the bedroom of his new bride, the bridegroom decided to sleep outdoors under some orange trees. The bride was greatly distressed and asked her father what she should do.

---

[4] genie—a supernatural creature who does one's bidding when summoned.

[5] sultan's—belonging to the sultan, the ruler of a Moslem country.

[6] wezir's—belonging to the wezir, a high officer in the Moslem government; also spelled vizier.

"Perhaps he is just tired from a long day of festivity," the sultan told her. "Give him another chance to be with you this evening."

On that evening, though, the wezir's son slept in the horse stables. The princess was very distraught. "I believe he does not love me," she told her father. "Is there no one who loves me enough to be my husband?"

Before the sultan could answer his daughter, a young man stepped from the courtyard. He was dressed in fine clothing and carried a magnificent sword of gold.

"I am Aladdin," he told the sultan, "a man of means and wealth. I have admired your daughter from afar. But, now, I believe the time is right to present myself to you, and ask for her hand in marriage."

The sultan looked at his daughter. He would have no trouble finding another suitor for her, for she was intelligent and beautiful, and the sultan's kingdom was worth a great deal. However, he saw something in his daughter's eyes that told him that she had found true love with the young man before her.

"Take my daughter and treat her well," he told Aladdin. "If you are kind and good to her, I will bestow[7] on you my kingdom and all my riches."

Aladdin promised he would love and cherish the princess. They were married in a wonderful ceremony, which was attended by his mother. And although Aladdin's evil uncle returned again to trick Aladdin into giving up the magic lamp, Aladdin was able to foil him, and keep it to the end of his days.

---

[7] bestow—to present as a gift or an honor.

QUESTIONS TO CONSIDER

1. In what ways is Aladdin a faithful son?

2. Why does the uncle bury Aladdin in the crevice?

3. What were Aladdin's first dreams, and what do they suggest that he valued?

4. In your opinion, is Aladdin selfish? Support your opinion.

Image Gallery

Women in Mythology

▲

Persephone
by Anthony Frederick Augustus Sandys, 19th century

In this portrait, the painter presents a highly detailed, though somewhat dreamlike view of the beautiful goddess Persephone. Here she is seen gathering leaves and flowers, which she so loved to do. The expression on her face, suggests Sandys may have captured her at the moment she first caught sight of Hades on his trip up from the Underworld.

Athena and the Centaur
by Sandro Botticelli, 15th century

A centaur was half-man and half-horse. Although most centaurs were vicious, they were also intelligent. The centaur Chiron was quite knowledgeable in the arts of hunting, healing, and prophecy. In this Botticelli painting, Athena, goddess of wisdom and the practical arts, consults with the centaur Chiron.

▼

Atalanta

This marble statue of the huntress Atalanta is unique because it shows a figure in motion. Most ancient Greek sculptors created statues that were *au repos*, or "at rest." Perhaps the sculptor reasoned that since Atalanta was unique among goddesses and mortals, it was only proper that she be depicted in a statue that was unique. ▶

Demeter Mourning for Persephone
by Evelyn de Morgan, 1907

Most paintings and sculptures of Demeter show her in a state of complete anger or utter despair. De Morgan's oil painting is no exception. Demeter spent so much time grieving over the kidnapping of her daughter that she was unable to enjoy the pleasures of life on Mount Olympus. ▶

▲

Pandora

H. Linton, late 19th century

In this line engraving, a lovely Pandora stands by the sea pondering whether or not she should open her box. In some paintings and sculptures, Pandora is shown as a confused or dim-witted young girl who is tricked into making a poor decision. In Linton's picture, however, Pandora clearly understands what she is about to do.

▲

The Ride of the Valkyries
by William T. Maud, late 19th century

In Norse mythology, the Valkyries were nine virgins who were
semidivine, meaning each was half-mortal, half-goddess. They
served as priestesses to the mother goddess Freya, who was
the goddess of beauty and love. Later, after Freya married Odin,
the Valkyries served the royal couple and waited on them at
their feasts. They also helped Freya in her important task of
deciding which mortals should live and which should die.

Isis

In Egyptian mythology, Isis was the mother goddess
of fertility and nature. She mourned the death of her
husband, Osiris, and protected her son, Horus, from his
enemies. Isis was also known for various magical abilities.
This ancient portrayal of the goddess, dated approximately
1300 B.C., is a painted relief from the Temple of King
Seti I at Abydos. ▶

▲

The Marriage Procession of Psyche
by Sir Edward Burne-Jones, 1894-1895
Because of her extraordinary beauty, Psyche won the love of the god Cupid and the jealousy
of Cupid's mother, Venus. This oil painting is Sir Edward Burne-Jones's vision of Psyche's wedding
procession. Her attendants are strewing rose petals.

▲

The Great Sphinx and the Pyramids of Giza
by David Roberts, 19th century
The sphinx, a mythological character with a lion's body and a human head, is an important figure in Greek and Egyptian legend. This lithograph portrays the Egyptians' vision of the character at Giza, Egypt. In Egyptian culture, the sphinx was often associated with images of royalty. In Greek mythology, the sphinx was an elegant, wise creature who tormented men with her infamous riddles.

▲

Goddess of the Underworld of Flames
by Bharat Kala Bhawan

In Hinduism, fire plays an important role in the act of sacrifice. In this image, the Goddess of the Underworld is surrounded by flames, raising her weapon as if waiting to receive an offering.

▲

Medusa
artist unknown, 19th century

Medusa was one of the three Gorgon sisters, whose gaze could turn a human or an animal into stone. Unlike her sisters Euryale and Stheno, Medusa was mortal. Her appearance, however, was otherworldly. She had serpents for hair, a huge, snake-like tongue, and teeth as long and sharp as the tusks of a boar.

◄ *Izanami*
artist unknown, late 19th century
In Japanese legend, Izanagi and Izanami were the god and goddess from whom Japan was created. In this silk scroll, they stand on the Floating Bridge of Heaven, stirring the waters of the sea with a magic spear, thereby creating the island of Onogoro. On Onogoro, they consummated their marriage, and then gave birth to the Japanese islands. Later, Izanami was burned to death while giving birth to the god of fire.

▲

Helen of Troy
by Sir Frederick Leighton, 19th century
Helen of Troy, thought to be the most beautiful woman in the world, was a daughter of Zeus and the wife of the powerful Greek King of Sparta, Menelaus. There are many variations of the story of Helen. Some myths say that she was quite happy to go off with the warrior Paris and leave Menelaus behind. Others say that she fought Paris desperately and had to be subdued before he could carry her off.

▲

Penelope

by Sir Frederick Leighton, 19th century

Penelope, wife of Odysseus, is often said to be the most faithful wife of all time. Shortly after they were married, Odysseus left to fight in the Trojan War. As soon as the ten-year war was over, Odysseus started for home, but the journey back took him another ten years. All told, Penelope waited twenty long years for her husband to return.

Part Four

True Love?

"He was the handsomest young man in all the land, while she was the most beautiful girl. As they grew older, it was almost inevitable that their childish friendship should turn into love."

◀ *African Man and Woman* by **Ashley Bryan**

Ashley Bryan used bold paint strokes and geometrical shapes to create this painting of young lovers. The closeness of the two figures suggests this might be a type of wedding portrait.

The Four Tasks: Cupid and Psyche

BY MARY POPE OSBORNE

Almost everyone knows about Cupid, the handsome god of love and desire. To be pricked by one of his arrows is to fall deeply in love with the first person you lay eyes on. "The Four Tasks" is unique, however, because it shows another side of Cupid. In Mary Pope Osborne's version of this story, Cupid accidentally turns one of his arrows upon himself and winds up falling hopelessly in love with a mortal named Psyche.

Long ago a king and queen had three lovely daughters. The two older ones were just a bit above ordinary. But the youngest, named Psyche, was the fairest and brightest girl in the kingdom. People began to desert the altars of Venus, the goddess of love and beauty, and worship Psyche instead. In fact, some were even beginning to call Psyche the second Venus.

Venus, furious about Psyche's fame, ordered her son Cupid to wound the princess with one of his arrows. "Avenge your mother!" she cried. "Make Psyche fall in love with the **vilest**[1] of men—the most miserable and meanest beast you can find!"

Cupid set out at once to do his mother's bidding. But when the god of love laid eyes on the fair maiden, he accidently pricked his own finger with one of his arrows—and he himself fell in love with Psyche.

Tormented by his sudden passion, Cupid immediately flew to Apollo, the god of light and truth, and asked for his help.

---

[1] **vilest**—most disgusting.

Soon afterwards all of Psyche's admirers mysteriously vanished. Her father couldn't understand why his daughter's suitors had stopped calling. Fearing the gods might be angry with him, he asked Apollo for advice.

"Perhaps it has been decreed your daughter is to marry a god," Apollo said. "Leave her alone on top of a mountain, and soon you will find out if a god wants her for his wife."

When Psyche's father returned home and reported what Apollo had said, a cry of grief went up from the household, for they all knew they would soon lose their beautiful Psyche. But since the commands of the gods must always be obeyed, the king and queen prepared their daughter for her lonely exile.[2]

The whole city lit torches. And to the sound of a lonely flute, people chanted a funeral hymn as they escorted the beautiful princess up a steep mountain. When they reached the topmost peak, Psyche spoke to her family and friends: "Fear not. Do not torment yourself with grief, but leave me now to meet my fate."

After her brave words, everyone bid her good-bye; and as they filed down the mountainside, their torches were nearly extinguished[3] by their tears.

Psyche also cried until she finally fell asleep on the deserted mountaintop. But while she slept, the gentle West Wind lifted her up and bore her down to a flowery plateau. And in the morning, when she woke, she found herself lying in a bed of grass before a great palace that had a roof of ivory and columns of gold. A chorus of sweet music filled the air, and the soft voices of invisible beings whispered in her ear, "All of this is yours now."

Psyche wandered about the golden, gleaming palace. She bathed herself in refreshing spring waters and ate a wonderful dinner, which invisible hands placed before her.

During the night, Cupid came to her. "You are my wife," he said in the dark. "I love you more than anything. But I must ask that you never try to look upon my face. I will only visit you in the night; but our nights will be glorious and filled with joy."

When Psyche asked why she could not look at him, Cupid only said, "Honor my request, for if you look upon me, we will be separated forever." Actually Cupid was afraid that if Psyche discovered he was the son of Venus, she would adore him as a god, rather than love him as an equal.

---

[2] exile—enforced removal from one's native place.

[3] extinguished—put out; quenched.

Psyche loved her nightly visits with Cupid, though during the day she was sad and lonely. One night, she asked her husband to allow her to send for her two older sisters.

"If they come here, it will be the beginning of our doom," Cupid said.

"Oh, no! Please, let them come!" Psyche begged. "If you won't allow me to see you, at least allow me to see my sisters!"

It saddened Cupid to hear these words, so he ordered the West Wind to bring Psyche's older sisters to her.

When the sisters arrived at the palace, they were overjoyed to find Psyche alive and well. But as soon as they began to look about and note the **splendor**[4] in which she lived, they grew envious. By the time they returned home, they were in a jealous rage because their own husbands were not as wealthy as Psyche's.

On their second visit to the palace, the sisters demanded to meet Psyche's husband.

"I'm afraid I cannot let you see him," she said.

"Why? Is he so ugly that you are ashamed?"

"No, he can't allow himself to be seen. Even I have not seen him in the daylight."

"What?" her sisters screamed.

"I try not to mind," said Psyche. "He's very gentle and kind, and he seems to love me more than life itself."

The two sisters grew more envious than ever when they heard how much Psyche's husband loved her. When they returned home, they tore their hair and wailed with sorrow because their own husbands were cold and unkind.

The sisters grew so jealous of Psyche, they decided to spoil her happiness. The next time they came to the palace, one said, "We don't believe your husband is so wonderful after all."

"Oh, but he is," said Psyche.

"Oh, but he is not!" said the other sister. "We've been to an oracle, and she said your husband is a **loathsome**,[5] horrible monster! And that's why he won't let you look upon him!"

"No! That's not true!" cried Psyche.

"It is! And what's more—she said he's just waiting for you to have his child, and then he plans to kill you!"

"No! No!" Psyche wept.

But finally her sisters persuaded her that her husband was indeed a horrible monster; and they convinced

---

[4] **splendor**—magnificence.
[5] **loathsome**—horrible; repulsive.

her that in the night, she must hold a lantern above him—and then cut off his head.

In the dark, all was quiet, except for the sound of Cupid's soft breathing as he slept. Psyche trembled as she slipped from their bed and fetched the oil lamp and knife she'd hidden earlier.

When she returned to bed, Psyche lit her lamp, then slowly lifted it above Cupid's head. She was stunned to see the flushed, shining face of Venus's son. Even her lamplight burned brighter with joy as it beheld the beautiful god.

In a daze, Psyche gently touched Cupid's golden curls and his white, shining wings and his quiver of arrows. When she touched one of his arrows, she pricked herself—and fell deeply in love with the god of love. Psyche felt such rapture she nearly swooned[6] to the floor. As she caught herself, a drop of oil fell from her lamp onto Cupid's shoulder.

Cupid woke up. When he saw Psyche staring wide-eyed at him, holding a knife in her hand, a look of sadness crossed his face. "My love, were you afraid that I was a hideous monster?"

Before Psyche could answer, he said, "There can be no love if there is not trust. I will never come to you again." And with those sad words, he started to fly away.

Crying out in grief, Psyche grabbed onto Cupid and clung to him as he soared high into the sky. But soon, overcome with weariness, she fell to the ground. Then she lay alone in the cold dark night, wishing she could die.

Thereafter, Psyche wandered the earth, searching for her lost husband. She didn't know that Cupid was as sad as she; and that he lay in bed at his mother's palace, wounded by his love for her.

Psyche desperately sought help from all the gods and goddesses, but none wished to incur the wrath of Venus. Only Ceres, the goddess of grain, would give her counsel.

"Seek Venus and beg her forgiveness," Ceres advised, "for her son now lies in her palace, mourning for you. And Venus tires of caring for him. Beg her to unite the two of you again."

But Venus let out a wild shriek when she saw Psyche humbly standing on her doorstep. The great goddess

---

[6] swooned—fainted.

ordered her handmaidens Trouble and Sorrow to fall upon the girl and tear her clothes and pull her hair.

When the dreadful attack was over, Venus smiled at Psyche who lay trembling on the ground. "Now, you want to see my son? Don't you know he loathes you and wishes to never lay eyes upon you again? Really, you are such a plain and unfortunate creature, I almost take pity on you. Perhaps I should train you to be more fitting for a god."

Venus then gave Psyche a task to perform. She led the girl to a storehouse filled with grains of many kinds. "Sort all these by evening," she said. And with that, she disappeared.

As Psyche stared hopelessly at the piles of barley, lentils, and poppy seeds, an amazing thing began to happen. An army of ants assembled; and within minutes, waves of ants crawled up the piles of grain. Each ant carried one tiny seed at a time—until all the seeds were sorted into three different piles.

When Venus returned at nightfall, she flew into a rage. "Someone has helped you!" she shrieked. "In the morning I demand you complete another task!" Then Venus threw Psyche a piece of hard black bread and left her to sleep on the cold threshing floor.[7]

The next morning, Venus pushed Psyche out into the rosy dawn. "Go to the pasture beside the flowing stream!" the goddess said. "There live the fierce rams with golden wool! Gather some of their fleece—and then you might be a person worthy of my son's love!"

Psyche stood by the flowing stream that bordered the pasture where the wild rams grazed. As she watched the beasts fight with one another, she knew she could never get near their wool without being killed. She felt such despair she wanted to drown herself in the stream.

But then a green swaying reed began to whisper melodically, "Do not slay yourself, Psyche. Nor approach those terrible sheep. In the noonday heat, when the sheep are napping, slip into the pasture and pick the golden wool that clings to the sharp briars[8] and thorny bushes."

At noontime when the drowsy rams lay down for a nap, Psyche crossed the stream and crept into the pasture. And within a short time, she had gathered all the golden wool that clung to the twigs and briars.

---

[7] threshing floor—place where the stems and husks of the grain were beaten to separate the grains or seeds from the straw.

[8] briars—prickly plants.

When Venus saw Psyche's wool, she smiled bitterly. "Someone must be helping you," she said, and she gave her yet another task. This time she wanted Psyche to fill a crystal goblet[9] with icy mountain water from the mouth of the Stygian[10] river.

Psyche took the goblet from Venus and began climbing the craggy rocks of the mountain. But when she got near the top, she realized this was the worst task yet, for the rocks near the mouth of the river were hopelessly steep and slippery. Just as she decided to fling herself off the mountain, an eagle flew over.

"Wait!" the eagle cried. "Give me the crystal goblet, and I will fly to the mouth of the black river and get water for you!"

Psyche gave her goblet to the eagle, and he held the vessel tightly with his fierce jaws as he flew to the mountain peak. After he'd filled the vessel and returned it to Psyche, she carried the dark water back to Venus.

When Psyche handed the goblet to Venus, the goddess accused her of being a sorceress. Then she gave Psyche the cruelest task of all: She ordered her to carry a box to the Underworld and ask Queen Proserpina for a small portion of her beauty.

Psyche knew this was the end, for never would she gain the courage to descend to the Underworld, the terrifying land of the dead. With great despair, she climbed to the top of a high tower and prepared to hurl herself to her death.

But just as she was about to jump, the tower spoke: "What cowardice makes you give up now, Psyche? Be kind to yourself, and I will tell you how to reach the Underworld and how to succeed in your quest."

After she promised not to kill herself, the tower told Psyche how to travel to the land of the dead. "Take two coins and two pieces of barley cake," the tower said. "A lame donkey driver will ask you for help, but you must refuse him.

"Then give one coin to Charon, the ferryman, and he will take you across the river Styx to the Underworld. As you cross the water, the groping hand of a dying man will reach out to you, but you must turn away. You must

---

[9] goblet—a stemmed drinking vessel.

[10] Stygian—of or pertaining to the River Styx or to Hades. The word *stygian* with a lowercase s can mean "evil" or "hellish."

also refuse to help three women weaving the threads of fate.

"When you come to Cerberus, the three-headed watchdog that guards the palace doors, give him a barley cake, and he will be friendly to you. Do all of this again on your way out. But most importantly, when you carry the box of beauty from Proserpina back to Venus, *do not open it*—whatever you do, *do not open the beauty box!*"

Psyche did as the tower told her, until finally she had secured the box of beauty from Proserpina, queen of the dead. Then she repeated her actions as she left the Underworld: She gave Cerberus a cake on her way out of the palace; she gave Charon a coin to take her across the river Styx; and she refused to stop for any who tried to ensnare her with cries for help.

But when Psyche was close to Venus's palace, a burning curiosity overtook her. She was dying to open the box and use a small portion of Proserpina's beauty.

Psyche gingerly lifted the lid of the box. But she did not find beauty inside—instead, she found a deadly sleep; and as the sleep overtook her, she crumpled to the road.

Meanwhile Cupid had escaped out the window of his palace room;

and as he was flying over the earth, searching for Psyche, he saw her lying unconscious beside the road.

Cupid hastened down to her and quickly gathered the sleep from her body and closed it back inside the box. Then he woke Psyche with a kiss.

Before Venus could catch them, Cupid lifted Psyche from the ground and carried her high into the heavens to Mount Olympus to the home of Jupiter, god of the skies; and he bid Jupiter to officially marry them.

After Jupiter married Cupid and Psyche, all of Mount Olympus celebrated the couple—except for Venus, of course. She raged about for weeks. But within the year, the aging goddess became the grandmother of a beautiful baby girl named Bliss.

QUESTIONS TO CONSIDER

1. Why does Cupid hide his face from Psyche?

2. What do you think of Cupid's proclamation, "There can be no love if there is no trust"? Explain your viewpoint.

3. Why does Venus dislike Psyche?

4. How do you feel about Psyche?

Pygmalion: Lover of Beauty

BY OLIVIA E. COOLIDGE

In classical mythology, there are two separate stories about Pygmalion. In the first, Pygmalion was a king who murdered his sister's husband in order to steal his wealth. In the second story, which the Roman poet Ovid tells in his Metamorphoses, *Pygmalion is a sculptor who falls in love with a statue he creates. To Pygmalion's great joy, Aphrodite brings the statue to life. "Pygmalion: Lover of Beauty" is a retelling of the myth that Ovid made famous.*

Pygmalion was a sculptor, a worker in marble, bronze, and ivory. He was so young and handsome that the girls as they went past his workshop used to look in and admire him, hoping that he would notice them. But Pygmalion was devoted only to his art. People seemed noisy and **trivial**[1] to him, and ugly too, for he had an image of beauty in his mind which caused him to work over his statues from morning to night, smoothing, re-working, always in search of a loveliness beyond his powers of expression. In truth the statues of Pygmalion were far more beautiful than human beings, and each statue was more nearly perfect than the last. Still in every one

Pygmalion felt that there was something lacking. While others would stand entranced before them, he never cared to look on anything he had finished, but was immediately absorbed in the next attempt.

At last, however, he was working on an ivory statue of a girl in which he seemed to have expressed his ideal in every way. Even before it was done, he would lay down the chisel and stare at his work for an hour or so together, tracing in his mind the beauty that was as yet only half unfolded. By the time

---

[1] **trivial**—not important.

the statue was nearly finished, Pygmalion could think of nothing else. In his very dreams the statue haunted him. Then she seemed to wake up for him and come alive. The idea gave him exquisite pleasure, and he used to dwell on it. The dreams passed into daydreams until for many days Pygmalion made little progress on his almost-finished statue. He would sit gazing at the maiden, whom he had christened Galatea, and imagining that perhaps he saw her move and the joy it would be if she actually were living. He became pale and exhausted; his dreams wore him out.

At last, the statue was actually finished. The slightest touch of the chisel now would be a change for the worse. Half the night Pygmalion gazed at the beautiful image; then with a hopeless sigh he went to bed, pursued as ever by his dreams. The next day he arose early, for he had something to do. It was the festival of Aphrodite, the goddess of beauty, to whom Pygmalion, since he was a seeker after beauty, had always felt a special devotion. Never once had he failed to give Aphrodite every possible honor that was due to her. In truth, his whole life was lived in worship of the goddess. There were many splendid gifts being given her,

snow-white bulls with their horns covered with gold, wine, oil, and incense, embroidered garments, carvings, offerings of gold and ivory. Both rich and poor came in turn to offer their gifts. As he approached the altar, Pygmalion prayed **earnestly**[2] and saw the fire that burned there leap suddenly in flame. Tense excitement stirred him; he could stay no longer; he must get back to his statue, though he did not quite know what he expected there. Galatea was as he had left her. He looked at her longingly once more, and again as he so often had, he seemed to see her stir. It was only a trick of imagination, he knew, because it had happened many times to him before. Nevertheless, on a sudden impulse, he went over to Galatea and took her in his arms.

The statue really was moving! He felt the hard ivory grow soft and warm like wax in his **clasp.**[3] He saw the lips grow red and the cheeks blush faintly pink. Unbelieving he took her hand and lifted it. As he pressed it, he felt the fingers gently tighten in his own. Galatea opened her eyes and looked at him. There was understanding in

---

[2] **earnestly**—sincerely.

[3] **clasp**—embrace.

her gaze. The red lips parted slightly, and as Pygmalion kissed them, they pressed against his own. Galatea stepped down from her pedestal[4] into Pygmalion's arms a living girl. The next day two lovers went to pray at Aphrodite's shrine, the one thanking her for the gift of life, the other that his dreams and prayers had been answered and his lifelong devotion to the goddess thus rewarded.

---

[4] pedestal—a base for a statue.

QUESTIONS TO CONSIDER

1. In what way is Pygmalion a "seeker of beauty"?

2. Why was Pygmalion unable to work on the statue of Galatea for a time?

3. What were Pygmalion's ideas of what is beautiful?

4. Why did Pygmalion and Galatea give thanks to Aphrodite?

Pyramus and Thisbe

BY SALLY BENSON

"Pyramus and Thisbe" first appeared in Ovid's Metamorphoses *in A.D. 8, many hundreds of years before Shakespeare wrote his* Romeo and Juliet, *and many thousands of years after Greek and Roman storytellers first began telling the myth. Ovid, who was perhaps the world's first great romantic, loved to write about love's complexities. In many of his stories, he explored this question: what are some of the ways that love can change us?*

In Babylon,[1] where Semiramis reigned as queen, there lived a youth named Pyramus and a maiden named Thisbe. He was the handsomest young man in all the land, while she was the most beautiful girl. Their parents occupied adjoining houses, and as children the two had been constant companions. As they grew older, it was almost **inevitable**[2] that their childish friendship should turn into love. Confronting their parents, they told them that they wished to marry, but the two families, for some reason, opposed the match. And Pyramus and Thisbe were forbidden to see, or even to speak to each other.

This was more than they could bear, and while they did not speak, they **conversed**[3] by signs and glances. Their love burned stronger and stronger every day, until one day, they discovered that the wall that divided the two houses had a small crack in it. Overjoyed by this discovery, they forgot what their parents had said, and whispered messages of love and encouragement through the tiny slit.

[1] Babylon—an ancient city of southwest Asia famed for its magnificence and culture.
[2] **inevitable**—impossible to avoid or prevent.
[3] **conversed**—talked.

As they stood, Pyramus on one side of the wall and Thisbe on the other, their breaths would mingle. "Cruel wall," they murmured softly, "why do you keep two lovers apart? But we will not be ungrateful. We owe you, we confess, the privilege of transmitting loving words to willing ears."

All day, they stood at the wall, whispering together, and when night came and they said goodbye, they pressed their lips to the stone.

Next morning, when Aurora, goddess of the dawn, had put out the stars and the sun had melted the frost from the grass, they met at the wall again. Rebelling against the cruelty of their parents, they decided they would slip away from their homes that very night and walk beyond the city's bounds, where they would meet at the Tomb of Ninus. The one who came first should await the other at the foot of a white mulberry tree that stood near a cool spring.

All day long, they waited impatiently for the sun to go down beneath the waters and the night to rise up from them. When it was dark, Thisbe crept out of the house, her head covered with a veil, and **stealthily**[4] making her way to the Tomb, she sat down under the mulberry tree to wait for Pyramus. As she sat alone, she saw a huge lioness, her jaws dripping with blood from a recent slaughter, approach the spring to drink. Thisbe fled in terror and hid in the hollow of a rock. As she ran, she dropped her veil, and the lioness, seeing the veil on the ground, tossed and tore it with her bloody mouth.

It was some time before Pyramus could leave his house without being observed, and when he arrived at the appointed meeting place, he was out of breath. There was no sign of Thisbe. In the sand, he saw the footprints of the lioness and he grew pale with fright. He followed the prints and came upon Thisbe's veil, torn and bloody. "O **hapless**[5] girl!" he cried in agony. "I have been the cause of thy death! Thou, more worthy of life than I, hast fallen first victim. I will follow. I am the guilty cause in tempting thee forth to a place of such **peril**,[6] and not being myself on the spot to guard thee. Come forth, ye lions, from the rocks, and tear this guilty body with your teeth!"

---

[4] **stealthily**—sneakily.

[5] **hapless**—luckless; unfortunate.

[6] **peril**—imminent danger.

He picked up the veil from the ground and carried it to a spot beneath the white mulberry tree, covering it with tears and kisses. For a while he lay there sobbing, then drawing his sword, he said, "My blood also shall stain your texture."

He plunged the sword into his heart. The blood spurted from the wound and tinged the white mulberries of the tree a dark red. It even sank into earth and the red color mounted through the trunk to the fruit.

Thisbe, hidden in the hollow of the rock, still shook with terror, but not wishing to keep her lover waiting too long, she **ventured**[7] forth and crept cautiously out. When she came to the spot where Pyramus was to meet her, she saw the changed color of the berries and doubted whether it was the same place. As she hesitated, she saw someone struggling on the ground in the **throes**[8] of death. Thinking the lioness had claimed another victim, she started to run away. Just then the moon appeared from behind a cloud and she recognized Pyramus dying at her feet.

She screamed and beat her breast. "O Pyramus," she cried. "What has done this? Answer me, Pyramus. It is your own Thisbe who speaks. Hear me, dearest, and lift your drooping head."

Pyramus opened his eyes and closed them again. Shuddering, he died.

Thisbe threw herself on his lifeless body. By his side she saw the empty scabbard[9] of his sword and, beneath it, her veil, torn and stained with blood.

She kissed him gently. "Thine own hand has slayed thee, and for my sake," she whispered softly. "I, too, can be brave for once, and my love is as strong as thine. I will follow thee in death, for I have been the cause. And death, which alone could part us, shall not prevent my joining thee. And ye, unhappy parents of us both, deny us not our united request. As love and death joined us, let one tomb contain us. And thou, tree, retain the marks of our slaughter. Let thy berries still serve for memorials of our blood."

She arose, and after a last look at Pyramus, plunged the sword into her breast.

When the distracted parents found the bodies of the beautiful maiden and the handsome youth, they were filled with **remorse**.[10] They appealed

---

[7] **ventured**—braved the dangers of.

[8] **throes**—agonizing struggle or trouble.

[9] scabbard—a sheath or case for the blade of a sword.

[10] **remorse**—moral anguish arising from repentance for past misdeeds; bitter regret.

to the gods, and the gods told them of Thisbe's dying wish. The two lovers were buried side by side in one **sepulcher,**[11] and the mulberry tree, forever after, brought forth dark red berries.

---

[11] **sepulcher**—a burial vault.

1. What was your first reaction to the story of Pyramus and Thisbe?

2. What does this story suggest about love?

3. At what point do Pyramus and Thisbe's parents allow the two lovers to be together?

Echo and Narcissus

BY HEATHER FOREST

Most myths about Echo and Narcissus usually are more like fables than other classical Greek and Roman myths. "Echo and Narcissus" was clearly intended to teach a lesson. In Heather Forest's retelling, two separate myths about Echo and Narcissus are combined into one, with Echo as the dominant character. It's interesting to note that from the stories about Narcissus comes the term narcissism, *which means "a love of self."*

Echo was a wood nymph, fond of forests and fields. Her only shortcoming was that she talked endlessly and always insisted on having the last word. One day as Zeus cavorted[1] in the forest with a group of lovely nymphs, his wife, Hera, came along the path. Echo intercepted Hera and diverted her with chatter while Zeus hastily left the woods.

Hera was not deceived, however. Infuriated[2] that Echo had prevented her from confronting Zeus's unfaithfulness, she said, "Echo, you will never speak another word of your own! From this moment forth you will only be able to repeat the last words of others."

In a rage, Hera returned to her home on Mount Olympus and left Echo **forlorn**[3] in the woods. Echo tried to speak, but to her horror, no sound came from her lips.

Before long, a handsome youth named Narcissus walked through the forest. Echo found him so attractive that her cheeks flushed red with passion. She pursued the sound of his footsteps and longed to express her love. Alas, she could not say the words she wished him to hear, for her tongue was silent.

---

[1] cavorted—jumped around.
[2] Infuriated—fiercely angry; enraged.
[3] **forlorn**—sad and lonely.

Narcissus stopped at the edge of a clear pool and bent over to take a drink. There in the water he saw his own image. He thought the beautiful face that gazed back at him was a water **sprite**.[4] He admired the soft, golden curls that curved around the radiant cheeks and **alluring**[5] eyes in the water. Soft lips, slightly parted, melted his heart. He said, "I love you."

Echo was ecstatic! He had said something she could repeat and yet truly mean to say. Standing in the bushes behind him and blushing, Echo repeated, "I love you."

When Narcissus heard these words, he thought that the face in the water had spoken. His fingers reached out to touch the image. The image reached out to him. But when he tried to caress his love, the image disappeared in the ripples. Filled with an unquenchable longing, he fell helplessly in love with himself. Unable to move, he gazed at his own reflection until he slowly withered away and died. Hermes came and led his sorrowful spirit across the River Styx to the Underworld.

A white flower with a deep purple center grew in the place where Narcissus had gazed at himself in the water. This flower still bears his name today.

Echo, meanwhile, lamented the loss of her love until she, too, faded away. Soon, nothing was left of her but her voice, which is still heard in hollow places, senselessly repeating the words of others.

---

[4] **sprite**—a small or an elusive supernatural being; an elf or a pixie.

[5] **alluring**—attractive; desirable.

QUESTIONS TO CONSIDER

1. Does Hera's punishment of Echo fit the crime? Explain.

2. From what you've read in this myth, what does it mean to be a narcissist?

3. What lessons did the Greek storytellers hope to convey with this myth?

Atalanta's Race

BY GERALDINE MCCAUGHREAN

Atalanta is a memorable character because there are so few classical myths about mortal women. Ancient storytellers often ignored women, unless the women happened to be goddesses. Atalanta, however, is a notable exception. Like Hercules, Atalanta first recognized her own strength when she was very young. As she grew older, she became faster and stronger and was known as a first-rate huntress. Unlike most of her male counterparts, however, Atalanta learned the importance of being patient and even-tempered.

On the island of Cyprus, in a lovely garden tended by Venus, the goddess of love, there grew an apple tree. It had yellow branches and yellow leaves but its apples were glittering gold.

Now, in the days when that tree was in fruit, there lived a beautiful girl called Atalanta. Men had only to see her to fall in love with her, but she had sworn never to marry. The young men pestered her to change her mind and grew tiresome. So she declared, "I will only marry the man who can race against me and *win*. But anyone who tries—and fails—must agree to die."

Despite the risk, many young men wanted to race Atalanta to win her hand. But she could run like the wind. The runners tried and the runners died, because they came in second.

A young man named Hippomenes had heard of Atalanta's races. He thought any boy must be stupid to throw his life away on a silly dare. But when one day Atalanta streaked by him, fast as a darting bird, he knew at once that he had to race for her.

When Atalanta saw Hippomenes, she did not want him to challenge her. He was too young and handsome to die. She half wanted him to win . . . but no! She had sworn never to marry.

A crowd gathered, impatient for another race, but Atalanta kept them waiting as she fretted about the result. And Hippomenes said his prayers.

"Oh, Venus!" prayed Hippomenes. "You plainly made me love this woman. So help me to win her!"

Venus heard him. She also thought Hippomenes too young and handsome to die. So she picked from the tree in her garden three golden apples and gave them to him. Now he was ready for the race.

"Ready, steady, go!" cried the starter.

Away went Hippomenes, as fast as he had ever run. Away went Atalanta, quick as a blink. She soon took the lead.

So Hippomenes threw one golden apple—beyond her, over her head. It caught the light. Atalanta ran to where it lay and picked it up. Hippomenes sped ahead.

But Atalanta caught up with him again and passed him, hair blowing like a flag. He ran faster than any of the other suitors, but it was not fast enough.

So Hippomenes threw another of the apples. Again Atalanta stopped to pick it up and again Hippomenes took the lead. But Atalanta was so much faster that she could stop, admire, pick up the shiny apple, and *still* catch up with him again.

Hippomenes ran faster than any man has ever run, but it was not fast enough. So he threw the third apple. Would Atalanta be fooled by the trick a third time? She saw—she slowed down—she glanced at the two apples in her hands . . . and she stopped for the third. The crowd cheered as Hippomenes dashed past her, lungs bursting, and threw himself over the winning line. He had won his bride!

And for a champion runner who has just lost a race for the first time, Atalanta looked extremely happy.

QUESTIONS TO CONSIDER

1. How would you describe Atalanta?

2. Is Atalanta someone to be admired?

3. Would Hippomenes have won the race without the help of Venus? Explain.

Frog and His Two Wives

(African folk tale)

BY ASHLEY BRYAN

"Frog and His Two Wives" is an age-old story retold by the incomparable Ashley Bryan, who has retold dozens of African folk tales in his career as a writer and storyteller. Bryan's "Frog and His Two Wives" is meant to be read or sung aloud. See if you can hear the beat of the drum and the tap of the dancer's feet as you read his musical narrative.

Listen, let me tell the story of Frog Kumbuto who married two wives.

"*Kuo-kua,*" he sang for one wife.

"*Kua-kuo,*" he sang for the other.

He sprang high into the air. *Whish!* Twirling both legs, he whirled himself about and came down. *Whump!* He jumped again into the skies. *Whee!* It was a wonder to have two wives.

Frog Kumbuto built each wife a good house of her own on his land.

The first wife chose the sycamore grove on the east of his land. There he built her house. *Bam!*

The second wife chose the palm grove on the west of Frog's land. There he built her house. *Bohm!*

The middle ground was where Frog liked to be. Berry bushes grew there with berries that Frog liked to lick, nibble, and bite for breakfast. And there was, as well, a tall nut tree for noonday shade and nuts; and nearby there lay a small rush marsh for an evening splash and bath. It was in the middle that Frog built his house. *Bosh!*

Well, the first wife cooked one meal for Frog each day. And the second wife cooked the other meal. The east house wife cooked for Frog as the sun rose in the east. The west house wife cooked for Frog as the sun set in the west. It was a fine plan. Frog swelled with pride when he saw how well it worked.

The sun shone day after day. And day after day for many months Frog ate at morning in the east and at evening in the west. But then the rainy season began.

Frog Kumbuto loved the rain. He sauntered about in delight. But by the thirteenth day of the rainy spell, Frog's two wives had become confused about the time of day. So it happened that one gray day, without knowing whether they were coming or going, the wives mixed up the mealtime plan. Well! Both began to cook for Frog at the same time.

Each wife fanned her fire and stirred her pot. Frog Kumbuto, not thinking about it, lay on his rush mat and smelled the delicious odor of juicy mush[1] from the east and the aroma of lush spicy mush from the west. *Haah!*

In time the mush was cooked. Both wives looked up to see if Frog was coming. But Frog had not moved. What!

The first wife called her little son and said, "Hop now and fetch your father!"

The second wife said to her small daughter, "Rush now and fetch your father!"

Both children left quickly to fetch Father Frog. Skipping and jumping and hopping from east and from west, they arrived at the same spot at the same time. *Thump!* They fell down on the rush mat beside Frog Kumbuto.

Regaining their feet and their breath, each child pulled one of Frog's arms as they sang out together, "Father come with me! Come with me! It's time to eat."

Now Frog was in a fix. He was pulled to the east. He was pulled to the west. Woe! He freed his arms and beat his breast.

"Oh, no!" he groaned as he spun around. He clutched his stomach. He pounded the ground.

"Both wives are calling, 'Come! Come! Come!' They are two, and I am one. If I go east to eat first, the west wife will **pester**[2] me. 'Aha,' she'll say, 'so east wife is your chief wife, eh?' If I decide to feast with the west wife first, then the east wife will cry, 'Aho, Kumbuto! From the start I thought the west wife was your best beloved!'"

Frog sat down and wailed. He was so upset that he **garbled**[3] his words. His cracked bass voice called out:

---

[1] mush—a thick porridge or pudding of cornmeal boiled in water or milk.

[2] **pester**—annoy; bother.

[3] **garbled**—mixed up or distorted.

"Rye bam in bubble! I tam tin tub-ble!" Till finally he croaked it right: "I am in trouble!"

Now friends, the story is as I have told it. Plucky Frog Kumbuto married two wives. All went well until the day that both called him to mush at once. To this day he does not know what to do.

He sits in the marsh and cries: *"Kuo-kua! Kua-Kuo!"*

It sounds funny, I know. Some people joke and say:

"Listen, Frog is croaking!"

But no! Frog is speaking. He is saying:

"I am in trouble!"

Pity poor Frog.

QUESTIONS TO CONSIDER

1. Why doesn't Frog Kumbuto simply pick one wife to eat with?

2. What clues do you have that "Frog and His Two Wives" began as an oral tale?

3. How do you feel about Frog Kumbuto? Do you admire or disapprove of him?

The Toad-Bridegroom

(Korean folk tale)

BY ZONG IN-SOB

"The Toad-Bridegroom" is a Korean folk tale similar to "The Frog Prince" and "Beauty and the Beast," although it's not nearly as well known. In this version of the story, an ugly-looking hero must be loved for who he is rather than what he looks like.

Long ago there lived a poor fisherman in a certain village. One day he went fishing in the lake as usual, but found he could not catch as many fish as he was accustomed to. And on each of the following days he found his catch growing smaller and smaller. He tried new baits, and bought new hooks, but all to no avail. At last even the water of the lake began to disappear, until in the end it became too shallow for fishing.

One afternoon in the late summer the bottom of the lake was exposed to view, and a big toad came out from it. The fishermen immediately thought that it must have eaten up all the

fish and angrily cursed the *samzog* or three families of the frog, its parents, brothers, wife and children, for it is popularly believed that the toad is a relative of the frog.

Then the toad spoke to him gently, rolling its eyes, "Do not be angry, for one day I shall bring you good fortune. I wish to live in your house, so please let me go with you." But the fisherman was annoyed that a toad should make such a request and hastened home without it.

That evening the toad came to his house. His wife, who had already heard about it from her husband, received it kindly, and made a bed for it in a corner of the kitchen. Then she brought it worms and scraps to eat. The couple had no children of their own, and decided to keep the toad as a pet. It grew to be as big as a boy, and they came to love it as if it were their son.

Nearby there lived a rich man who had three daughters. One day the toad told the fisherman and his wife that it would like to marry one of the three daughters. They were most alarmed at this unreasonable request and **earnestly**[1] advised it to forget such an impossible ambition. "It is utterly **absurd**,"[2] they said. "How can poor people like us propose marriage to such a great family? And you are not even a human being."

So the toad replied, "I don't care what the rank of the family is. The parents may object, but yet one of the daughters may be willing to accept me. Who knows? Please go and ask, and let me know what answer you receive."

So the fisherman's wife went and called on the mistress of the rich man's house and told her what her toad-son had asked. The lady was greatly displeased and went and told her husband. He was furiously angry at such a **preposterous**[3] suggestion and ordered his servants to beat the toad's foster-mother. So the poor woman returned home and told the toad of her painful experience.

"I'm very sorry that you have been treated like that, Mother," the toad said to her, "but don't let it worry you too much. Just wait and see what will happen." Then he went out and caught a hawk and brought it home. Late that night he tied a lighted lantern to its foot, and crept stealthily to the rich man's house. He tied a long string to the hawk's foot and then climbed a tall persimmon tree[4] which stood by the house. Then he held the end of the string in his hand and released the hawk to fly over the house. As it flew into the air he solemnly declared in a loud voice, "The master of this house shall listen to my words, for I have been dispatched by the Heavenly King. Today you rejected a proposal of marriage, and now you shall be punished for your arrogance. I shall give you one day to reconsider your decision.

---

[1] **earnestly**—sincerely.

[2] **absurd**—ridiculous.

[3] **preposterous**—contrary to nature, reason, or common sense; ridiculous.

[4] persimmon tree—a chiefly tropical tree, having hard wood and orange-red fruit that is edible only when completely ripe.

I advise you to accept the toad's proposal, for if you do not, you, your brothers, and your children shall be utterly destroyed."

The people in the house were startled by this **nocturnal**[5] proclamation from the sky, and they opened the windows to see what was going on. When they looked up into the sky they saw a dim light hovering overhead. The master of the house went out into the garden and kneeled humbly on the ground looking up into the sky. Then the toad let go of the string he held in his hand, and the hawk soared skywards with the lantern still tied to its foot. The rich man was now convinced that what he had heard was spoken by a messenger from Heaven, and at once resolved to consent to the toad's marriage to one of his daughters.

Next morning the rich man went and called on the toad's foster-parents, and apologized humbly for his discourteous refusal on the previous day. He said now that he would gladly accept the toad as his son-in-law. Then he returned home and asked his eldest daughter to marry the toad, but she rushed from the room in fury and humiliation. Then he called his second daughter, and suggested that she be

the toad's wife, but she too rushed from the room without a word. So he called his youngest daughter and explained to her that if she refused she would place the whole family in a most difficult position indeed, so stern had been the warning from Heaven. But the youngest daughter agreed without the slightest hesitation to marry the toad.

The wedding took place on the following day, and a great crowd of guests attended, consumed by curiosity at such an unusual happening. That night, when they retired, the toad asked his bride to bring him a pair of scissors. She went and got a pair, and then he asked her to cut the skin off his back. This strange request startled her greatly, but he insisted that she do so without delay, and so she made a long cut in his back. Then, lo and behold, there stepped forth from the skin a handsome young man.

In the morning the bridegroom put on his toad skin again, so that nobody noticed any difference. Her two sisters sneered **contemptuously**[6] at the bride with her repulsive husband, but she took no notice of them. At noon all the men of the household

---

[5] **nocturnal**—of, relating to, or occurring in the night.
[6] **contemptuously**—scornfully, hatefully.

went out on horseback with bows and arrows to hunt. The toad accompanied them on foot and unarmed. But the party had no success in the hunt and had to return empty-handed. The bridegroom stripped off his toad skin and became a man when they had gone, and waved his hand in the air. Then a white-haired old man appeared, and he bade him bring one hundred deer. When the deer came he drove them homeward, once more wearing his toad skin. Everyone was most surprised to see all the deer, and then he suddenly stripped off the toad skin and revealed himself as a handsome young man, at which their astonishment knew no bounds. Then he released all the deer and rose up to Heaven, carrying his bride on his back and his parents on his arms.

QUESTIONS TO CONSIDER

1. Why do the poor fisherman and his wife agree to let the toad live with them?

2. How does the toad convince the rich man to consider the marriage proposal?

3. What happens once the third daughter agrees to marry the toad?

4. What would you say is the storyteller's message in "The Toad-Bridegroom"?

What Does Woman Want?

(British myth)

BY BARBARA STANFORD WITH GENE STANFORD

The real King Arthur was most likely a Celtic British king or chieftain of 500 B.C. who led the Saxons in their successful invasion of England. However, the King Arthur you've heard most about is an imaginary character who lived during the Age of Chivalry. This is the King Arthur that Sir Thomas Malory describes in his prose epic, Morte d'Arthur. In Sir Malory's retelling of the King Arthur stories, Arthur is born to Igraine and King Uther Pendragon. He is tutored by the magician Merlin and assumes the throne of England after he pulls the Excalibur sword from a rock. According to Sir Malory, Arthur began a round table for his knights of Camelot, a group that included his nephew, Sir Gawaine (or Gawain).

"What Does Woman Want?" is a retelling of one of the Arthurian legends. It has a more contemporary feel than most King Arthur stories, perhaps because the storyteller felt the legend needed a little modernizing.

King Arthur one day was hunting in the woods when suddenly he met a well-armed knight who stopped him and challenged him to fight.

"But I am not armed," protested Arthur.

"All right, then," replied the knight, "I will give you a chance to escape according to your rules of chivalry.[1] I will give you a riddle to solve and a year in which to solve it.

Next year at this time you must return to the same spot, again unarmed, and give me the answer to my riddle. If you fail, then I can kill you without violating your code. The riddle is, 'What is the thing that women desire most?'"

Arthur pledged to return and went back to his castle quite disturbed.

---

[1] chivalry—qualities of an ideal knight, such as bravery, honesty, and courtesy.

Sir Gawaine noticed how upset he was and asked what the problem was. Arthur explained what had happened.

"That is no problem at all," said Sir Gawaine. "All we have to do is ask some women. Surely we will get the answer very quickly."

"That is a very good idea," said King Arthur. "Let's both travel throughout the country and ask for answers. We can write down all of the answers in a book so that we will not forget any."

So both traveled through the country for several months. But the **quest**[2] turned out to be more difficult than it had appeared at first. All of the women said something different. The young women wanted husbands, married women wanted to be rich, sick women wanted to be well, and old women wanted to be young again. There did not seem to be anything that all women wanted.

---

[2] **quest**—search or hunt.

So when only one month remained in the year, King Arthur set off again. This time he came to a forest and found within it the ugliest hag that had ever been seen on the earth. King Arthur was so repelled by her appearance that he was going to ride right past her instead of asking for her answer, but she stood in the road and stopped him.

"Why are you riding so fast through the woods that you do not have time to greet a lonely woman?" she demanded.

"I am on an important quest," replied Arthur **curtly**,[3] trying to get around her.

"And I know the only answer to the question you have been asked that can save your life," replied the hag slyly.

"Then tell me quickly," said Arthur.

"On one condition only. I would like to have a husband. And I think one of your knights would do fine. So I will tell you the answer to your question when you obtain the promise of one of your knights to marry me." With that she laughed and went into her cabin.

Arthur returned to the castle more dejected than ever. And again Gawaine asked him what the trouble was. As soon as Arthur had told him, he immediately agreed to marry the hag.

"But you would not believe how ugly she is!" protested Arthur.

"It would be but a small price to pay for the life of my king," replied Gawaine. At last Arthur accepted his offer and returned to the hag.

"The answer is very simple," she replied. "What every woman wants is to have her way with men."

When the year was up, Arthur returned to the knight and first gave him all of the answers that he and Gawaine had collected.

"All of these answers are wrong," laughed the knight. "Are you ready to die?"

"Wait, I have one more answer," said Arthur. "What every woman wants is to have her way with men."

The knight walked away in fury. "It must have been my sister who told you," he muttered.

Arthur returned to Camelot rejoicing, but Sir Gawaine was forced to go to the forest to claim his bride.

---

[3] **curtly**—rudely; abruptly.

As much of a gentleman as he was, Sir Gawaine had to use all of the self-control he had to keep from vomiting at the sight of his bride-to-be. But he greeted her courteously and returned with her to the court. There he submitted bravely to the mockery of the other knights and the townspeople, and took the hag to the chapel and married her.

Sir Gawaine maintained his knightly and courteous behavior until nighttime when he lay in bed with his bride. Then he could not bring himself to kiss her or even to look at her.

"What is the matter, my lord, that you do not do your duty as a husband?" asked the hag.

Sir Gawaine, who was truthful as well as courteous, replied, " I am very sorry, but I am upset by your age, your ugliness, and your low birth."

"You do wrong to be upset by these things," she replied. "For age brings discretion, and ugliness provides you security from all your rivals, and true quality does not depend upon birth but character."

Sir Gawaine was impressed by the wisdom of her reply and turned to face her again. But instead of the old hag who had been there before, he now saw a beautiful young lady.

"I see you are surprised," she laughed. "I have been enchanted by my evil stepmother. The enchantment could not be broken until a knight of the Round Table would wed me."

"But the charm is only half-broken now," she went on. "I can only have my natural form for half of the day. I can either be a hag by night and beautiful during the day for the court to see, or I can be a hag by day and beautiful for you at night."

Sir Gawaine mused over this choice for a long time. Finally he said, "There are advantages to both and I cannot decide between them. I will let you make the choice. Let it be the way you desire, for my body and soul are yours."

Then the lady rejoiced. "Now I am free of the charm altogether. For the final test to break the spell was that the knight who married me must be willing to let me have my way with him."

QUESTIONS TO CONSIDER

1. What are the two parts of the charm the evil stepmother cast on the beautiful girl?

2. Which part or parts of this statement do you agree with: "Age brings discretion, ugliness provides . . . security, . . . and true quality does not depend upon birth but character"? Explain your answer.

3. Whom do you admire most: Sir Gawaine or King Arthur? Explain.

Part Five

Wise or Foolish?

"He passed the birds. He passed the clouds. He passed into the realm of the sun. Too late he felt the wax run down his arms; too late he smelled the singe of feathers."

◀ *Daedalus and Icarus* **by Albrecht Dürer, 1493**

Dürer's woodcut shows Icarus's tragic fall from the sky, which was the result of the boy's foolish decision to fly too close to the sun. Icarus's father, Daedalus, who used wax and feathers to make the boy's wings, watches in horror as the boy plunges to his death.

Wings

BY JANE YOLEN

The ancient Greeks considered Daedalus the most talented of their artists, sculptors, and architects. According to their myths, Daedalus was an apprentice to Athena, goddess of wisdom, practical arts, and war. During his most creative period, Daedalus enjoyed tremendous success, although he never stopped worrying that his nephew, Talos, would surpass him in originality. In a fit of jealousy, he murdered Talos and then fled to Crete, where he was eventually imprisoned, along with his son, Icarus. Determined to escape, Daedalus decided to learn to fly.

Once in Ancient Greece, when the gods dwelt on a high mountain overseeing the world, there lived a man named Daedalus who was known for the things he made.

He invented the axe, the bevel, and the awl.[1] He built statues that were so lifelike they seemed ready to move. He designed a maze whose winding passages opened one into another as if without beginning, as if without end.

*But Daedalus never understood the **labyrinth**[2] of his own heart. He was clever but he was not always kind. He was full of pride but he did not give others praise. He was a maker—but he was a taker, too.*

The gods always punish such a man.

A man who hears only praise becomes deaf. A man who sees no rival to his art becomes blind. Though he grew rich and he grew famous in the city, Daedalus also grew lazy and careless. And one day, without thought for the consequences, he caused the death of his young nephew, Prince Talos, who fell from a tall temple.

Even a prince cannot kill a prince. The king of Athens punished Daedalus by sending him away, away from all he loved: away from the colorful pillars of the temples, away from the noisy,

---

[1] bevel . . . awl—A bevel is a tool used for drawing angles or for adjusting the surfaces of work to a particular angle. An awl is a sharp-pointed tool used for making small holes in leather or wood.

[2] **labyrinth**—maze.

winding streets, away from the bustling shops and stalls, away from his smithy,[3] away from the sound of the dark sea. He would never be allowed to return.

And the gods watched the exile from on high.

Many days and nights Daedalus fled from his past. He crossed strange lands. He crossed strange seas. All he carried with him was a goatskin flask, the clothes on his back, and the knowledge in his hands. All he carried with him was grief that he had caused a child's death and grief that Athens was now dead to him.

He traveled a year and a day until he came at last to the island of Crete,[4] where the powerful King Minos ruled.

The sands of Crete were different from his beloved Athens, the trees in the meadow were different, the flowers and the houses and the little, dark-eyed people were different. Only the birds seemed the same to Daedalus, and the sky—the vast, open, empty road of the sky.

But the gods found nothing below them strange.

Daedalus knew nothing of Crete but Crete knew much of Daedalus, for his reputation had flown on wings before him. King Minos did not care that Daedalus was an exile or that he had been judged guilty of a terrible crime.

"You are the world's greatest builder, Daedalus," King Minos said. "Build me a labyrinth in which to hide a beast."

"A cage would be simpler," said Daedalus.

"This is no ordinary beast," said the king. "This is a monster. This is a prince. His name is Minotaur and he is my wife's own son. He has a bull's head but a man's body. He eats human flesh. I cannot kill the queen's child. Even a king cannot kill a prince. And I cannot put him in a cage. But in a maze such as you might build, I could keep him hidden forever."

Daedalus bowed his head, but he smiled at the king's praise. He built a labyrinth for the king with countless corridors and winding ways. He devised such cunning passages that only he knew the secret pathway to its

---

[3] smithy—a blacksmith's shop; a forge.
[4] Crete—a Greek island in the Mediterranean.

heart—he, and the Minotaur who lived there.

Yet the gods marked the secret way as well.

For many years Daedalus lived on the island of Crete, delighting in the praise he received from king and court. He made hundreds of new things for them. He made dolls with moving parts and a dancing floor inlaid with wood and stone for the princess Ariadne. He made iron gates for the king and queen wrought with cunning designs. He grew fond of the little dark-eyed islanders, and he married a Cretan wife. A son was born to them whom Daedalus named Icarus. The boy was small like his mother but he had his father's quick, bright ways.

Daedalus taught Icarus many things, yet the one Daedalus valued most was the language of his lost Athens. Though he had a grand house and servants to do his bidding, though he had a wife he loved and a son he adored, Daedalus was not entirely happy. His heart still lay in Athens, the land of his youth, and the words he spoke with his son helped keep the memory of Athens alive.

One night a handsome young man came to Daedalus's house, led by a lovesick Princess Ariadne. The young man spoke with Daedalus in that Athenian tongue.

"I am Theseus, a prince of Athens, where your name is still remembered with praise. It is said that Daedalus was more than a prince, that he had the gods in his hands. Surely such a man has not forgotten Athens."

Daedalus shook his head. "I thought Athens had forgotten me."

"Athens remembers and Athens needs your help, O prince," said Theseus.

"Help? What help can I give Athens, when I am so far from home?"

"Then you do not know. . . ," Theseus began.

"Know what?"

"That every seven years Athens must send a tribute of boys and girls to King Minos. He puts them into the labyrinth you devised and the monster Minotaur devours them there."

Horrified, Daedalus thought of the bright-eyed boys and girls he had known in Athens. He thought of his own dark-eyed son asleep in his cot. He remembered his nephew, Talos, whose eyes had been closed by death. "How can I help?"

"Only you know the way through the maze," said Theseus. "Show me the way that I may slay the monster."

"I will show you," said Daedalus thoughtfully, "but Princess Ariadne must go as well. The Minotaur is her half-brother. He will not hurt her. She will be able to lead you to him, right into the heart of the maze."

The gods listened to the plan and nodded gravely.

Daedalus drew them a map and gave Princess Ariadne a thread to tie at her waist, that she might unwind it as they went and so find the way back out of the twisting corridors.

Hand in hand, Theseus and Ariadne left and Daedalus went into his son's room. He looked down at the sleeping boy.

"I am a prince of Athens," he whispered. "I did what must be done."

If Icarus heard his father's voice, he did not stir. He was dreaming still as Ariadne and Theseus threaded their way to the very center of the maze. And before he awakened, they had killed the Minotaur and fled from Crete, taking the boys and girls of Athens with them. They took all hope of Daedalus's safety as well.

Then the gods looked thoughtful and they did not smile.

When King Minos heard that the Minotaur had been slain and Ariadne taken, he guessed that Daedalus had betrayed him, for no one else knew the secret of the maze. He ordered Daedalus thrown into a high prison tower.

"Thus do kings reward traitors!" cried Minos. Then he added, "See that you care for your own son better than you cared for my wife's unfortunate child." He threw Icarus into the tower, too, and slammed the great iron gate shut with his own hand.

The tiny tower room, with its single window overlooking the sea, was Daedalus's home now. Gone was Athens where he had been a prince, gone was Crete where he had been a rich man. All he had left was one small room, with a wooden bench and straw pallets[5] on the floor.

Day after day young Icarus stood on the bench and watched through the window as the seabirds dipped and soared over the waves.

---

[5] pallets—small or poor beds.

"Father!" Icarus called each day. "Come and watch the birds."

But Daedalus would not. Day after day, he leaned against the wall or lay on a pallet bemoaning his fate and cursing the gods who had done this thing to him.

The gods heard his curses and they grew angry.

One bright day Icarus took his father by the hand, leading him to the window.

"Look, Father," he said, pointing to the birds. "See how beautiful their wings are. See how easily they fly."

Just to please the boy, Daedalus looked. Then he clapped his hands to his eyes. "What a fool I have been," he whispered. "What a fool. Minos may have forbidden me sea and land, but he has left me the air. Oh, my son, though the king is ever so great and powerful, he does not rule the sky. It is the gods' own road and I am a favorite of the gods. To think a child has shown me the way!"

Every day after that, Daedalus and Icarus coaxed the birds to their windows with bread crumbs saved from their meager meals. And every day gulls, gannets, and petrels, cormorants and pelicans, shearwaters and grebes,[6] came to the sill. Daedalus stroked the feeding birds with his clever hands and harvested handfuls of feathers. And Icarus, as if playing a game, grouped the feathers on the floor in order of size, just as his father instructed.

But it was no game. Soon the small piles of feathers became big piles, the big piles, great heaps. Then clever Daedalus, using a needle he had shaped from a bit of bone left over from dinner and thread pulled out of his own shirt, sewed together small feathers, overlapping them with the larger, gently curving them in great arcs. He fastened the ends with molded candle wax and made straps with the leather from their sandals.

At last Icarus understood. "Wings, Father!" he cried, clapping his hands together in delight. "Wings!"

At that the gods laughed, and it was thunder over water.

They made four wings in all, a pair for each of them. Icarus had the smaller pair, for he was still a boy.

---

[6] gulls . . . grebes—all sea birds.

They practiced for days in the tower, slipping their arms through the straps, raising and lowering the wings, until their arms had grown strong and used to the weight. They hid the wings beneath their pallets whenever the guards came by.

At last they were ready. Daedalus kneeled before his son.

"Your arms are strong now, Icarus," he said, "but do not forget my warning."

The boy nodded solemnly, his dark eyes wide. "I must not fly too low or the water will soak the feathers. I must not fly too high or the sun will melt the wax."

"Remember," his father said. "Remember."

The gods trembled, causing birds to fall through the bright air.

Daedalus climbed onto the sill. The wings made him clumsy but he did not fall. He helped Icarus up.

First the child, then the man, leaped out into the air. They pumped once and then twice with their arms. The wind caught the feathers of the wings and pushed them upward into the Cretan sky.

Wingtip to wingtip they flew, writing the lines of their escape on the air. Some watchers below took them for eagles. Most took them for gods.

As they flew, Daedalus concentrated on long, steady strokes. He remembered earlier days, when the elements had been his friends: fire and water and air. Now, it seemed, they were his friends once more.

But young Icarus had no such memories to steady his wings. He beat them with abandon, glorying in his freedom. He slipped away from his father's careful pattern along a wild stream of wind.

"Icarus, my son—remember!" Daedalus cried out.

But Icarus spiraled higher and higher and higher still. He did not hear his father's voice. He heard only the music of the wind; he heard only the sighing of the gods.

He passed the birds. He passed the clouds. He passed into the realm of the sun. Too late he felt the wax run down his arms; too late he smelled the singe[7] of feathers. Surprised, he hung solid in the air. Then, like a star in nova,[8] he tumbled from the sky, down, down, down into the waiting sea.

---

[7] singe—slight burn.

[8] nova—star that gradually becomes brighter and then fades.

And the gods wept bitterly for the child.

"Where are you, my son?" Daedalus called. He circled the water, looking desperately for some sign. All he saw were seven feathers afloat on the sea, spinning into different patterns with each passing wave.

Weeping, he flew away over the dark sea to the isle of Sicily. There he built a temple to the god Apollo, for Apollo stood for life and light and never grew old but remained a beautiful boy forever. On the temple walls Daedalus hung up his beautiful wings as an offering to the bitter wisdom of the gods.

QUESTIONS TO CONSIDER

1. What sort of person is Daedalus?

2. Why does Daedalus agree to help Theseus?

3. How is young Icarus like his father?

4. Why do the gods feel bitter when Icarus falls to his death?

Midas

BY THOMAS BULFINCH

Thomas Bulfinch's myths have been read and loved for generations. Bulfinch, who was born in 1796, was the son of the famous architect, Charles Bulfinch. Young Thomas learned from his father to love all things classical, including the myths and stories of ancient Greece and Rome. In 1855, he wrote an enormously popular account of classical world mythology entitled The Age of Fable. *"Midas" is from that anthology.*

Bacchus,[1] in return for a kindness done him, offered King Midas his choice of a reward, whatever he might wish. Midas asked to have everything he should touch changed into gold. Bacchus consented, though sorry he had not made a better choice. Midas went his way, rejoicing in his new-acquired power, which he **hastened**[2] to put to the test. He could scarcely believe his eyes when he found a twig of an oak, which he plucked from the branch, become gold in his hand. He took up a stone; it turned to gold. He touched a **sod**;[3] it did the same. He took an apple from the tree; you would have thought he had robbed the garden of the Hesperides.[4]

His joy knew no bounds, and as soon as he reached home, he ordered the servants to set a splendid feast on the table. Then he found to his dismay that whenever he touched bread, it hardened in his hand, or put a morsel to his lips, it **defied**[5] his teeth. He took a glass of wine, but it flowed down his throat like melted gold.

Worried by this **affliction**,[6] he tried to get rid of the power; he hated the

---

[1] Bacchus—the god of wine.

[2] **hastened**—hurried.

[3] **sod**—a section of grass or ground.

[4] Hesperides—the nymphs who guarded the golden apples of Hera.

[5] **defied**—opposed.

[6] **affliction**—a condition of pain, suffering, or distress.

gift he had lately **coveted.**[7] But all in vain. Starvation seemed to await him. He raised his arms, all shining with gold, in prayer to Bacchus, begging to be delivered from his glittering destruction. Bacchus, merciful deity, heard and consented. "Go," he said, "to the River Factolus, trace the stream to its source, and there plunge your head and body in and wash away your fault and its punishment."

He did so, and scarcely had he touched the waters before the gold-creating power passed into them, and the river sands were changed into gold, as they remain to this day.

---

[7] **coveted**—wished for longingly.

QUESTIONS TO CONSIDER

1. At what point does Midas realize that his wish was foolish?

2. Why is Bacchus sorry that Midas had not made a better choice?

3. What would be your wish if, like Midas, you could have anything you asked for?

Prometheus

BY MOLLIE MCLEAN AND ANN WISEMAN

The Greeks thought of the Titan Prometheus (his name means "forethought") as the creator of humankind. According to many myths, it was Prometheus who first fashioned humans from clay and water. He was the champion of all men and women and came to their defense on many separate occasions. In one memorable story, Prometheus volunteers to defy Zeus and take back the fire that the mighty god stole from humankind. As punishment, Zeus chains Prometheus to a rock in the hope that the vultures will tear him apart.

There were many Greek gods. Zeus, their king, was the most powerful of all. At one time, he called all the gods and goddesses to a meeting at his palace on Mount Olympus. They came as fast as they could because they heard that Zeus was angry. When he came before them, he had a fierce look on his face.

"I am not pleased with the kingdom of Man," roared Zeus. "Men forget their gods, and use their time looking for riches."

The gods and goddesses were angry when they heard this. They had given Man many gifts and did not want the people of the world to forget them.

"What shall we do to make Man more thankful for the things he has been given?" asked Artemis, goddess of the moon.

"We shall take away one of the gifts he uses the most," answered Zeus.

The gods and goddesses began to think of the gifts they had given the world.

"We could take back my gift," said beautiful Artemis. "Without my light the people would find the nights very black."

"The moon is very pretty, but men do not use it much," said Poseidon, god of the sea. "They would not miss your gift as they would mine. Were the sea to dry up, men would be very unhappy."

"You are right," said Apollo, god of the sun, "but think of what the world would be like without my gift. There would be no daylight. Trees and flowers would not grow. The world would be cold. No one could live without the sun.

"Apollo forgets one thing," said Zeus. "I do not want to kill the people of the world. I only wish to teach them a lesson. If we took the sun from Man, he would soon die."

"There is one thing we can take away from Man which he will miss very much," said Hephaestus. "Let us take away my gift, fire. Without it, he will be unhappy, but he will not die."

"Good!" roared Zeus. "It shall be as you have said, Hephaestus. From this day on, there will be no fire for men."

As he said this, the warm day became cold and black. A strong wind shook the trees. All the fires on earth began to go out. Soon only one was left. This, Zeus put in a hollow tube which he carried back to Mount Olympus.

"Now," said Zeus fiercely. "I shall keep this hollow tube with me always. Man will never have fire again."

After Zeus took fire away, the world was sad. When the sun went down, there was no light. Men could not find their way. Many people were lost in the black night. There was no fire to warm the people. They would try to sleep and forget how cold they were. There was no cooking. Men would bring home animals which they had killed, only to find they must eat them as they were. They remembered the feasts they had had before.

Now fierce monsters who once had been afraid of the fire carried off sheep, chickens, and cows. Sometimes they even took a little child.

Year by year, the people of the world became more unhappy. Over and over again they asked Zeus to give them back the gift of fire. They said they would not forget the gods again. They said that they would thank the gods every day for the many gifts they had been given.

The gods and goddesses did not think Zeus should keep fire from Man for so long a time. They wanted people to be happy again. They asked Zeus to give fire back to the world.

Zeus roared, "I am the king of the gods. I took fire from Man and I will give it back when I wish."

The gods and goddesses could not make Zeus forget his anger. But they did not like to look down on a world so cold and black.

When the people of the world found that Zeus would not forget, they called a meeting. They met in an underground cave where the farseeing eyes of Zeus could not find them. They said how unhappy they were without fire. They said that they had done everything they could to please Zeus but that he would not give fire back to them.

"We must find a way to take fire back from Zeus," said one man.

"Yes," said another. "We cannot live without it any longer."

"Who would be so brave as to try to take something from the king of the gods?" asked a girl.

The people looked at one another. Their faces were sad. Every man wanted to help the world, but none was brave enough.

All at once a man stood up in the crowd.

"I will steal the fire from Zeus," he said.

Everyone at the meeting looked at him.

Then a man asked, "Who are you?"

All the people shouted, "Yes, tell us your name!"

"I am Prometheus," he said.

"I have heard of you," one man said, "and I know you are brave. But how will you take fire from Zeus? The king of the gods can see all the world from where he sits. You could not steal it, for he would see you."

Prometheus gave a laugh and said, "He can see nothing when he sleeps! I shall steal it at night."

The people looked at one another. They had not known there was so brave a man in all the world.

"When will you go?" they asked.

"I shall go now," said Prometheus. He put on his sword and walked out into the black night.

As Prometheus came near Mount Olympus, he heard the gods and goddesses laughing and singing. He saw the bright palace of Zeus where all had come to eat and drink. He heard fierce Zeus telling the story of how he had taken fire from Man. He saw the king of the gods laugh as he held over his head the hollow tube in which he had put the fire. As Zeus laughed, the walls of the palace shook, but Prometheus was not afraid.

For a long time Prometheus watched the bright windows of the palace. At last, one by one, the lights went out as the gods and goddesses went home. All was dark. Prometheus knew his time had come. Quietly, he opened the golden door of the palace. Without a sound he walked to the room where the king of the gods was sleeping. He saw the hollow tube in which Zeus had put the fire. He picked it up. Just then, powerful Zeus turned over. Prometheus jumped back and, still holding the hollow tube, put his hand on his sword. He stood quietly watching. Soon Zeus was sleeping soundly again. Prometheus ran from the palace, the hollow tube in his hand. When he reached the earth, he gave fire to everyone. The night which had been black was bright, and once again the world was happy.

In the morning Zeus found that the hollow tube was gone. His anger was so great that even Mount Olympus shook. He sent his messenger, Hermes, to earth to find out who had taken the fire. Hermes came back and said, "A man named Prometheus came in the night and took the fire back to earth."

"Who is this Prometheus that steals from the gods?" roared Zeus. "Bring him here at once!"

Hermes went back to earth as fast as he could. Soon Prometheus was standing before the king of the gods.

Zeus looked hard at him. "Did you think you could steal from me, little man?" he said. As he spoke, the ground shook and the sky grew black. "I will teach you not to steal from the king of the gods," he roared.

"I am not afraid," said Prometheus. "I would steal from you again to help Man. It was not right to keep fire from him so long."

"You will never steal from anyone again," shouted Zeus. He pulled Prometheus to the window of the palace. From there they could see the whole world.

"Look down, little man," he said. "Do you see that far-off rock that over-looks the angry sea? That will be your home until the world ends. "

The king of the gods went to another room in the palace and came back carrying an ugly black vulture.

"This bird will be your guard. He will watch you day and night." Zeus turned to Hermes and said, "Take this man to the place I have shown you. Chain him to the rock so he cannot move. Let the vulture fly around him." Turning to Prometheus he said, "Now, little man, we will see how brave you are." He gave a cruel laugh and left the room.

Hermes took Prometheus to the far-off place. He chained him to the rock. Leaving the vulture to guard him, he went back to Olympus.

For many years Prometheus stayed chained to the rock. In the day, the hot sun beat down on him. At night, the cold rain fell on him. All he could hear was the roaring of the wind and sea. All he could see was the ugly black bird flying around him. No one came near him. The people of the world wanted to help, but they were afraid of the anger of Zeus.

QUESTIONS TO CONSIDER

1. Why does Zeus take fire from the mortals?

2. Why do the gods and goddesses want it returned?

3. In what ways is Prometheus a champion of the "little people"?

4. In your opinion, was Prometheus wise or foolish? Explain your answer.

Pandora

BY BERNARD EVSLIN, DOROTHY EVSLIN, AND NED HOOPES

After Prometheus returned fire to Earth (see pages 185–189), Zeus set about getting his revenge. He condemned Prometheus to a lifetime of torture on a rock far away from civilization. But Zeus also wanted to punish humans for asking Prometheus to give them fire. With the creation of Pandora, he discovered the perfect revenge.

After Zeus had condemned Prometheus to his long torment for having given man fire, he began to plan how to punish man for having accepted it.

Finally, he hit upon a scheme. He ordered Hephaestus to mold a girl out of clay, and to have Aphrodite pose for it to make sure it was beautiful. He breathed life into the clay figure, the clay turned to flesh, and she lay sleeping, all new. Then he summoned the gods, and asked them each to give her a gift.

Apollo taught her to sing and play the lyre.[1] Athene taught her to spin, Demeter to tend a garden. Aphrodite taught her how to look at a man without moving her eyes, and how to dance without moving her legs. Poseidon gave her a pearl necklace and promised she would never drown. And, finally, Hermes gave her a beautiful golden box, which, he told her, she must never, never open. And then Hera gave her curiosity.

Hermes took her by the hand and led her down the slope of Olympus. He led her to Epimetheus, brother of Prometheus, and said, "Father Zeus grieves at the disgrace which has fallen upon your family. And to show you that he holds you blameless in your brother's offense, he makes you

---

[1] lyre—a stringed instrument of the harp family.

this gift—this girl, fairest in all the world. She is to be your wife. Her name is Pandora, the all-gifted."

So Epimetheus and Pandora were married. Pandora spun and baked and tended her garden, and played the lyre and danced for her husband, and thought herself the happiest young bride in all the world. Only one thing bothered her—the golden box. First she kept it on the table and polished it every day so that all might admire it. But the sunlight lanced through the window, and the box sparkled and seemed to be winking at her.

She found herself thinking, "Hermes must have been teasing. He's always making jokes; everyone knows that. Yes, he was teasing, telling me never to open his gift. For if it is so beautiful outside, what must it be inside? Why, he has hidden a surprise for me there. Gems more lovely than have ever been seen, no doubt. If the box is so rich, the gift inside must be even more fine—for that is the way of gifts. Perhaps Hermes is waiting for me to open the box and see what is inside, and be delighted, and thank him. Perhaps he thinks me ungrateful. . . ."

But even as she was telling herself this, she knew it was not so—that the box must not be opened—that she must keep her promise.

Finally, she took the box from the table, and hid it in a dusty little storeroom. But it seemed to be burning there in the shadows. Its heat seemed to scorch her thoughts wherever she went. She kept passing that room, and stepping into it, making excuses to dawdle[2] there. Sometimes she took the box from its hiding place and stroked it, then quickly shoved it out of sight, and rushed out of the room.

She took it then, locked it in a heavy oaken chest, put great **shackles**[3] on the chest, and dug a hole in her garden. She put the chest in, covered it over, and rolled a boulder on top of it. When Epimetheus came home that night, her hair was wild and her hands were bloody, her tunic[4] torn and stained. But all she would tell him was that she had been working in the garden.

That night the moonlight blazed into the room. She could not sleep. The light pressed her eyes open. She

---

[2] dawdle—linger.

[3] **shackles**—metal fastenings, used for encircling and confining the ankle or wrist of a prisoner or captive.

[4] tunic—a loose-fitting garment, sleeved or sleeveless, extending to the knees and worn by men and women especially in ancient Greece and Rome.

sat up in bed and looked around. All the room was swimming in moon-light. Everything was different. There were deep shadows and swaths[5] of silver, all mixed, all moving. She arose quietly and tiptoed from the room.

She went out into the garden. The flowers were blowing, the trees were swaying. The whole world was adance in the magic white fire of that moonlight. She walked to the rock and pushed it. It rolled away as lightly as a pebble. And she felt herself full of wild strength.

She took a shovel and dug down to the chest. She unshackled it, and drew out the golden box. It was cold, cold; coldness burned her hand to the bone. She trembled. What was inside that box seemed to know the very secret of life, which she must look upon or die.

She took the little golden key from her tunic, fitted it into the keyhole, and gently opened the lid. There was a swarming, a hot throbbing, a wild meaty rustling, and a foul smell. Out of the box, as she held it up in the moonlight, swarmed small scaly lizardlike creatures with bat wings and burning red eyes.

They flew out of the box, circled her head once, clapping their wings and screaming thin little jeering screams—and then flew off into the night, hissing and cackling.

Then, half-fainting, sinking to her knees Pandora, with her last bit of strength, clutched the box and slam-med down the lid—catching the last little monster just as it was wriggling free. It shrieked and spat and clawed her hand, but she thrust it back into the box and locked it in. Then she dropped the box, and fainted away.

What were those deathly creatures that flew out of the golden box? They were the ills that beset mankind: the **spites**,[6] disease in its thousand shapes, old age, famine, insanity, and all their foul kin. After they flew out of the box they scattered—flew into every home, and swung from the rafters—waiting. And when their time comes they fly and sting—and bring pain and sorrow and death.

At that, things could have been much worse. For the creature that Pandora shut into the box was the most dangerous of all. It was forebod-ing, the final spite. If it had flown free, everyone in the world would have

---

[5] swaths—strips.

[6] **spites**—malicious feelings, ill will.

been told exactly what misfortune was to happen every day of his life. No hope would have been possible. And so there would have been an end to man. For, though he can bear endless trouble, he cannot live with no hope at all.

QUESTIONS TO CONSIDER

1. How would you describe Pandora?

2. Why did Zeus want Pandora and Epimetheus to marry?

3. How did Zeus achieve revenge on mankind through Pandora?

4. Was Pandora wrong to open the box? Explain your opinion.

5. In your opinion, is the worst ill to know "exactly what misfortune was to happen every day"? Why or why not?

The Boatman, The Smuggler, and Looking for the Key

(Middle-Eastern folk tales)

BY HEATHER FOREST

These three Middle-Eastern tales are about both wise and foolish people. The third tale is one of many about Mulla Nasrudin. Storyteller Heather Forest explains that "Mulla is sometimes portrayed as a wise man offering sage advice to his followers, while in other tales he is a bumbling fool whose charm lies in the thought-provoking, zany solutions he finds for his problems."

The Boatman

A scholar asked a boatman to row him across the river. The journey to the other shore was long and slow. Before they reached midway, the scholar grew bored and began a conversation.

"Boatman," he called out, "let us pass the time by speaking of interesting matters. Have you ever studied phonetics[1] or grammar?"

"No," replied the boatman. "I've no use for those tools."

"What a pity," snickered the scholar. "You've wasted half of your life! It is useful to know the rules."

Suddenly, the boat struck a sharp rock in the middle of the river and began to fill with water. The boatman turned to the scholar and said, "Pardon my humble mind, which appears to you so dim. Wise man, tell me, have you ever learned to swim?"

"No!" scoffed the scholar. "I have immersed myself in thinking."

"In that case," said the boatman, "you've wasted all your life. Alas, the boat is sinking!"

---

[1] phonetics—the branch of linguistics that deals with the sounds of speech and their production.

The Smuggler[2]

A clever smuggler led a donkey burdened with bundles of straw to the border between two lands. The inspector at the border eyed the donkey's bundles with suspicion.

"You must allow me to search your bundles!" the inspector said. "I think that you have hidden a valuable treasure that you wish to sell at the market. If so, you must pay me a border fee!"

"Search as you wish," said the man. "If you find something other than straw, I will pay whatever fee you ask."

The inspector pulled apart the straw bundles until there was straw in the air, straw on the ground, straw, straw, straw all around. Yet not a valuable thing in the straw was found.

"You are a clever smuggler!" said the inspector. "I am certain that you are hiding something. Yet so carefully have you covered it, I have not discovered it. Go!"

The man crossed the border with his donkey. The suspicious inspector looked on with a scowl.[3]

The next day the man came back to the border with a donkey burdened with straw. Once again the inspector pulled apart the bundles. There was straw in the air, straw on the ground, straw, straw, straw all around.

"Not one valuable thing have I found!" the exasperated inspector said. "Go!" The man and the donkey went across the border. "Bah!" cried the inspector once again, scowling.

The next day and the next day, for ten years, the man came to the border with a donkey burdened with straw. Each day the inspector carefully searched his bundles, but he found nothing.

Finally, the inspector retired. Even as an old man, he could not stop thinking about that clever smuggler. One day as he walked through the marketplace, still trying to solve the mystery at the border, he muttered to himself, "I am certain that man was smuggling something. Perhaps I should have looked more carefully in the donkey's mouth. He could have hidden something between the hairs on the donkey's tail!"

As he mumbled to himself, he noticed a familiar face in the crowd. "You!" he exclaimed. "I know you! You were the man who came to the border every day with a donkey burdened with straw. Come and speak with me!"

---

[2] Smuggler—person who brings in or takes out without paying lawful charges or duties.

[3] scowl—frown.

When the man walked toward him, the old inspector said, "Admit it! You were smuggling something across the border, weren't you?"

The man nodded and grinned.

"Aha!" said the old inspector. "Just as I suspected. You were sneaking something to market! Tell me what it was! What were you smuggling? Tell me, if you can."

"Donkeys," said the man.

Looking for the Key

Mulla Nasrudin, the wise sage,[4] crept around in the dust, inspecting the ground. His persistence caused another man to stop and ask, "What are you doing?"

Mulla replied, "I have lost the key to a great treasure and am trying to find it here."

"A great treasure?" exclaimed the man. "Let me help you search for it."

A woman passed on her way to market. Seeing two men crawling around in the dust, she asked, "What are you doing?"

The man replied, "We are searching for the key to a great treasure. It has been lost. I am helping this sage to find it."

"A great treasure?" exclaimed the woman. "Let me help you search for the key too."

A large caravan[5] came along. The head camel driver stopped and, seeing three people crawling around in the dust, inquired, "Why are you crawling on the ground?"

The woman replied, "We are searching for the key to a great treasure. It has been lost, and I am helping this sage and this man to find it."

"A great treasure?" exclaimed the camel driver. Like the others he thought, "Perhaps when it is found we can share it!" He invited everyone in the caravan to help. "Let us all assist you in this important task!"

A large crowd now crawled around in the dust, looking for the key. After a long while of unsuccessful searching, a young boy asked Mulla Nasrudin, "Are you certain that you dropped the key right here?"

Mulla stopped poking in the dust and replied, "No. I lost the key somewhere inside my house."

The crowd stopped searching, stood up and asked, "Then why

---

[4] **sage**—one who is admired for experience, judgment, and wisdom.

[5] caravan—a company of travelers journeying together.

are we wasting our time looking for it outside?"

"That is an excellent question!" Mulla replied. "Your insight is clear! It is too dark to look for the key in my house. There is far more light out here."

1. What is the message or lesson of "The Boatman"?

2. What can be learned from the smuggler?

3. Who would you say is most foolish in "Looking for the Key"?

4. Which of these three stories did you enjoy most? Explain.

5. Which of these three characters—the boatman, the scholar, or the smuggler—reminds you most of yourself?

A Wolf and Little Daughter and Ol' Gally Mander

(United States folk tales)

Award-winning author Virginia Hamilton says that myths, folk tales, and legends can help keep the past close to us. Folklorist Nancy Van Laan would probably agree. The two stories that follow have been told and retold for generations, although both stories seem fresh and new. This is because Hamilton and Van Laan have succeeded in breathing new life into these "ancient" characters and plots. Sometimes it is thanks to the talents of the storytellers that a story can survive for hundreds or even thousands of years.

A Wolf and Little Daughter
by Virginia Hamilton

One day Little Daughter was pickin some flowers. There was a fence around the house she lived in with her papa. Papa didn't want Little Daughter to run in the forest, where there were wolves. He told Little Daughter never to go out the gate alone.

"Oh, I won't, Papa," said Little Daughter.

One mornin her papa had to go away for somethin. And Little Daughter thought she'd go huntin for flowers. She just thought it wouldn't harm anythin to peep through the gate. And that's what she did. She saw a wild yellow flower so near to the gate that she stepped outside and picked it.

Little Daughter was outside the fence now. She saw another pretty flower. She skipped over and got it, held it in her hand. It smelled sweet.

She saw another and she got it, too. Put it with the others. She was makin a pretty bunch to put in her vase for the table. And so Little Daughter got farther and farther away from the cabin. She picked the flowers, and the whole time she sang a sweet song.

All at once Little Daughter heard a noise. She looked up and saw a great big wolf. The wolf said to her, in a low, gruff voice, said, "Sing that sweetest, goodest song again."

So the little child sang it, sang,

"Tray-bla, tray-bla, cum qua, kimo."

And, *pit-a-pat, pit-a-pat, pit-a-pat, pit-a-pat,* Little Daughter tiptoed toward the gate. She's goin back home. But she hears big and heavy, PIT-A-PAT, PIT-A-PAT, comin behind her. And there's the wolf. He says, "Did you move?" in a gruff voice.

Little Daughter says, "Oh, no, dear wolf, what occasion have I to move?"

"Well, sing that sweetest, goodest song again," says the wolf.

Little Daughter sang it:

"Tray-bla, tray-bla, cum qua, kimo."

And the wolf is gone again.

The child goes back some more, pit-a-pat, pit-a-pat, pit-a-pat, softly on tippy-toes toward the gate.

But she soon hears very loud, PIT-A-PAT, PIT-A-PAT, comin behind her. And there is the great big wolf, and he says to her, says, "I think you moved."

"Oh, no, dear wolf," Little Daughter tells him, "what occasion have I to move?"

So he says, "Sing that sweetest, goodest song again."

Little Daughter begins:

"Tray-bla, tray-bla, tray-bla, cum qua, kimo."

The wolf is gone.

But, PIT-A-PAT, PIT-A-PAT, PIT-A-PAT, comin on behind her. There's the wolf. He says to her, says, "You moved."

She says, "Oh, no, dear wolf, what occasion have I to move?"

"Sing that sweetest, goodest song again," says the big, bad wolf.

She sang:

"Tray bla-tray, tray bla-tray, tray-bla-cum qua, kimo."

The wolf is gone again.

And she, Little Daughter, *pit-a-pat, pit-a-pat, pit-a-pattin* away home. She is so close to the gate now. And this time she hears PIT-A-PAT, PIT-A-PAT, PIT-A-PAT comin on *quick* behind her.

Little Daughter slips inside the gate. She shuts it—CRACK! PLICK!— right in that big, bad wolf's face.

She sweetest, goodest safe!

Ol' Gally Mander
by Nancy Van Laan

Ol' Gally Mander was a stingy ol' hag and nasty to boot. She was so lazy, she kept hirin' girls all the time to come in and clean. Most didn't stay but a second, 'cause they couldn't stand her.

But one day a girl came along who was as stingy and nasty as ol' Gally Mander. Fact is, they took to each other right well. After a time, ol' Gally Mander decided she could trust to leave this gal alone to clean house while she went off a-visitin'. Just before she went out the door, ol' Gally Mander said,

"You can scrub-a-dub and rub-a-rub,

But don't peek up my chimney!"

"I wouldn't think of doin' somethin' like that," said the girl.

Course, as soon as ol' Gally Mander went out, that's the first thing this hag of a girl did. She got down on her hands and knees and peeked up the chimney.

"What's that?" she said, poking around with a stick. Then with a *plop*, a long leather purse fell, *drop*, right into her hands.

Why, it was full of gold and silver!

"Whoo-ee!" Off she ran as fast as her two skinny legs would take her.

Directly, she passed an old cow. It called out,

"Hey, pretty gal, don't act like a hag,

Come milk my sore ol' milkin' bag."

But the girl said,

"I've got no time to fool with you, honey.

I'm goin' round the world with all this money!"

Then off she ran. Went on a little way and met a horse. It called out,

"Hey, pretty gal, don't run anymore.

Please rub my back 'cause it's mighty sore."

But the girl said,

"I've got no time to fool with you, honey.

I'm goin' round the world with all this money!"

Off she ran some more. Further down the road she met a peach tree. It called out,

"Hey, pretty gal, before you go,
Come pick my peaches 'cause my limbs hurt so."

But the girl said, "I've got no time to fool with you, honey.

I'm goin' round the world with all this money!"

Then off she ran.

Meanwhile, ol' Gally Mander had come back and found the girl gone and her purse gone. She took off down the road, hollerin',

"Gally Mander, Gally Mander, what could be worse!

That gal's run off with my long leather purse!"

She loopdy-looped down the road and met the old cow.

"Ol' cow," said she, "did a gal run by?

She stole my purse, and that's no lie!"

The cow shook her bony head and said, "She went thataway."

Ol' Gally Mander ran off, hollerin',

"Gally Mander, Gally Mander, what could be worse!

That gal's run off with my long leather purse!"

She stumbly-bumbled down the road and met the old horse.

"Ol' horse," said she, "did a gal run by?

She stole my purse, and that's no lie!"

The horse swatted his tangly tail and said, "She went thataway."

Ol' Gally Mander ran off, hollerin',

"Gally Mander, Gally Mander, what could be worse!

That gal's run off with my long leather purse!"

She ran lickety-split down the road and met the peach tree.

"Ol' tree," said she, "did a gal run by?

She stole my purse and that's no lie!"

The peach tree wriggled its topmost limb and said, "She went thataway."

Ol' Gally Mander ran off, hollerin',

"Gally Mander, Gally Mander, what could be worse!

That gal's run off with my long leather purse!"

Soon she came to the ocean where, at last, she found the girl. She grabbed her purse, then tossed the screaming hag of a girl into the salty sea.

Before you know it, ol' Gally Mander had gone and hired a new girl. This one was much too nice to work for the likes of her. But she did. By and by, ol' Gally Mander left the girl alone while she went off a-visitin'. 'Course, she told her the same thing she'd told t'other.

"You can scrub-a-dub and rub-a-rub,

But don't peek up my chimney!"

"I wouldn't think of doin' some-thin' like that," said the girl—and she meant it. Only thing was, ol' Gally Mander didn't come back for the longest time, and this poor girl thought somethin' terrible had happened. So she started a-cleanin' like crazy and without thinkin' stuck her broom up the chimney.

Plop! Drop! Down fell the long leather purse.

"Oh, dear!" said she. "No wonder ol' Gally Mander hasn't come home! She's done forgot to take her money with her!"

So off ran the girl with the long leather purse to give back the money to nasty ol' Gally Mander. But when the cow she met asked to be milked,

this girl milked it. And when the horse asked to have his back rubbed, this girl rubbed it. And when the tree asked her to pick peaches to ease its sore limbs, this girl picked them all off.

And when ol' Gally Mander came hollerin' down the road,

"Gally Mander, Gally Mander, what could be worse!

That gal's run off with my long leather purse," the cow said, "T'ain't seen nobody a-tall." The horse said, "T'aint seen nobody a-tall." And the tree said,

"That gal's got no time to fool with you, honey.

She's gone clear 'round the world with all yer money!"

Nasty ol' Gally Mander hollered and boo-hooed all the way home. There she stayed with nothin' but ash cakes to eat for the rest of her life.

Stingy ol' cuss got what she deserved. And the girl sailed off to London, where she lived like a queen.

1. How does Little Daughter outsmart the wolf?

2. What effect does the repetition of "pit-a-pat" and "tray-bla, tray-bla" have on the story?

3. In "Ol' Gally Mander," what is the difference between the first girl and the second?

4. Do you agree with the narrator that the second girl was nicer than the first? Explain.

5. How is the language in these stories different from what you've read so far?

The Trojan War

▲

The Siege of Troy II: The Wooden Horse
by Biagio di Antonio, 15th century
The Trojan Horse was Odysseus's secret weapon for winning the war. With Athena's
help, Epeius, a Greek artisan, constructed an enormous wooden horse with a hollow
underbelly that was large enough to hold several Greek warriors.

◀ *Helen Abducted by Paris*
by R. V. Deutsch
In this painting of the famous abduction scene, Helen, wife of Menelaus, and the Trojan
prince Paris both appear exhilarated at the thought of escape. In other paintings, Helen
appears terrified, and Paris looks grim and resolute.

▲

The Trojan Horse
engraving from a painting by Henri Motte
Once inside the horse, the warriors waited for a signal from the Greek soldier Sinon, who managed to convince the Trojans to take the horse inside the walls of Troy. At Sinon's signal, the Greek warriors climbed out of the underbelly (pictured here), and attacked the Trojans in the middle of the night.

The Trojan Horse
by Raoul Lefevre, 15th century
Thanks to cunning Odysseus, the Trojan Horse bore an inscription dedicated to the goddess Athena. Not wanting to offend Athena, the Trojans agreed to accept the horse as a gift. ▶

▲

The Burning of Troy
by Louis de Caullery, 16th century
Before the siege of Troy actually began, Menelaus and Odysseus made a personal
appeal to the king of Troy, King Priam, to return Helen. Priam wanted to return her
to Greece, but his sons, who were also Paris's brothers, said they would defend
their brother to the last. Thus began the ten-year war.

◄ *Hector and Andromache*
**by Giovanni Antonio Pellegrini,
c. 1708-1710**
This oil painting shows Hector, mightiest of the Trojan warriors, and Andromache, his wife. Hector holds their infant son Astyanax, who was brutally murdered by Odysseus or Neoptolemus at the end of the war.

King Priam and Achilles
by Aleksandr Andreevich Ivanov, 1824
In this painting, King Priam of Troy begs Achilles to return his son Hector's body after Hector is murdered. Surprisingly, Achilles agreed to Priam's request. After the body was returned, both sides called an eleven-day truce in order to properly mourn Hector, who was thought to be the finest Trojan warrior.

▼

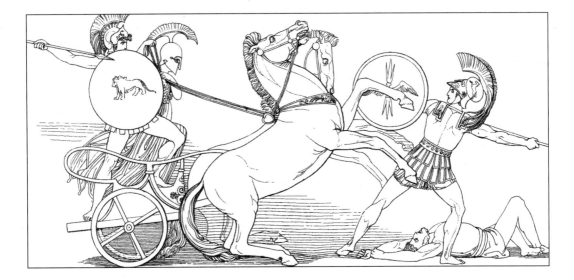

▲

Diomedes

Diomedes, in the chariot, aims his spear at Ares, the god of war. Diomedes was perhaps the most daring of the Greek warriors, second only to Achilles. He and Odysseus often fought side by side in the heat of battle. Together they wounded or killed countless Trojans. Diomedes managed to injure Aphrodite and Ares, both of whom were fighting on the side of Troy.

▲

War Heroes

The warriors of the Trojan war appear in profile. From left to right, they are Menelaus,
husband of beautiful Helen of Troy; Paris, who kidnapped Helen of Troy and eventually killed
Achilles; Diomedes, Greek leader who wounded Aphrodite during the battles; Ulysses, or
Odysseus, the great Greek warrior and adventurer; Nestor, a Trojan king who barely escaped
the sword of Hercules; Achilles, the greatest warrior of the Trojan War; and Agamemnon,
the commander in chief of the Greek forces. These characters intermingled to create many
exciting episodes of the Trojan War.

▲

The Blinding of Polyphemus
by Pellegrino Tibaldi, 16th century
Polyphemus was the leader of the Cyclopes, a group of one-eyed giants. He devoured several of
Odysseus's crew before Odysseus managed to blind him, thereby allowing the others to escape.

**Odysseus and the Sirens
by Edmund Dulac, 20th century**

The Sirens, who were quite ugly, sang melodies
so beautiful that sailors passing their rocky island
were lured to shipwreck. Odysseus's crew was
able to pass by because their ears were plugged
with wax. ▶

Scylla and Charybdis

Scylla and Charybdis were two sea monsters who
lived in caves on opposite sides of the Strait of
Messina, which separates Italy and Sicily. Scylla had
six heads, twelve feet, and a group of barking dogs
for a torso. Charybdis was actually a dreadful
whirlpool that sucked in and spewed out the sea
three times a day.
▼

Part Six

Triumph and Defeat

"The final labor was to fetch Cerberus, the three-headed monster dog, from Hades. My labors were finished, my earlier shame and horror put to rest. My glory complete. But my story was not over."

◀ Hercules Chaining Cerberus, artist unknown

This late-18th-century line engraving shows Hercules wrestling with the hound Cerberus, a three-headed watchdog who stood guard at the gates to the Underworld. After subduing Cerberus, Hercules freed his friend Theseus, who stands here with his father, King Aegeus.

Hercules

BY KATHRYN LASKY

So many stories have been told about Hercules that it's hard to figure out which tales come from classical mythology and which come from other storytellers. Still, most versions of Hercules have a few things in common. First, according to almost any version of the Hercules story, Hercules was the greatest, strongest, and most skillful of the Greek heroes. Second, as a young man, he undertook a series of twelve labors that were designed to test his strength and skill. Third, Hercules's skill earned him a place among the gods on Mount Olympus. In Kathryn Lasky's "Hercules," he is a kind but troubled man who is willing to search the world over for the peace and happiness he feels he deserves.

Listen to my tale, one of cunning and glory. A story of a monster and a man, a hero and a man. But all with one name: Hercules.[1] It is *my* story.

Once long ago I was not called Hercules but Palaemon. Although my mother was mortal, my father was the mightiest of all the gods, Zeus: king of Olympus. His queen was Hera. But Zeus often took other wives, mortal ones who gave him children. This poisoned Hera with jealousy.

As a baby I did not sleep in a cradle but in the curve of a shield. One night I saw something **slither**[2] silently toward me across the floor. With weaving heads and flickering tongues, two serpents slid over the shield's edge. I sat up and waved my hands happily, not knowing that these were deadly serpents sent by Hera. I let them coil around my arms and chest. At first they tickled. But then the serpents squeezed hard, until my breath came short. So I squeezed back. They twisted. I pinched. When both serpents went limp and lifeless in my hands, the game was over.

---

[1] Hercules—In most classical mythology, *Hercules* is called *Heracles*. Hercules and Heracles are the same man.

[2] **slither**—move along by gliding.

"Hera!" my mother screamed. The nurse and other servants raced in after her and gaped at the sight of me with the two limp bodies. "Hera! Hera!" they all whispered.

For many years Hera left us in peace. I learned boxing and archery, astronomy and philosophy, fencing and riding. Music too—how to sing and play the lyre.[3] I did not learn the awesome power of my strength, however, until one day when my music teacher made me do the scales[4] again and again. Becoming impatient, I hit him with my lyre. The man crumpled. My teacher was dead!

"I didn't mean to kill him. I really didn't," I cried to my mother. She looked at me as if I were not her son but some terrible monster. I felt hot with shame.

That was when I began to understand that I was neither quite a man nor a god. What was I? Perhaps what my mother saw—a monster. I was sent away.

"Go, Palaemon," she said. "Go to where there are wild animals to kill and not teachers." I was sent to the rugged mountain country.

Soon I had rid the countryside of lions and wolves. The farmers offered me gifts of food and wine and beds in their small homes. They even offered me their daughters in marriage. But I preferred to sleep under the stars. As for a wife, it seemed impossible. Ever since I had accidentally killed my music teacher, I was frightened to be around people. My own strength scared me except when I fought a ferocious animal. There were, however, other enemies besides wild animals.

For years my city, Thebes, had suffered under attacks from the Minyans. Our king, hearing of how I had rid the countryside of **marauding**[5] animals, asked me to help with this human **menace**.[6]

I sent scouts to watch at a narrow pass through which the approaching Minyans had to march. As soon as the last of the enemy had entered the pass, we ambushed them from above— a glorious victory! The kingdom of Thebes was safe.

The people of Thebes loved me as Palaemon: a man, a victor of battles, and a **cunning**[7] warrior—not a monster. So they gave me their most precious gift—Megara, daughter of the king, in marriage. I accepted.

---

[3] **lyre**—ancient stringed instrument related to the harp.

[4] **scales**—an ascending or descending series of tones.

[5] **marauding**—roaming about in order to conduct raids and attacks.

[6] **menace**—threat or danger.

[7] **cunning**—clever.

We married, had children, and were very happy. I never thought of Hera. It was as if she had vanished.

One afternoon in the courtyard I felt a shadow slide across my mind. Then a deep despair. From the window of the nursery of my children came a terrible hissing, an echo of the two serpents that Hera had sent when I was a baby. I raced inside. I could not see my children, nor two serpents, but at least ten! And wild boars and a lion, its fangs dripping blood. I drew my sword and lunged and slashed until nothing moved. My children were safe.

I blinked, and the shadow and despair slipped away. Beasts did not lie at my feet but my own wife and children. And another voice from a distant time echoed and then pounded in my head. "Hera! Hera!" This time Hera had not sent serpents but madness. I was drowning in my horror and shame.

The people had been wrong: I was a monster! I went to a sacred place, the shrine of Apollo at Delphi, to ask the oracle how I could ever purify myself and be forgiven.

"You shall no longer be called Palaemon," the priestess said. "You are from this moment forth *Hercules*, 'Hera's glory,' since it is from Hera

that you shall have everlasting fame. Now, go to Tiryns and serve your cousin King Eurystheus, performing the twelve labors he asks of you. If you successfully do his bidding, you shall be forgiven."

I had no choice and set forth.

"You are to kill the terrible lion of Nemea who preys on people and the flocks of farmers," demanded Eurystheus upon my arrival. He paused as if listening to a voice only he could hear. I realized that Hera, though invisible, was present. "Not just kill," he continued, "but **flay**[8] the lion." This had to be Hera's idea, for the beast had a skin like stone.

I went straightaway to the mountain where the lion was known to live. He was splattered and dripping with blood from a day of killing. I shot a flight of arrows but they merely bounced off his flanks.[9] Next I struck with my sword. It bent double. Fie![10] I flung the weapons down, seized the great cat, and clamped his muzzle shut so he could not breathe. After a few minutes the lion was dead. Knowing no blade would pierce his flanks, I skinned the beast with his

---

[8] **flay**—strip the skin from.
[9] flanks—sides, located between the hips and ribs.
[10] Fie—an expression of disgust.

own sharp claws. The armor-like pelt made a good cloak and the head became my helmet. I returned to see the king.

Eurystheus had never expected me to kill the lion. When he saw me coming, he became frightened and dived into a large pot to hide.

From the pot this cowardly king issued the command for the second labor. I was to slay the nine-headed hydra[11] of Lerna. I found her quickly—for her foul breath made the swamp stink—and easily chopped off one of her heads. But three grew in its place! I beheaded these only to have nine more sprout. How could I stop this now huge and raging beast? Suddenly I had an idea. Around me flames erupted, caused by the poisonous gases of the hydra's breath. I took a firebrand.[12] As I chopped each new head I seared its roots so it couldn't grow further. Finally, I sliced off the hydra's biggest head and buried it still hissing in the ground.

My third labor was to capture but not kill the Cerynitian hind.[13] It required great cunning and took me a year of stalking. My fourth labor was to bring a terrible boar which had ravaged the countryside back to Eurystheus alive.

"You failed!" Eurystheus shrieked when I returned with my hands and clothes spotless from my fifth labor. With Hera's help, he had devised what they believed to be an impossible and shameful task. I was to clean out the filthy stables of King Augeas, where dung was piled high as mountains.

"The stables are clean," I answered. "By moving huge boulders I changed the course of two rivers so the water swept through the stables and washed the filth away."

For the sixth labor I had to destroy a flock of flesh-eating birds. For the seventh, I captured the bull of Crete.

I stole the horses of King Diomedes for the eighth labor, and for the ninth I brought back the golden girdle of the Amazon queen. Then I sailed far to seize the cattle of a monster named Geryon.

For the eleventh labor I traveled west. There, guarded by a horrible dragon was Hera's tree that bore golden apples. I killed the dragon, but was wary[14] to pluck the fruit myself, as Eurystheus had ordered. Seeing Atlas nearby gave me an idea.

---

[11] hydra—a serpent with many heads.

[12] firebrand—piece of burning wood.

[13] hind—female red deer.

[14] wary—careful.

"You look weary, my friend. I shall hold the sky for you, if you fetch Hera's golden apples from her garden."

"Here are your apples," Atlas said, returning in a short time. "But let me take them to Eurystheus for you."

He doesn't wish to take back the burden of the sky, I thought. "All right," I said. "Just hold the sky a moment while I make a pad of my lion skin to ease the weight." Atlas was tricked, and I ran off with the apples.

The final labor was to fetch Cerberus, the three-headed monster dog, from Hades.

My labors were finished, my earlier shame and horror put to rest. My glory complete. But my story was not over.

Shortly afterward I visited an old friend. All through dinner I felt another presence in the room. My host—a quiet, peaceful man—suddenly jumped up and falsely accused me of stealing his horses. I grew incensed. Just before I saw her shadow, the shadow of Hera, my anger exploded. I struck out at my host, but his son stood between us. I was sorry before the boy's body hit the ground but it was too late. I then heard her terrible laughter. "Hera!" I screamed. "Fie on you! You are my shame."

Once more I went to the oracle at Delphi. "You have murdered the son of your host!" she cried. "Slave you shall now be called—slave for Queen Omphale of Lydia, and you shall wear a dress instead of your lion's pelt and a woman's turban instead of a helmet, and you shall spin and embroider. And by this you shall tame the monster within you." The shame stung me like the bite of a thousand wasps. And in the distant clouds I heard not a rumble of thunder but the laughter of Hera.

I served Queen Omphale obediently. When my service was done I put on my pelt and helmet again. I prayed that the monster within me slept, and I prayed that I might find a new wife. I did. Her name was Deianira.

One day Deianira and I came to a river in full flood. I saw a **centaur**[15] frolicking in the shallows and in the **glinting**[16] light I thought for a moment he swam with a woman. My breath locked. Was it Hera? But it must have been the play of the light on the water, for the centaur, named Nessus,

---

[15] **centaur**—a creature who is half-man and half-horse.
[16] **glinting**—brilliantly reflecting.

rose out of the river quite alone and offered to carry Deianira across.

Once on the other side, however, he tried to run off with her. Taking careful aim I shot an arrow. The centaur dropped and blood poured from his wound. I saw him whisper something to my wife. I thought nothing of it until many years later. . . .

I returned home last night after several weeks away. Deianira seemed different to me; she acted suspiciously. She brought me a shirt she had woven herself with rusty streaks in it. "A gift for my husband," she said. Pleased, I put it on. Immediately the cloth began to **chafe**[17] my skin, burning worse with each passing second.

"What have you done?" I cried.

"Forgive me!" she wailed. "It is stained with the blood of the centaur from long years ago. He said it would make you faithful to me always. I heard you loved another. It was a trick."

I remembered Nessus and the fleeting figure of a woman that I thought was mere light on water. Hera. Hera again. Invisible flames flared within me. I had never known such pain. And yet I felt no rage. For the first time I did not want to strike out. Hera could not rouse my anger.

I knew there was no cure, save mortal death. A **pyre**[18] was built for me on the highest mountain. There I spread my lion's pelt, and resting my head on my olive club, I told my servants to set a torch to the pyre.

The flames shot high into the sky. The monster within became ashes, replaced by peace and calm. My spirit rose from my pelt.

I am no longer mortal and my trials on earth are over. The anger is gone, the shame is finished; there is only glory—now and forever. My father, Zeus, opens his arms for me. "Come to me, Hercules! Come to me, my son!"

---

[17] **chafe**—rub and wear away.
[18] **pyre**—a pile of material for burning a dead body.

QUESTIONS TO CONSIDER

1. Why is Hercules "neither man nor god"?
2. Why did Hercules have trouble finding someone to marry?
3. In what ways did the gifts of Hercules make him a monster?
4. Who was the final winner of the battle of wills—Hercules or Hera? Support your answer with evidence from the story.
5. Do you think Hercules was a hero? Explain your opinion.

The Story of Theseus

BY WILLIAM F. RUSSELL

Theseus is said to be the man who organized Athens into a true metropolis. A strong and heroic warrior, Theseus was unafraid of adventure and never hesitated to risk his own safety to help others. In this way he was like another Greek warrior—Hercules. Like Hercules, Theseus's parentage is a little uncertain. Some storytellers say he is the son of Aegeus, king of Athens, while others say he is the son of Poseidon, brother of Zeus. Also like Hercules, Theseus performs a series of labors involving mortals and monsters alike. Eventually Theseus, known for his bravery, is crowned king of Athens.

There was once a man named Aegeus, who, although he was still a young man, was king of the great city of Athens. Now, because he was still quite young for a king, Aegeus found more pleasure in travel than he did in remaining at home and governing his own people. And it happened that, while he was on one of his lengthy stays in southern Greece, Aegeus met a beautiful woman in a village there, a woman named Aethra, and they fell in love, and they were married. After some time, Aegeus grew restless, and he longed to return to Athens and govern his own people once again.

So, in spite of his love for Aethra, and in spite of the fact that she had just given birth to their infant son, Aegeus decided to leave the village, alone, and to leave the task of raising the child to Aethra.

Before he went back to Athens, though, Aegeus buried his sword and sandals under a heavy boulder, and he said to his wife, "When our boy is old enough and strong enough to lift this stone, let him take the sword and the sandals and make his way to Athens, for then he will be man enough to succeed me on the throne." Then, kissing his wife and baby, Aegeus walked away, never to return to that village again.

Aethra named her son Theseus, and as he grew, she taught him many things, for she knew that he would someday be a king. Theseus learned the lessons of nature and also the wisdom of the world's great thinkers; he learned to be brave, but he also learned to respect the gods. And all the while Theseus improved his body and his strength, longing for the day when he could lift the giant stone his mother had told him about and thereby prove himself a man.

It was not many years before that day arrived. Theseus had grown tall, and though he was still quite young, his muscles were like iron. He had become an expert swordsman and such a skillful boxer and wrestler that no one in all the land around dared to challenge him. His mother knew that the time had come for him to join his father in Athens, and so, much as she feared losing her son forever, she led him to the massive boulder under which Aegeus had placed the sword and sandals. Theseus put his bulging arms around it, and his hands grasped it firmly on the sides. Then, with his knees bent and his back arched, he gave the huge rock a mighty upward jerk, and up it rose, as though it had been made of paper instead of stone. Theseus raised the boulder above his head and heaved it deep into the surrounding woods. Then he looked down at the sword of bronze, its hilt glittering with gold, and at the pair of golden sandals that had been placed there by his father long ago.

Tears filled Aethra's eyes as she told Theseus that the time had come for him to take the sword and sandals to his father in Athens. Theseus, too, wept now, for he suddenly realized that, although he had longed for the day when he could join his father, that day would also be the last he would ever see his mother. But Aethra comforted him, saying, "Weep not, my son, for that which has been fated must come to be. We cannot know what the gods intend, and so we must do as they command and try to live a good life as best we can." And then she kissed Theseus one last time, and she began to make her way back to the village. Theseus gathered up the sword and placed the sandals on his feet. Still weeping, he turned and began to walk in the opposite direction, but he never once looked back.

Now, all along his way, Theseus had many thoughts, and some fears, come to him about what it would be like to meet his father. What if the king has other sons whom he loves, thought Theseus, and what if he does not accept me? After all, he has forgotten me since I was born, so why should he welcome me now? What have I done that he would want to look upon me as a son? These thoughts saddened him greatly, until at last he thought of a plan, and he cried aloud, "Yes, I will make my father love me by proving myself worthy of his love. I will win such honor and renown[1] and do such deeds that Aegeus shall be proud of me no matter how many sons he may have!" And so he determined to take the long way to Athens, over the mountains and through many strange lands where he could find adventure and where monsters and robbers preyed upon helpless people. And this is just what he did.

Along his way, Theseus was set upon by robbers who lay hidden behind every turn in the road and by cruel giants that set all kinds of traps to **ensnare**[2] unwary travelers. First there was Sciron, a robber who would throw his victims over a cliff where they would be eaten by a giant tortoise who lived at the bottom. Theseus not only wrestled this robber into **submission**,[3] but then he threw Sciron over the cliff so that the tortoise could put a fitting end to this evildoer. Then there was another savage robber, Sinis, who was called "the pine-bender" because he tortured his victims by bending down two tall pine trees and tying his prey between them. When the trees were allowed to spring back, the bodies of the poor travelers would be torn to pieces. Theseus rid the countryside of this monster, too, and he gave to Sinis the same death between the trees with which Sinis had tortured so many others.

There were many other monsters and barbarians that Theseus defeated on his journey, too, and all along the way his fame among the people in the surrounding lands grew and grew. He had made the hills safe to live upon and the roadways safe to travel.

Now, as he came ever nearer to the Athenian countryside, he met an old man who was trying to gather a load of driftwood, but his burden was far greater than his weary old bones could carry. Theseus did not ignore the old

---

[1] renown—fame.

[2] **ensnare**—catch as if in a trap.

[3] **submission**—a state of giving in.

man's plight,[4] as so many others who had passed along the road had done. And when Theseus picked up all the wood and carried it upon his own shoulders, the stranger blessed him and asked where he was bound. Theseus told him that he was following the road to Athens, and with that a look of terror came over the old man's face as he warned Theseus to beware of a wicked robber named Procrustes, who preyed upon people who traveled that road.

"He invites his victims into his home," the old man warned, "and he offers them a bed to rest on for the night. He boasts that this bed fits people of all sizes, and surely it does, but none ever rose from it alive. For if a man be too tall for it, Procrustes lops off the legs of his guest till they fit just right. And if a man be too short, then he is stretched from head and foot until he, too, is the perfect size for the bed. Oh, the pain and horror of it all! Fly from this murderous beast," cried the old man to Theseus. "He will have no pity on you because of your youth or kindness. Even yesterday he brought a young man and a maiden to rest at his house, and he fitted them both upon his bed. The young man's hands and feet he cut off, but the maiden's limbs he stretched until she died, and so both perished in a most miserable way. Turn back, my friend, and do not be another of his victims."

"I have no need to flee," replied Theseus, "now that you have warned me what I may expect from Procrustes. Besides, this land must be rid of such monsters, and I will see to it that it is."

Thus prepared, Theseus was not surprised when he later encountered another stranger along the road, who called to him in a friendly voice and offered him the hospitality of his home for the night. "And might you have a special bed for me as well?" answered Theseus. Then did the face of the stranger, who was none other than Procrustes himself, take on the look of fear, for his would-be victim was not to be taken by surprise. Procrustes reached for his sword, but Theseus leaped upon him and encircled the monster's body with his mighty arms. Tighter and tighter he closed his embrace, all the while accusing and **berating**[5] Procrustes for the crimes he had committed, until at last, with one powerful constriction, he squeezed the very life out of the vicious beast.

---

[4] plight—difficult situation.

[5] **berating**—criticizing or scolding angrily.

Then he bore the body to Procrustes's home, where he found great wealth and treasure, all of which had been stolen from passersby. He called all the people of the surrounding country together, and he divided up the treasure among them. And then he resumed his journey once again, but his fame and honor became legend among the people, and they spread the word of his heroic deeds far and wide, so that there was no corner of Greece that had not heard of the mighty Theseus or of his many noble achievements.

At last, weary and footsore, but looking like a king's son, every inch of him, Theseus came to the gates of his father's palace. He went up the steep stairs and made his way to the great hall, where he saw many young men feasting and drinking wine. Soon he learned that these were not the king's sons, but the king's nephews, and he was told that because the king had no son to reign after he died, one of these foolish fellows would someday be king of Athens. "It is no wonder," Theseus muttered to himself, "that the land is full of robbers, if the like of these are destined to rule."

Then he strode into the midst of the feast, and he announced that he was Theseus, slayer of many monsters, and he wished an audience with the king. Well, Theseus's fame had arrived in Athens long before he did, and so everyone knew and honored the name as soon as it was spoken. King Aegeus came running from his chamber into the great hall to meet the man who had rid his kingdom of so many evils, and when Theseus saw the king, the young man's heart leaped into his mouth. He wanted so much to hold his father in his arms, but he realized that Aegeus had no idea at all that it was his son who stood before him. And so Theseus took off his sword and sandals, and, bowing low, he presented them to his father, saying, "You left these for me under a large rock long ago, and I have come here to return them."

Aegeus stepped back a pace, and he looked at the lad until his eyes grew dim, and then he threw his arms around Theseus's neck and he wept, and Theseus wept on his neck, till they had no strength left to weep anymore. Then Aegeus turned to all the people, and he cried, "Behold my son, who has come to me after all these years, a better man than his father was before him." And all the people cheered to see their king and his son united again, and they made Theseus welcome in their land, which would be his land, too, from this time on.

Theseus stayed with his father all the winter, and when the spring equinox[6] drew near, all the Athenians grew sad and silent, and Theseus saw this and asked why it should be, but no one would explain it to him. Then he went to his father, and he asked about why the people were sad, but Aegeus turned his face away and wept. "Do not ask, my son, about evils that must come to pass," he said. "It is enough to wait for them and face them when they arrive."

And when the spring equinox did come, there also came to Athens a black-sailed ship, which put into the harbor, and a **herald**[7] came from the ship and made his way to the market-place. Here he cried aloud, "O people of Athens, hear me well. It is time for your yearly tribute, so assemble your youths and maidens at once, for we sail with the tide to Crete."

Then Theseus went to the herald and said, "I am a stranger here. Pray, tell me the meaning of your message so that I might know why mighty Athens should pay a tribute to anyone."

And the herald related to Theseus the whole story of the war between Athens and Crete, and how King Minos of Crete had laid siege to Athens and would have let all the people there starve to death if they had not agreed to pay him a tribute each year. But what a terrible price the Athenians agreed to pay for their lives: Every year, at the spring equinox, the people of Athens must send seven youths and seven young maidens to King Minos, who then feeds them, alive, to a terrible monster called the Minotaur. So once each year, all the boys and girls of Athens are called together in the marketplace, and there they draw lots[8] to see which fourteen unlucky ones will be sent away to Crete, there to be given to the Minotaur for food.

Now when Theseus heard this incredible tale, he knew why there was so much sorrow in the city, and he went to his father and said, "I will go myself with these youths and maidens, and I shall slay the Minotaur and rid Athens of ever having to pay this tribute again."

But Aegeus shuddered at this and cried, "You shall not go, my son, for

---

[6] equinox—time when day and night are of equal length. The spring equinox is about March 21.

[7] **herald**—messenger.

[8] lots—chances.

you are the light of my old age and the person who must rule this land when I am dead and gone. If you go to fight the Minotaur, you will surely die a horrible death, for the beast is kept inside the **Labyrinth,**[9] which the cunning architect Daedalus built with so many winding and bewildering paths that no one who enters it can ever find his way out again. Here, entangled in the winding corridors, lives a monster who is half man and half bull and who feeds on human flesh. No, my son, I beg you not to give up your life this way."

But Theseus was only the more convinced that it was his duty to slay the horrid beast, and he told his father that somehow he would find a way to kill the Minotaur and escape the Labyrinth as well. Aegeus clung to his son's knees and, weeping bitterly, pleaded for him to stay, but Theseus had made up his mind. Finally, seeing that Theseus would not be swayed from his course, his father asked him one favor, saying, "Promise me that if you do come back alive and well, you will strike the black sail of the ship and hoist a white one instead, for I will be watching every day from the cliffs, and if only white sails I see, then I will know that you are well and will someday return to my side.

Promise me this, my son, and may the gods be with you on your quest."

And Theseus promised he would honor his father's request, and went out to the marketplace where the herald stood, watching the drawing of lots that would decide who was to sail in that **doleful**[10] crew. And the people stood wailing and weeping as first one was chosen, then the next, and the next. But Theseus strode into the midst, and cried, "Here is a youth who needs not be chosen by lot; I will be one of the seven." Then did the people give a great cheer, for they now had hope that perhaps mighty Theseus could put an end to their yearly misery.

The townspeople followed Theseus and the thirteen unfortunates down to the black-sailed ship, and the herald from Crete was with them and so was King Aegeus. Theseus tried to comfort Aegeus, saying, "Father, I am young and strong, and I have overcome many monsters and giants before this. Fear not, for this Minotaur is not immortal, and if he can be slain, then I shall do it." But his words cheered neither his father nor his companions, for they knew that even if the monster could be slain, whoever accomplished

---

[9] **Labyrinth**—maze.
[10] **doleful**—very sad.

the feat could never find the way back to the entrance of the Labyrinth. So there was much sobbing both on the ship and on the dock as the tide came in and the fairest of all Athens sailed off toward their deaths on Minos's island kingdom.

After several days, the ship reached Crete, and the young people were led into the king's presence. Minos looked at each one to assure himself that the exact tribute had been paid, and then he commanded his guards to take them to a prison cell and lock them up this night, for in the morning they would be fed to the monster one by one. Then Theseus stepped forward and cried, "A favor, O King! Let me be thrown first to the beast, for I came here of my own will, and it is only right that I should precede those who were forced here by lot."

Minos, then, could see that this was no ordinary youth standing before him, and when he learned that it was, in fact, the prince of Athens, he said, "It is wrong that one so brave should meet such an **inglorious**[11] end, and so I say to you, brave prince, go back to your home this night; the Minotaur will be satisfied with your companions alone."

But Theseus would not leave the others, and he repeated his demand that he be the first of all to face the monster. Now Minos was angered at having his kindness refused, and he said to Theseus, "You have sealed your own fate, rash prince; tomorrow you shall have your wish. Now, guards, away with them!"

It happened that King Minos's daughter, the beautiful and tender-hearted Ariadne, had witnessed this encounter, and her beating heart was filled with love for the courage that Theseus had displayed. "He shall not die, if there is some way I can save him," she said to herself.

Later that night, Ariadne crept down to the dungeon[12] beneath the palace, and she unlocked the cell in which Theseus was being held. "Flee to the ship at once," she said to him, "for I have bribed the guards to look the other way. Take your friends with you, but I beg you to take me, too, for my father will cause me to die a miserable death when he finds out what I have done."

Theseus stood silent for a while, for he was stunned by her beauty.

---

[11] **inglorious**—shameful.
[12] dungeon—dark underground room.

At last he said to her, "Dear princess, I cannot go home in peace until I have slain this Minotaur and **avenged**[13] the deaths of the youths and maidens he has so cruelly devoured. Help me in this quest and I shall gladly take you home with me in triumph."

Then she loved him all the more, and she said, "Fair prince, you are too bold, but I can be of help to you. Here is a sharp sword for you to carry, so that you won't have to face the beast unarmed. And here is a ball of string, the end of which you must fasten tightly to the gate of the Labyrinth, and the string must unwind without breaking through all the twisting passageways so that, after you have slain the monster, you can follow the string back to the entrance."

Now Theseus smiled, for he knew that he would be safe. He kissed Ariadne for a long while, and she wept for fear that her plan might fail. Then the princess led him, quietly, out of the palace and toward the great Labyrinth that lay some distance away. At the gate, Theseus made sure to fasten one end of the string tightly, and he played out the rest of the ball as he wandered through the many dark and winding passages.

After encountering a seemingly endless set of blind corridors and blocked passageways, and after doubling back his course so many times that he had lost all sense of direction, he at last came into an open court. There lay the Minotaur, fast asleep, for he expected no food until the next morning. Theseus stopped short, for he had never seen such a strange beast. His body was that of a man, but his head was the head of a bull, and his teeth were like those of a lion, so sharp and strong that they could tear apart any prey. The monster sensed the presence of someone nearby, and he awoke with a roar that sent a shiver through Theseus's body and weakened his knees. Still the prince knew his duty, and he raised the sword Ariadne had given him, just as the Minotaur charged headlong toward him. Theseus stepped nimbly aside, avoiding the monster's charge, and he struck the body of the passing beast with his sword, wounding the Minotaur and causing it to bellow even louder. Again it charged, with its head down and its sharp horns ready to rip apart the body of the man who had caused him this pain. But this time Theseus brought his sword above his head with both hands, and as the beast

---

[13] **avenged**—taken revenge for.

rushed blindly by, down came the blade with such a force that the monster's head was severed completely from its body, and its life's blood gushed out all around.

Now, weary from his adventure, Theseus turned to locate the ball of string he had brought with him, and finding it nearby, he followed its course through all the passageways he had traversed[14] before, until at last it led him to the gate of the Labyrinth. Here, waiting for him, was none other than Ariadne, and Theseus held her tightly in his arms as he whispered, "It is done! The terrible beast is dead!"

Together they returned to the dungeon, where they opened the cells of all the Athenians who had expected to die on the following morning. Then Theseus led them all, including the lovely Princess Ariadne, down to the black-sailed ship on which they had come to Crete. He lifted the anchor, and before morning could alert King Minos to the events that had taken place that night, they were well out to sea and rejoicing at their great good fortune.

Ah, but great tragedy lay just ahead, for in his haste to return to Athens, Theseus forgot the promise he had made to his father, and he did not replace the black sail with a white one. Aegeus, therefore, who watched the sea day after day from high atop an overlooking cliff, straining his tired old eyes to see the color of every sail in the distance, now was filled with terror at the sight of the black-sailed vessel he had feared so. Knowing by this sign that his dear son Theseus had perished in Crete, Aegeus felt that his own life was no longer worth living, and so he leaped from the cliff and fell to his death in the sea below. From that day on, the water that claimed Aegeus's life became known by the name of the old king, and still today it is called the Aegean Sea.

---

[14] traversed—passed through.

QUESTIONS TO CONSIDER

1. How did Aethra prepare Theseus for his future role as king?

2. Why does Theseus decide to take the long way to Athens?

3. Why are the people of Athens so sad and silent each spring?

4. How do you suppose Theseus reacted when he heard the news of Aegeus's suicide?

5. What are some of the qualities that make Theseus a hero?

The Apple of Discord

BY THOMAS BULFINCH

In Greek and Roman mythology, the Trojan War pitted a group of Greek kingdoms against Troy, a city located on the coast of what is now Anatolia in Turkey. According to the Greek epic poets, Paris, who was the son of King Priam, brought Helen, wife of King Menelaus of Sparta, back to Troy with him. To recover Helen, the Greeks sent an army to Troy. The army was led by the brave warrior Agamemnon, who was the brother of Menelaus. The war lasted ten years, although the first nine years seem to have been indecisive. Only in the tenth year, after Achilles had killed Hector, the most powerful of the Trojan warriors, were the Greeks able to win a victory. Here is Thomas Bulfinch's retelling of the events leading up to the declaration of war.

Athena was the goddess of wisdom, but on one occasion she did a very foolish thing; she entered into competition with Hera and Aphrodite for the prize of beauty.

It happened thus: At the wedding of Peleus and Thetis all the gods were invited with the exception of Eris, or Discord. Enraged at her exclusion, the goddess threw a golden apple among the guests, with the inscription, "For the fairest." Hera, Aphrodite, and Athena each claimed the apple. Zeus, not willing to decide in so delicate a matter, sent the goddesses to Mount Ida, where the beautiful shepherd Paris was tending his flocks, and to him was committed the decision. The goddesses accordingly appeared before him. Hera promised him power and riches, Athena glory and **renown**[1] in war, and Aphrodite the fairest[2] of women for his wife, each attempting to bias his decision in her own favor. Paris decided in favor of Aphrodite and gave her the golden apple, thus making the two other goddesses his enemies. Under the protection of

---

[1] **renown**—fame.

[2] fairest—most lovely.

Aphrodite, Paris sailed to Greece, and was hospitably received by Menelaus, king of Sparta.

Now Helen, the wife of Menelaus, was the fairest of her sex and the very woman whom Aphrodite had destined for Paris. She had been sought as a bride by numerous suitors, and before her decision was made known, they all, at the suggestion of Odysseus, one of their number, took an oath that they would defend her from all injury and avenge her cause if necessary. She chose Menelaus, and was living with him happily when Paris became their guest. Paris, aided by Aphrodite, persuaded her to elope[3] with him, and carried her to Troy, whence[4] arose the famous Trojan war, the theme of the greatest poems of antiquity,[5] those of Homer[6] and Virgil.[7]

---

[3] elope—run away to get married.

[4] whence—from where; from what place.

[5] antiquity—ancient times.

[6] Homer—a much-admired Roman poet who lived between 70–19 B.C. Homer was a major figure of ancient Greek literature and the author of the earliest and finest epic poems, the *Iliad* and the *Odyssey*.

[7] Virgil—a Roman poet born Publius Vergilius Maro on Oct. 15, 70 b.c., in Andes, a village in northern Italy. He is remembered most for his epic poem, the Aeneid.

QUESTIONS TO CONSIDER

1. What decision is Paris supposed to make?

2. What promise do Odysseus and the other suitors make to Helen?

3. What is the cause of the Trojan War?

4. What does the saying "Helen had a face that launched a thousand ships" mean to you?

The Trojan War: Paris and Helen

BY PAUL FLEISCHMAN

Paul Fleischman, the award-winning author of this retelling, says that he became interested in mythology and the Trojan War one night while reading the myth of Hercules to his children. This war, between the Greek invaders and the defenders of Troy, prompted him to write a book that would help contemporary readers see how and why a war that took place thousands of years ago still might be of interest today. The result is his book, Dateline: Troy, *from which this excerpt is taken.*

It began with a nightmare.

Hecuba, queen of Troy, was with child. The night before the birth, she awoke shrieking. "The fire!" she cried out. "It spreads!"

King Priam bolted up. There was no fire. Hecuba had been dreaming. Shaking, she stammered what she'd dreamt: that instead of bearing a child, she'd brought forth a tangle of flaming snakes.

"Send for Calchas!" commanded Priam.

Old feet shuffled through the palace. Priest of Apollo, interpreter of omens, reader of dreams and the future, Calchas gave ear to the queen.

"The vision speaks plainly," he pronounced. "The child will bring fire and ruin upon Troy. There's but one course of action." He peered at the queen, then the king. "When it's born, cut the infant's throat."

At first light, Hecuba gave birth to a boy. She held him until noon, weeping all the while. Priam at last took the baby from her arms, but couldn't bring himself to kill him. Still, he knew what must be done. He had a herdsman brought to the palace and entrusted him with the child and the deed. "Take him high on Mount Ida," he instructed. "Seek an untraveled spot—and leave him." He touched his son's face, then the rattle his wife had pressed into his tiny hand. He turned away.

The herdsman obeyed and left the infant to die. Five days later he returned to the place—and **gaped.**[1] No crow-pecked corpse lay before him, but a living baby, being **suckled**[2] by a she-bear. Amazed, sure the boy was fated to live, the man carried him home to his wife.

The next day, he walked to Troy and presented Priam with a dog's tongue as proof that the prince was dead. He returned to his hut. He would raise the child in secret. He and his wife named him Paris.

The lad grew up hardy, handsome, and as quick with his wits as his feet. He tended cattle, unaware that he was a prince. When the herdsmen set their bulls to fight, fair-minded Paris was often asked to judge the winner. Zeus, chief among all the gods, watching from his palace on Mount Olympus, took note of the young man.

It was at this time that the gods attended the wedding of the sea goddess Thetis. They'd all been invited, with one exception. Eris, the spiteful goddess of strife, had been shunned. Incensed, she plotted her retaliation,[3] and in the midst of the festivities she flung a golden apple into the throng.

Written upon it were the words: FOR THE FAIREST. Zeus's wife Hera assumed it was meant for her. Athena, goddess of wisdom and battle, boasted that her own beauty outshone Hera's. Appalled, Aphrodite, the goddess of love, insisted that the apple should be hers. Their quarrel grew vicious, halting the feast. Watching, Eris grinned. Finally, Zeus had to be called on to choose the most **comely**[4] of the three. He eyed them, knowing that the two he passed over would make his life a misery. He longed to pass the task to another.

It was then that he remembered Paris.

"How can I choose without favor?" asked Zeus. "Hera is my wife, and Athena my own daughter." He handed the apple to Hermes, the gods' messenger, and set him winging away. "The Trojan herdsman Paris will judge instead. He's much admired for his impartial[5] decisions. You'll find him on Mount Ida."

---

[1] **gaped**—stared stupidly.

[2] **suckled**—nursed.

[3] retaliation—return of evil for evil.

[4] **comely**—attractive.

[5] impartial—fair; just.

Grazing his cattle, Paris was **agape**[6] when Hermes appeared and announced Zeus's will. He humbly tried to decline, but was refused. A moment later the goddesses **alit**.[7]

They disrobed before a dumbstruck Paris. Nervously, he regarded Hera first. "Award me the apple," she coaxed, "and I'll make you emperor of all Asia." Athena, next, promised to make him the wisest of men and invincible in war. Then he came to Aphrodite. "I can make you emperor as well—of the heart, and invincible in love. Name the woman and she shall be yours."

Paris paused, distracted by this offer.

"Queen Helen of Sparta, for instance," Aphrodite continued. "The most beautiful woman in all the world, whose looks approach even my own."

Paris gazed upon the goddess's body, imagining she were Helen and his. Then he remembered. "But Helen is married."

"My magic will make her as a moth, and you a lantern. She'll follow you, entranced with passion, leaving her husband and home without a thought."

Paris's judgment buckled beneath the weight of this bribe. He took a step back. "I find Aphrodite the fairest," he announced, and placed the golden apple in her palm.

She nodded at him, sealing their pact, and gave her rivals a superior smile. Hera fumed. Athena's eyes blazed. Furious with Paris, the two stalked off, vowing revenge on him and all Trojans.

The following day, his mind whirling with thoughts of Helen, Paris strode off toward Troy. An athletic competition was to be held there that afternoon. His foster father tried to **dissuade**[8] him but ended up walking with him to the city. It was the first time Paris had set foot in Troy.

He began the competition by entering the boxing contest, and to the surprise of all, defeated Priam's sons. The proudhearted princes were unaccustomed to losing. Yet Paris flew past them in the footrace as well. At once they demanded a second race to be run. Paris left them behind again. Infuriated, they decided to kill him and drew their swords. Paris dashed for his life. His foster father threw himself before Priam. "Stop them, Your Majesty!" he cried. "That youth is your own lost son!"

---

[6] **agape**—in a state of wonder.

[7] **alit**—came down or settled on something.

[8] **dissuade**—persuade not to do something.

Priam recognized the old man, halted his sons and rushed up to Paris. He stared into his face. Hecuba followed. The herdsmen produced the silver rattle he'd found in the infant's hand years before. The king and queen knew it at once. Both burst out weeping, clutching Paris.

The old herdsmen had feared he'd be punished. But that night, Priam invited him to a magnificent banquet to mark his son's return. When the seer Calchas heard the news, he and Apollo's other priests again warned the king to put Paris to death.

"Never!" replied Priam. "Better that Troy should burn than my precious son should die!"

Paris exchanged his dirt-floored hut for a room of polished stone in the palace. Soon afterward, Menelaus, king of Sparta, chanced to visit Troy. Knowing that he was Helen's husband, Paris prodded him, heart pounding, to describe his bewitching wife. He so **shrewdly**[9] cultivated the king's friendship that Menelaus invited the prince to accompany him home and be his guest in turn. Feverish with joy, Paris accepted.

Aphrodite sent their ship fair winds. They reached Sparta and marched up toward the palace. A woman stood in wait. Paris approached then halted in awe. Flesh bested fancy. She had the grace of a deer and a dewdrop's radiance. He feared that such an earthly wonder would take no notice of a cowherd-prince. Had Aphrodite cast her promised spell? He watched as the queen embraced her husband. The goddess, however, had been true to her word. Helen set her eyes upon Paris and fell instantly, irresistibly in love.

For nine days Paris feasted with his hosts. He yearned to shout out his love for Helen and wrote her name in wine spilled on the table. Menelaus, cast down by the news that his father had just died in Crete, took no notice. On the tenth morning, he departed for the funeral.

The lovers exulted at their good fortune. Paris had first imagined Helen, then beheld. At last he'd be able to touch her. Love-maddened, the two decided to leave Sparta that night and never return.

In darkness the pair carried the palace treasures aboard their ship and set off. They headed for Troy, but Hera, pouncing on the chance to punish Paris for denying her the golden apple, raised a great storm that blew them

---

[9] **shrewdly**—cunningly; intelligently.

far off course. Landing at Cyprus, they stayed several months, fearing Menelaus lay in wait off Troy. They then sailed to the city of Sidon, whose king Paris murdered and whose coffers he emptied, adding vast stores of gold to their hold.

At last they reached Troy, welcomed by cheers and celebrations. The Trojans were dazzled not only by the riches but by Helen, more exquisite than any gem. Entranced, they swore never to see her returned. Hadn't the Greeks refused to send back Priam's own sister, carried away from Troy by a band of Greeks years before? As for the priests who'd joined Calchas in urging that Paris be killed, Paris silenced them with generous gifts of gold to Apollo's temple.

Only one voice was raised against Paris. It came from his own sister, Cassandra, a prophetess who'd been doomed by the god Apollo never to be believed. Over and over she'd warned Priam not to let Paris travel to Sparta. Now she declared that a frightful war would result unless Helen were sent back at once. The king listened patiently to his daughter. Then, as he had many times before, he sent her away, ignoring her words.

QUESTIONS TO CONSIDER

1. Why does Aphrodite help Paris?

2. Is Paris a likeable person? Explain your opinion.

3. Whom do you think is most responsible for causing the Trojan War? Explain your answer.

The Trojan War: Odysseus

BY ALICE LOW

The Greek hero Odysseus (who was called Ulysses by the Romans) was immortalized by Homer, the most famous of the ancient poets. Not much is known about Homer. He was probably Greek and may have been blind, but it's generally believed that during the ninth century B.C. he wrote two epics ("lengthy poems") about Odysseus. The Iliad describes the warrior's exploits during the final year of the decade-long Trojan War. The Odyssey tells the story of Odysseus's trip back home to Ithaca—a frightening journey that took another ten long years to complete.

The city of Troy was well fortified by a strong, high wall. The Greeks and the Trojans fought countless battles outside the wall, but neither side could win. The bitter war went on for ten long years. It might have continued for many more, had not Odysseus thought up a clever plan.

"We have not been able to break down the strong wall of Troy by force," said Odysseus to the Greek soldiers. "Therefore we must trick the Trojans into opening the gates, so that our army can enter the city and destroy it."

First Odysseus directed the construction of an enormous, hollow wooden horse. It had a trapdoor on the underside, and an inscription dedicating it to the goddess Athena.

Next he instructed the Greeks to abandon their camp outside the wall of Troy. He told them to sail their ships away from the port and hide behind a nearby island. "The Trojans will think that our army has accepted defeat and gone home," he said. "But a group of our men will stay behind, hidden in the wooden horse. We will place the horse by the shore, outside the wall of Troy. And one man, Sinon, will stay behind in the camp to trick the Trojans into bringing the horse inside the gates."

Odysseus had the bravest Greek warriors climb up a rope ladder through the trapdoor and into the hollow horse. Menelaus, Helen's husband, was among them. Odysseus and his companions spent the long night waiting inside the wooden horse.

Early the next morning, one of the Trojan guards sighted something strange. "A huge wooden horse!" he shouted to the other guards. "Come quickly! Is it real, or is it my imagination?"

Just then a Trojan scout came running up, shouting, "The Greeks have abandoned their camp and sailed away."

The people of Troy heard their shouts and streamed out of the gates to the enemy camp. "It is true!" they cried. "The Greek army has gone. We have won the war!"

"But what is the meaning of this horse?" asked one.

"It is a gift meant for Athena," said another. "We must bring it into our city and take it to her temple."

"No! No!" cried Laocoön, a seer. "I fear Greeks, even when they bear gifts."

At that moment a group of Trojans dragged Sinon the Greek into their midst. Sinon told the tale that Odysseus had instructed him to tell: "The Greeks were going to kill me as a sacrifice to the goddess Athena, but I escaped. Now I wish to live as a Trojan."

The Trojans believed him, and they believed the rest of his story, too. "The huge wooden horse was made and left by the Greeks as an offering to Athena."

"But why did they make it so big?" asked a Trojan soldier.

"To discourage you Trojans from taking it into your city. They hope that you will destroy it and make Athena angry with you."

"Do not believe him," cried Laocoön. But just then, two huge serpents emerged from the sea and slithered toward Laocoön. They coiled themselves around him and squeezed him to death while the people watched helplessly.

"Laocoön has been punished by the gods," they cried. "The gods wish us to bring the wooden horse into our city and offer it to Athena."

"Yes! Yes!" cried the others. They acted quickly, dragging the heavy horse through the gates and up the hill to Athena's temple.

"Now," they said, "the war is over, and Athena will bless us with peace after ten years of terrible **strife.**"[1] They went to bed and slept soundly for the first time in all those years.

Inside the horse, Odysseus said to the men hidden there, "Our plan is working. All is quiet now. This is the moment we have been waiting for."

He opened the trapdoor, and he and the other Greek warriors climbed down the rope ladder. They crept to the gates of Troy and opened them. Then they signaled to the Greek army.

The Greeks marched into Troy and took the Trojans by surprise. In the terrible fighting that followed, most of the Trojan leaders lost their lives. At last the Greeks were victorious.

Aphrodite saved Helen and led her to her husband, Menelaus. They sailed for Greece, thankful that the long, bloody war was over.

---

[1] **strife**—bitter conflict.

QUESTIONS TO CONSIDER

1. Why are the Greek soldiers so desperate for the war to end?

2. What is the purpose of the Trojan Horse?

3. Why is the inscription to Athena on the Trojan horse so important?

The Trojan War: Aeneas

BY WILLIAM F. RUSSELL

In the year 19 B.C., the poet Virgil was commissioned to write an epic poem that would glorify the Roman Empire in much the same way that Homer's Iliad *and* Odyssey *brought glory to Greece. It took Virgil eleven years to write his great epic, which he called the* Aeneid. *Although the* Aeneid *opens in medias res ("in the middle of things"), as was the custom in epic poetry, Aeneas's wanderings actually begin with the destruction of Troy by the Greeks. Virgil's account of the terror and bloodshed that took place once the Trojan Horse was brought into the city serves to show not only the savagery of the Greeks, but also the concern that Aeneas had for his family and his people as well. For the Romans, Aeneas was the true hero of the Trojan War.*

The wooden horse had fooled the men of Troy, who had taken it into their city as a captured prize from their ten-year war with the Greeks. While the Trojans slept after their wild celebrations that night, however, Sinon unlatched a secret door in the belly of the beast, and out came an armed band of Greek chiefs, led by Ulysses, who opened the city's gates to the rest of their army, and the sack of Troy began with a **vengeance.**[1] Soon the Greeks were setting fire to every home and temple in the city, and they were slaughtering the sleeping and unsus-pecting citizens. The city became filled with cries of horror, and the streets flowed with a crimson tide of blood.

All this while, Aeneas—a handsome Trojan prince whose mother was the goddess Venus—lay sleeping in his house, for it was in a less populated part of Troy, enclosed by a dense row of trees. It was not long, though, before the din of the slaughter reached his ears and awakened him from his sleep. Springing up from his bed, he

---

[1] **vengeance**—a great force.

quickly ascended to the roof of his house to see what was causing such commotion.[2] He stood there, almost in shock, for he could see the flames rising from hundreds of buildings, and he could hear the shouts of men and the call of trumpets.

Seizing his armor, he rushed out into the streets, shouting to his neighbors who were still asleep to arm themselves and follow him. He was soon joined by a **frenzied**[3] band of comrades, and together they rushed toward the place where the din of combat was loudest. Aeneas assumed that the hated Greeks had somehow gained entrance to the city, and he was determined to make them pay a dear price for their **treachery**.[4] Around him burst the flames of burning buildings, while the shrieks of the dying pierced the very skies.

No words can describe the scenes of terror and confusion or the **strife**[5] and carnage[6] of that fateful night. Not just the Trojans, but many Greek heroes as well perished in the bloody conflict. In the midst of the fighting, Aeneas and his companions heard a shriek, and looking up saw Cassandra, the young daughter of King Priam, being torn away from the temple where she had sought refuge. With her eyes raised to heaven, she was dragged through the streets by cords that bound her tender hands.

Now Aeneas's thoughts turned to old King Priam himself, and to Queen Hecuba, for surely the Greeks would be at their palace by now. He hurried to the palace gate, which had already been broken down, and on to the king's bedchamber. But the Greeks had been there, too, especially young Pyrrhus, the son of Achilles, who was bent on avenging the death of his father. Aeneas found the bodies of Priam, Hecuba, and one of their sons there on the floor, and he was overcome with grief. He staggered to the balcony, tears streaming from his eyes, and he looked down on his burning city with darkest despair in his heart.

It was hopeless to think that Troy could be saved now, and so Aeneas turned his thoughts to saving himself and his family. His mind raced with anxiety about the fate of his aged father, Anchises, and his wife, Creusa, who had been left at home with his little son, Ascanius. Had the Greeks

---

[2] commotion—agitation.

[3] **frenzied**—excited with panic.

[4] **treachery**—betrayal, lies.

[5] **strife**—bitter conflict.

[6] carnage—slaughter of a great number of people.

already slain them, too, and flung their bodies into the flames? He hurried back toward that part of the city where he had left them only a few hours ago, and hope of escape revived in his breast when he found that the area was not in flames.

As he crept through the streets, not wanting to attract the attention of any Greeks, he spied a female figure lurking in the shadow of an altar near which he had to pass. Coming nearer, he saw that it was Helen, the woman who had been the cause of all the strife and woes of his country, and who now hid in fear that the Trojans would take vengeance upon her. The flame of hatred rose within him, and he said to himself, "Is it right that this woman should be carried back to Sparta as a queen, and be waited upon by captured Trojan slaves? No, and though there is no honor in killing a woman, yet the sons of Troy must be avenged!" And drawing his sword, he was about to rush upon her when, all of a sudden, in his path stood his mother, the goddess Venus, **arrayed**[7] in glorious and heavenly splendor. "Why, my son, are you so filled with rage?" she said, taking him by the hand. "Think of your aged father, and your loving wife, and your little son, and fly to them before the Greeks can slay them or carry them away into captivity. As for Helen, it is not she, nor Paris, that is to blame for the destruction of Troy, for the immortal gods had decreed that the city must fall. Therefore, my son, make haste to those who are dear to you, and fear not, for I will stand by you in every danger." So saying, she vanished into the shadows of the night.

Then Aeneas, heeding his mother's advice, ran through the crowded streets toward his home. When he arrived, he gave thanks to Venus that his family was still alive, and he announced to them all that there was no hope of saving Troy, and that their only chance was to flee up into the mountains. But Anchises, who was broken-hearted at the loss of his homeland and the destruction of his city, refused to flee, saying, "You who are in the flower of your days may run if you choose, but I am old and will not attempt to save the little remnant[8] of life that remains to me. If the gods had wished me to live any longer, they would have spared this city, which has been my only home. No, here will I stay, and

---

[7] **arrayed**—dressed.

[8] remnant—small part left.

here will I die by my own hand before I allow my life to be taken by any Greek."

At these words, both Aeneas and Creusa burst forth into tears, and they pleaded with Anchises to flee with them, but their appeals were in vain. Seeing that his father's mind was made up, Aeneas said to him, "Can you, my father, expect that I would ever leave you behind? If you are determined to stay, then so shall we all, and we shall all perish here together as a family."

Then Anchises, who wished no harm to come to anyone on his account, raised his eyes to heaven and, stretching out his arms, uttered a prayer to Jove. He asked the god of gods to send down some sign to show him what to do. No sooner had he spoken than the roar of thunder was heard and a star was seen to fall from its place in heaven and shoot through the darkness like a shaft, as though marking the pathway for their flight. Now Anchises, seeing that it was the will of the gods that he should leave the city, gave his consent, saying, "Delay no more; whither you goest, I shall follow, for the gods must not be disobeyed."

Meanwhile, the noise and uproar in the city was drawing nearer and nearer, and the light of burning buildings breaking out at new points showed that no time was to be lost. Anchises was too old to run, so Aeneas carried him upon his shoulders, and he held the hand of little Ascanius, and Creusa, his wife, followed close behind, so that she would not lose the others in the darkness. He instructed his servants and the comrades he met to leave the city in different directions, so that one blocked gate would not prevent their escape, and to meet him at an old, deserted temple that stood in the mountains, not far from Troy.

Through the gloomy streets of the city, **illuminated**[9] occasionally by flashes of light from the flames of burning houses, Aeneas and his family moved steadily toward the city gates. For a time they seemed to escape all danger, but just as they neared the gates and began to think they were safe at last, a sound of rushing feet fell upon their ears and filled them with alarm. "Fly, fly, my son!" yelled Anchises. "They are upon you, for I see their gleaming weapons as they rush to destroy us!"

---

[9] **illuminated**—lit.

Aeneas was terrified by the shouts and the uproar around him, and he became confused and hardly knew which way to proceed. But, pressing forward, still with his father on his shoulders and his son in tow, he began to run, first this way, now that, wherever there seemed to be a chance of escape. Finally, he saw a small opening in the frantic mob of Trojans, with the Greeks behind them, and through it he could see the open city gates. Gripping his son's hand hard, he dashed headlong through this gap, and he soon found himself outside the city, heading up into the mountains. Nor did he stop to look back, either, until he reached the meeting place he had designated—the old, deserted temple. Then, lifting his father from his shoulders, he placed him on the ground and turned to embrace his wife. But she was nowhere to be seen! Whether she had gotten separated in the confusion at the gate, or whether she had become weary along the way and had stopped to rest, no one could say.

Almost frantic with grief at the loss of his wife, Aeneas hid his father and son away in a small cave near the temple, and, buckling on his armor, he hastened back to the city to search for his beloved Creusa. He found the gate through which he had just passed, and, re-entering the city, he began to retrace, as well as he could with only the light of the flames to guide him, the path of his escape. On every side a scene of horror met his eyes, and at times a sudden silence sent a chill into his heart. He tried to think of what Creusa would do when she found herself separated from him, and he decided that she would probably go back to their house and wait there for Aeneas to return. But when Aeneas did return, he found the house already enveloped in flames, its treasures **strewn**[10] around the grounds. Nearby he saw a long line of boys and women who had been taken captive and would from now on be Greek slaves, and he so feared that this fate had befallen his wife that he cried out "Creusa! Creusa!" many times, even though these cries turned the heads of the Greek soldiers who guarded the slaves.

Just then a miraculous thing happened, for an image of Creusa suddenly appeared, standing right

---

[10] **strewn**—tossed.

in front of him. Aeneas knew it was not her mortal self, for the image was vast in size and had shadowy features, though its expression was calm and full of affection. He stood aghast, his hair almost on end, as this image of his wife said to him in a gentle voice, "My dearest husband, do not grieve or blame yourself for losing me. It was not the will of the gods that I should accompany you in your flight. You are destined to wander for many years, over the land and the sea, and you will meet with many dangers and difficulties. But at last you will reach a peaceful and happy home, where the River Tiber flows softly through a fertile land, and there you will build a kingdom. Even now a princess is waiting for you and will become your bride. Weep not, then, for Creusa, but rejoice that I was not captured and carried away as a slave. I am now at peace, and so you must not lament my fate. Farewell, dear Aeneas, and always love our son Ascanius as you loved me."

With these words the vision began to fade away and vanish into the air. Three times did Aeneas try to throw his arms around her neck, and three times did he grasp only vapor. With a heavy heart he turned and slowly made his way toward the gates of the city.

Having made a second escape from Troy, he soon came to the cave where he had left Anchises and his son. Now, however, he found gathered there a large number of companions—men, women, and children—who had come to join Aeneas and were glad to follow him wherever he might lead.

They could see the flames of their city below them in the distance, and the morning star, the herald of the dawn, rising overhead. Aeneas uttered a prayer to Janus, the god of beginnings and endings, and all in the group understood that, although the world of Troy had come to an end, they themselves were **embarking**[11] upon a new beginning. And Aeneas led them deeper into the mountains, where they could no longer see the flames of Troy, and here they camped and prepared for their journey.

---

[11] **embarking**—setting out for, as on a journey.

QUESTIONS TO CONSIDER

1. What are Aeneas's feelings toward his city?

2. What advice does the goddess Venus have for Aeneas?

3. Why did Anchises wish to end his life?

4. Were you surprised that Aeneas returned to the city to attempt a rescue of Creusa? Why or why not?

5. How are the Greek soldiers portrayed by Virgil?

Beowulf

(Anglo-Saxon epic)

BY THOMAS BULFINCH

Beowulf, the prince of Geatland (the area now known as southern Sweden) is the hero of an eighth-century epic poem of the same name. No one is sure who wrote Beowulf, although scholars have been researching the poem's origin for centuries.

Some people think the most interesting question about Beowulf is this: Why did this particular story survive all these years, when countless other poems and stories were lost? One reason might be because Beowulf is so well written. In its original form, Beowulf is filled with metaphors and imagery that make the writing very vivid and the action very lively. Another answer might be because Beowulf's adventures are so exciting. Even young children enjoy hearing about the exploits of this mighty mortal.

In his boyhood Beowulf gave evidence of the great feats of strength and courage which in manhood made him the deliverer of Hrothgar, King of Denmark, from the monster, Grendel, and later in his own kingdom from the fiery dragon which dealt Beowulf a mortal blow.

Beowulf's first renown followed his conquest of many sea-monsters while he swam for seven days and nights before he came to the country of the Finns. Helping to defend the land of the Hetware, he killed many of the enemy and again showed his prowess[1] as a swimmer by bringing to his ship the armor of thirty of his slain pursuers. Offered the crown of his native land, Beowulf, just entering manhood, refused it in favor of Heardred, the young son of the queen. Instead, he acted as guardian and counselor until the boy-king grew old enough to rule alone.

---

[1] prowess—unusual skill or ability.

For twelve years, Hrothgar, King of Denmark, suffered while his kingdom was being **savaged**[2] by a devouring monster, named Grendel. This Grendel bore a charmed life against all weapons forged by man. He lived in the wastelands and nightly prowled out to visit the hall of Hrothgar, carrying off and slaughtering many of the guests.

Beowulf, hearing from mariners of Grendel's murderous visits, sailed from Geatland with fourteen **stalwart**[3] companions to **render**[4] Hrothgar the help of his great strength. Landing on the Danish coast, Beowulf was challenged as a spy. He persuaded the coastguards to let him pass, and he was received and feasted by King Hrothgar. When the king and his court retired for the night, Beowulf and his companions were left alone in the hall. All but Beowulf fell asleep. Grendel entered. With a stroke he killed one of Beowulf's sleeping men, but Beowulf, unarmed, wrestled with the monster and by dint of his great strength managed to tear Grendel's arm out at the shoulder. Grendel, mortally wounded, retreated, leaving a bloody trail from the hall to his lair.

All fear of another attack by Grendel **allayed**,[5] the Danes returned to the hall, and Beowulf and his companions were sheltered elsewhere. Grendel's mother came to **avenge**[6] the fatal injury to her monster son and carried off a Danish nobleman and Grendel's torn-off paw. Following the blood trail, Beowulf went forth to **dispatch**[7] the mother. Armed with his sword, Hrunting, he came to the water's edge. He plunged in and swam to a chamber under the sea. There he fought with Grendel's mother, killing her with an old sword he found in the sea cavern. Nearby was Grendel's body. Beowulf cut off its head and brought it back as a trophy to King Hrothgar. Great was the rejoicing in the hall and greater was Beowulf's welcome when he returned to Geatland, where he was given great estates and many high honors.

Shortly afterward, Heardred, the boy-king, was killed in the war with the Swedes. Beowulf succeeded him to the throne.

For fifty years Beowulf ruled his people in peace and serenity. Then

---

[2] **savaged**—attacked ferociously.

[3] **stalwart**—strong and steadfast.

[4] **render**—to give or make available; provide.

[5] **allayed**—set to rest.

[6] **avenge**—to inflict a punishment or penalty in return for; revenge.

[7] **dispatch**—to put to death summarily.

suddenly a dragon, furious at having his treasure stolen from his **hoard**[8] in a burial mound, began to ravage Beowulf's kingdom. Like Grendel, this monster left its den at night on its errand of murder and **pillage.**[9]

Beowulf, now an aged monarch, resolved to do battle, unaided, with the dragon. He approached the entrance to its den, whence boiling steam issued forth. **Undaunted,**[10] Beowulf strode forward shouting his defiance. The dragon came out, sputtering flames from its mouth. The monster rushed upon Beowulf with all its fury and almost crushed him in its first charge. So fearful grew the struggle that all but one of Beowulf's men deserted and fled for their lives. Wiglaf remained to help his aged monarch. Another rush of the dragon shattered Beowulf's sword and the monster's fangs sunk into Beowulf's neck. Wiglaf, rushing into the struggle, helped the dying Beowulf to kill the dragon.

Before his death, Beowulf named Wiglaf his successor to the throne of Geatland and ordered that his own ashes be placed in a memorial shrine at the top of a high cliff commanding the sea. Beowulf's body was burned on a vast funeral pyre, while twelve Geats rode around the mound singing their sorrow and their praise for the good and great man, Beowulf.

---

[8] **hoard**—a hidden fund or supply stored for future use; a cache.

[9] **pillage**—robbery of goods by force, especially in time of war; plunder.

[10] **undaunted**—not discouraged or disheartened; resolutely courageous.

QUESTIONS TO CONSIDER

1. Why does Beowulf go to Hrothgar's kingdom?

2. What can you infer from this myth about the society in which Beowulf lived?

3. What makes Beowulf such a great leader?

Gassire's Lute

(African myth)

BY LEO FROBENIUS

"Gassire's Lute" is at least 2,000 years old. The story was first told by the African Soninke people, who are ancestors of the Fasa, a sophisticated nation of people who lived around the third century B.C. The Soninke are credited with creating the first empire in West Africa— ancient Ghana—during the fourth or fifth century. The kingdom of Ghana was located on major caravan routes across the Sahara in present-day Mauritania. Trade in salt and other goods made the Soninke an extremely wealthy and powerful group.

"Gassire's Lute" offers an unusual view of what it means to be a hero to one's people. Gassire, who wants nothing more than to be a wise and worshipped king of the Fasa, knows that the only way to fulfill his wish is to wreak havoc upon the kingdom. Unlike other heroes—who spend much of their time preserving the safety of those around them—Gassire must destroy his family and at least a part of his kingdom.

Four times beautiful Wagadu[1] has existed and four times Wagadu has disappeared from sight: the first time because her children were vain, the second because they were deceptive, the third because they were greedy, and the fourth because they were **quarrelsome.**[2] Four times Wagadu has changed her name: first to Dierra, next to Agada, then to Ganna, and finally to Silla.[3] Four times Wagadu has changed the direction she faces: first to the north, next to the west, then to the east, and finally to the south.

Wagadu receives the strength to endure from the four directions, which is why she has had four gates

---

[1] Wagadu—the legendary city of the Fasa and the capital of Ghana. Wagadu was a cosmopolitan, bustling city filled with artists, musicians, and craftspeople.

[2] **quarrelsome**—given to quarreling; fond of fighting.

[3] Dierra, Agada, Ganna, Silla—ancient cities in Africa.

to her city: first to the north, next to the west, then to the east, and finally to the south. She has endured when her children have built her of earth, of wood, or of stone, or when she has existed only as a vision in the imaginations and desires of her children.

Wagadu actually is the strength that is in the hearts of her children. She is visible in times of war, when the air **resounds**[4] with the clash and clamor of battle as sword meets sword or shield. She is invisible when the errors in the hearts of her children tire her and make her fall asleep. Wagadu has fallen asleep four times: the first time because her children were vain, the second because they were deceptive, the third because they were greedy, and the fourth because they were quarrelsome.

If her children ever find Wagadu a fifth time, the vision of her beauty will shine so radiantly within their minds that they will never again lose her. Then, even if her children suffer from vanity, deception, greed, and **dissension**,[5] these will never be able to harm her.

Hoooh! Dierra, Agada, Ganna, Silla! Hoooh! Fasa![6]

Each time the errors in the hearts of her children have caused Wagadu to disappear, she has reappeared possessing an even greater beauty. Her children's vanity created the great songs of heroes that bards[7] sang in the second Wagadu and have continued to sing for countless generations, songs that all peoples of the Sudan[8] still value today. Her children's deception brought forth showers of gold and pearls in the third Wagadu. Her children's greed created the need for writing in the fourth Wagadu, writing that the Burdana still use today.

Her children's quarrels will produce a fifth Wagadu that will continue as long as it rains in the south and rocks **jut**[9] from the Sahara Desert. Then every man will carry a vision of Wagadu within his heart, and every

---

[4] **resounds**—fills with sound.

[5] **dissension**—difference of opinion; disagreement.

[6] Fasa—ancestors of the African people known as the Soninke. The Fasa were an aristocratic group with a large nobility and complicated class structure. On the battlefield they fought with spears and swords, although Fasa warriors would only fight those who were their social equals. This meant that kings fought kings, princes fought princes, and so on.

[7] bards—ancient poets who composed and recited verses celebrating the adventures of chieftains and heroes.

[8] the Sudan—vast region south of the Sahara Desert and extending from the Atlantic Ocean to the Red Sea.

[9] **jut**—to extend outward or upward beyond the limits of the main body; project.

woman will carry a vision of Wagadu within her womb.

Hoooh! Dierra, Agada, Ganna, Silla! Hoooh! Fasa!

Her children's vanity led Wagadu to disappear for the first time. Then she was called Dierra, and she faced north. The last king of Dierra was Nganamba Fasa. The Fasa were strong warriors and great heroes, but they were growing old. Every day of every month they had to fight their enemies. Day after day, month after month, without ceasing, they had to fight their enemies. Yet the Fasa remained strong. Each man was a hero in his own right, and each woman was proud of the heroic strength of each man.

King Nganamba was old enough to have a son, Gassire, who was the father of eight grown sons. Even these sons were the fathers of sons, making King Nganamba a great-grandfather among men. It was at the end of King Nganamba's rule that Wagadu disappeared for the first time. Would this have happened if Nganamba had died, and Gassire had ruled in his place?

Hoooh! Dierra, Agada, Ganna, Silla! Hoooh! Fasa!

Yet Gassire never had the opportunity to rule in his father's place.

Gassire longed for his father's death and his own kingship. He listened for some sign of weakness in his father, and he searched for a sign of impending death as a lover searches the sky at dusk for the evening star, the first sign of night. Day after day and month after month passed, and still Nganamba did not die.

Each day Gassire raised his sword and shield and rode into battle against the Burdama, fighting like the great hero that he was. Each night, when evening shrouded the land in shadow, Gassire rode into Dierra and took his place in the circle among the men of the city and his eight grown sons. His ears listened to the praises the other heroes sang of his great deeds upon the battlefield, but his heart was jealous of his father's power.

Deep within, night after night and month after month, Gassire wept with longing for his father's death and his own kingship. He longed to carry his father's sword shield, but they belonged to the king alone. His anger grew into **wrath,**[10] his wrath grew into rage, and he could no longer sleep at night. So late one night Gassire quietly

---

[10] **wrath**—forceful, often vindictive, anger.

arose, dressed, left his house, and visited the oldest wise man in the city.

"Can you tell me when I shall become king of the Fasa?" Gassire asked.

"Ah, Gassire," the old wise man replied, "your father, King Nganamba, will die but you will not inherit his shield and sword. That is for others, not for you. You will carry a **lute,**[11] and your lute will cause the disappearance of Wagadu! Ah, Gassire!"

Gassire said, "You lie, old man! It is clear that you are not wise at all. As long as her heroes can defend her, we shall not lose Wagadu!"

"Although you do not believe me, Gassire," the old wise man answered, "your path is not that of the warrior and hero. You will find the partridges[12] in the fields, and when they speak to you, you will understand them. They will reveal your path and the path of Wagadu."

Hoooh! Dierra, Agada, Ganna, Silla! Hoooh! Fasa!

The next morning Gassire set out to prove that his path was indeed that of the warrior and hero. He said to the other Fasa heroes, "Today there is no need for you to fight the Burdama. I shall take them upon my spear and my sword without your help."

So it came to pass that Gassire fought against the Burdama, one against many. As a farmer's sickle cuts down the wheat in the field, so Gassire's sword cut down the Burdama.

The Burdama felt terror enter their hearts. "We are fighting more than a hero, and more than a Fasa!" they cried. "Against such a being, we have no strength and no skill." So each Burdama tossed away his two spears, turned his horse in retreat, and fled in fear.

As the Fasa heroes entered the field to gather the spears of their enemies they sang, "Gassire has always performed the greatest deeds of any Fasa. He has always been the greatest of our heroes. Yet by winning so many swords, as one against many, Gassire has outdone himself today! Wagadu smiles with pride."

That night, when evening **shrouded**[13] the land in shadow and the men gathered into their circle, Gassire wandered into the fields. He heard a partridge that was resting

---

[11] **lute**—a stringed instrument having a body shaped like a pear sliced lengthwise and a neck with a fingerboard that is usually bent just below the tuning pegs.

[12] partridges—any of several game birds belonging to the same family as quail and pheasant.

[13] **shrouded**—covered; screened.

beneath a bush sing, "Hear the song of my deeds!" And then the partridge sang of its battle against a snake. "In time, all who live will die, will be buried, and will decay," the partridge sang. "Like all creatures, I too will die, will be buried, and will decay. But the song of my battles will live! Bards will sing my battle song again and again, long after heroes and kings have died and decayed. Wagadu will disappear, but my battle song will live on and on. Hoooh, that my deeds will become such a song! Hoooh, that I will sing such battle songs!"

Hoooh! Dierra, Agada, Ganna, Silla! Hoooh! Fasa!

Gassire returned to the old wise man. "I heard a partridge in the field brag that the songs of its deeds will live long after Wagadu has disappeared. Do humans also know great battle songs? And do these battle songs live long after heroes and kings have died and decayed?"

"Yes, they do, Gassire," the old wise man replied. "Your path is to be a singer of great battle songs rather than a great king of the Fasa. Ah, Gassire! Long ago the Fasa lived by the sea. They were great heroes then, too. They fought against men who played the lute and sang great battle

songs. And those men were heroes also. Often they caused terror to enter the hearts of the Fasa. You too will play battle songs on the lute, but Wagadu will disappear because of it."

"Then let Wagadu disappear!" Gassire exclaimed.

Hoooh! Dierra, Agada, Ganna, Silla! Hoooh! Fasa!

The next morning Gassire visited the Fasa smith and said, "Master Smith, I want you to make a lute for me."

The smith replied, "Make a lute I will, but it will not sing!"

Gassire responded, "Master Smith, just make the lute. I will make it sing!"

When the smith had finished the lute, Gassire immediately tried to play it, but he found that it would not sing.

"Master Smith, what good is this lute to me! I cannot make it sing," Gassire complained. "Tell me what I should do."

The smith answered, "Gassire, until it develops a heart, a lute is only a piece of wood. If you wish to make it sing, you must help it develop a heart. When you next go into battle, carry your lute upon your back. Let it feel the thrust of your sword, and let it absorb the blood of your wounds. Right now, your lute is still part of the tree from which it was made. It must become a part of you, your sons, and your people. It must share your pain as well as your fame. It must absorb the lifeblood of your sons. Then the feelings of your heart will enter the lute and develop its heart. Your sons will die and decay, but they will continue to live in your lute. However, I must warn you. You will play battle songs on the lute, but Wagadu will disappear because of it."

"Then let Wagadu disappear!" Gassire exclaimed.

Hoooh! Dierra, Agada, Ganna, Silla! Hoooh! Fasa!

The next morning Gassire called his eight sons together and said, "Today, when we fight the Burdama, our sword thrusts will live forever in my lute. May we fight with such courage, strength, and skill that our deeds will create a battle song that surpasses the battle songs of all other heroes! You, my eldest son, will lead the charge with me today."

So it came to pass that Gassire hung his lute upon his shoulder and rode into battle with his eldest son at his side. They fought against the Burdama as more than heroes and more than Fasa. Together they fought against eight Burdama. As a farmer's sickle cuts down the wheat in the field, so Gassire's sword and the sword of his eldest son cut down four of the Burdama heroes.

Then a Burdama thrust his sword into the heart of Gassire's eldest son. He fell from his horse, his lifeblood pouring from him. Gassire sadly **dismounted,**[14] lifted the corpse of his son upon his back, and returned to the other heroes and the city of Dierra. As he rode, the blood of his eldest son poured over the lute and was absorbed into the wood.

Hoooh! Dierra, Agada, Ganna, Silla! Hoooh! Fasa!

Gassire's eldest son was buried, and the city was solemn with mourning. That night Gassire tried to play his lute, but no matter how hard he tried, it would not sing. He called his seven sons together and said, "Tomorrow we again ride into battle against the Burdama."

Each of the next six days passed as the first day had passed. Each day, in the order of their birth, a different one of Gassire's sons joined his father in leading the charge against the Burdama. Each day, one of the enemy thrust his sword into the heart of that

---

[14] **dismounted**—to get off or down, as from a horse.

son and he fell from his horse, his lifeblood pouring from him. Each day, Gassire sadly dismounted, lifted the corpse of his son upon his back, and returned to the other heroes and the city of Dierra. Each day, as he rode, the blood of his son poured over the lute and was absorbed into the wood.

By the end of the seventh day of fighting, the men of Dierra were angry, the women were weeping with fear and grief, and everyone was mourning the dead. That night, when evening shrouded the land in shadow and the heroes had gathered into their circle, they said, "Gassire, enough is enough. You are fighting out of anger, and without good reason. Gather your servants and your cattle, take those who would join you, and leave our city. Let the rest of us live here in peace. We too want fame but we choose life over fame when the cost of fame is death."

The old wise man exclaimed, "Ah, Gassire! Today, for the first time, Wagadu will disappear."

Hoooh! Dierra, Agada, Ganna, Silla! Hoooh! Fasa!

So Gassire gathered his wives, his youngest son, his friends, and his servants and rode off into the Sahara Desert. Only a few of the Fasa heroes accompanied Gassire on his journey.

Gassire and his companions rode far into the lonely wilderness. They rode day and night, sleeping only when they could ride no farther.

One night Gassire sat awake and alone by the fire. The world around him was lonely and silent, for everyone else was asleep: his youngest son, the heroes, the women, and the servants. Gassire had just dozed off himself when a sudden sound awakened him. Next to him, as though he were singing himself, Gassire heard a voice singing. It was his lute, and it was singing his great battle song.

When the lute finished singing his great battle song for the first time, back in Dierra, King Nganamba died, and Wagadu disappeared for the first time. When the lute finished singing his great battle song for the second time, Gassire's anger disappeared and he wept. He wept with grief and with joy: grief over the death of his seven sons and the disappearance of Wagadu, and joy over the great battle song that would bring everlasting fame to him and his sons.

Hoooh! Dierra, Agada, Ganna, Silla! Hoooh! Fasa!

Four times beautiful Wagadu has existed. And four times Wagadu has disappeared from sight: the first time because her children were vain, the second because they were deceptive, the third because they were greedy, and the fourth because they were quarrelsome. Her children's quarrels will produce a fifth Wagadu that will continue as long as it rains in the south and rocks jut forth from the Sahara Desert. Then every man will carry a vision of Wagadu within his heart, and every woman will carry a vision of Wagadu within her womb.

Hoooh! Dierra, Agada, Ganna, Silla! Hoooh! Fasa!

QUESTIONS TO CONSIDER

1. What does Gassire want most in his life?

2. Why is he jealous of his father?

3. Why does Gassire insist that each of his sons accompany him into battle?

4. How do Gassire's actions harm Wagadu?

5. In your opinion, what is the lesson of this story?

How War Was Ended

(Arctic—Central Yupik Eskimo myth)

BY HEATHER FOREST

The Eskimo are the natives of the Arctic and sub-Arctic coastal regions of North America and the northeastern tip of Siberia. Eskimos (also called the Inuit, Inupiat, and Yuit people) live in a land that is mostly tundra—flat, barren plains where the ground remains frozen except for a few inches below the surface during the short summer season. Most Eskimo live as hunters of sea mammals (seals, walrus, and whales). They also rely on the sea to supply materials for just about all their basic needs, including food and materials for clothing, shelter, and weaponry. Like many other cultures of the world, the Eskimo are known for their songs, dances, and stories. The Yupiks are a group of Eskimo peoples. "How War Was Ended" is one of their most important myths.

Five hundred years before the first outsiders came to central Alaska, there lived a powerful Yupik warrior named Apanugpak. He was renowned by the Yupik people for his skill with the harpoon and bow and arrow.

It was a time of great madness and terror among the Yupik. Warring groups attacked each other across the tundra. People lived in fear within their **subterranean**[1] sod houses, unable to safely light fires or to cook food. Each band of warriors had a "smeller" who traveled with them. The "smellers" had such keen noses they could sense even one particle of smoke in the pristine[2] air of the cold tundra and direct the warriors to the source of the fire. People were cold, hungry, and afraid.

It came to pass that one day Apanugpak had a vision. In the vision he saw houses in villages everywhere

---

[1] **subterranean**—underground.
[2] pristine—clean.

vanishing into the sky as curling wisps of black smoke. He saw a **crimson**[3] lake of blood, made from the dripping wounds of slain warriors. As he gazed at these strange sights, Apanugpak, the bravest of warriors, was struck with terror. He trembled as he watched the ghosts of dead warriors slowly rise up to do battle with the living.

At that moment, Apanugpak knew that war was futile. No side could win, for as warriors killed more and more people, the vast army of ghosts would continue to increase. Like memories of horror driving people to revenge, the ghosts of war would **vanquish**[4] the living and cause great suffering to continue endlessly. Apanugpak knew then that war must end.

He was the most respected of all the fierce warriors. People were surprised when he held up his harpoon[5] and his bow and arrows and said, "These things were created to help us hunt for food, not to cause death to each other. I will not use these tools to fight people any longer." When Apanugpak, the greatest warrior, put down his weapons, all the others followed. The time of madness was over. The killing was finished.

Discord[6] between people found a different expression. People created new kinds of contests. Instead of killing each other in battle, warring bands began to compete energetically with each other in singing contests, dancing contests, and insulting contests. Colorful gatherings rich in music, movement, and pointed, clever words settled disputes.

Peace prevailed and people were able to light their hearth fires again. The sweet smell of savory food, cooking in subterranean homes, signaled the return of sanity to the land of ice and cold.

---

[3] **crimson**—deep or vivid red.

[4] **vanquish**—to defeat or conquer in battle.

[5] **harpoon**—a barbed spear with a rope tied to it, used for catching sea animals.

[6] **discord**—tension or strife.

QUESTIONS TO CONSIDER

1. What does Apanugpak "see" in his vision?

2. Why does Apanugpak lay aside his weapons?

3. Why were the contests a good replacement for war?

Part Seven

Journeys

"The men bent to their oars and rowed more swiftly, for they saw the mast bending like a tall tree in a heavy wind, and they feared that Ulysses, in his fury, might snap it off short and dive, mast and all, into the water to get at the Sirens."

◀ *Ulysses and the Sirens* by John William Waterhouse, 1891

This painting shows the mighty Ulysses tied to the mast of his ship. Ulysses's crew is making a desperate attempt to row past the Sirens, whose seductive singing might cause them to wreck their ship.

Jason and the Golden Fleece

BY INGRI AND EDGAR PARIN D'AULAIRE

The story of Jason and the mighty Argonauts is probably the first great quest story in English literature. In a quest story, the hero (who is almost always a man) must leave his home and embark on a journey filled with danger and excitement. The purpose of the hero's quest varies from story to story, but the intent is almost always to right some wrong or do away with some evil being. In "Jason and the Golden Fleece," the quest is a simple one. Jason must travel to the land of the Golden Fleece, grab the fleece, which is hanging on a branch, and then give it to the evil King Pelias of Iolcus. Once he has done this, Pelias will give up the throne and the kingdom will belong to Jason. Pelias believes that Jason will never be able to complete the task. Jason, as you will see, feels differently.

The muses sang about handsome Jason and his quest for the Golden Fleece.

Jason of Iolcus was as strong and well bred as he was handsome, for he had been raised by the wise centaur[1] Chiron. Jason's father had brought the boy to the centaur and had asked him to bring him up, for he feared that his own brother, Pelias, who had taken from him the throne of Iolcus, might harm his heir. In Chiron's lonely mountain cave young Jason was raised to be a hero, skilled in all manly sports. When he was grown he left his foster father to go to Iolcus and reclaim his father's throne.

Hera, who was paying a visit to earth, saw the handsome youth as he walked down from the mountain. His golden hair hung to his shoulders and his strong body was wrapped in a leopard skin. Hera was taken by his fine looks. She quickly changed herself into an old crone[2] and stood

---

[1] centaur—one of a race of monsters having the head, arms, and trunk of a man and the body and legs of a horse.

[2] crone—an ugly, withered old woman; a hag.

helplessly at the brink of a swollen stream as if she did not dare to wade across. Jason offered politely to carry her and lifted her on his strong shoulders. He started to wade and at first she was very light. But with each step she grew heavier, and when he reached midstream, she was so heavy that his feet sank deep into the mud. He lost one of his sandals, but struggled bravely on, and when he reached the other side, the old crone revealed herself as the goddess Hera.

"Lo," she said. "You are a mortal after my liking, I shall stand by you and help you win back your throne from your uncle Pelias." This was a promise the goddess gladly gave, for she had a grudge against Pelias, who had once forgotten to include her when he sacrificed to the gods.

Jason thanked her and went on his way in high spirits. When he arrived in Iolcus, people crowded around him, wondering who the handsome stranger might be, but when King Pelias saw him, his cheeks paled. An oracle had predicted that a youth with only one sandal would be his undoing. Pelias **feigned**[3] great friendship when Jason said who he was and why he had come, but underneath he held dark thoughts and planned to do away with his guest. Pelias feasted Jason and flattered him and promised him the throne as soon as he had performed a heroic deed to prove himself worthy of being a king.

"In the kingdom of Colchis, at the shores of the Black Sea," said Pelias, "on a branch in a dark grove, there hangs a golden **fleece**[4] shining as brightly as the sun. Bring the fleece to me and the throne shall be yours."

The Golden Fleece was once the coat of a flying ram, sent by Zeus to save the life of young Prince Phrixus of Thessaly. The crops had failed and Phrixus's evil stepmother had convinced his father that he must sacrifice his son to save his country from famine. Sadly the king built an altar and put his son on it, but Zeus hated human sacrifice, and as the king lifted his knife, a golden ram swooped down from the skies and flew off with Phrixus on his back. They flew far to the east and landed in the kingdom of Colchis. The King of Colchis understood that Phrixus had been sent by the gods. He gave him his daughter in marriage and sacrificed the ram. Its glittering fleece was hung

---

[3] **feigned**—pretended.

[4] **fleece**—the coat of wool of a sheep or similar animal.

in a sacred grove and it was the greatest treasure of the country.

King Pelias was certain that Jason would not return alive, for he knew that the warlike king of Colchis would not part with the fleece and that a never-sleeping dragon was guarding it. But Pelias did not know that Jason had Hera's help.

"Give me timber and men to build for me a sturdy ship and I shall sail off at once," said Jason. The king gave him what he asked for and a great ship, the *Argo*, was built. It was the most seaworthy ship ever seen. Athena, herself, prodded by Hera, put a piece of sacred oak in its prow. The oak had the power to speak in time of danger and advise Jason what to do.

With a ship like that it was not hard for Jason to gather a crew of heroes. Even Heracles came with his young friend Hylas. Calaïs and Zetes, winged sons of the North Wind, joined, and Orpheus came along to inspire the crew with his music. Soon each of the fifty oars of the ship was manned by a hero who swore to stand by Jason through all dangers.

Before they set sail, the heroes, who called themselves the Argonauts, sacrificed richly to the gods and made sure to forget no one. Poseidon was in a good mood. He called for the West Wind and under full sail the *Argo* sped toward the east. When the wind grew tired and died down, the Argonauts put out their oars and rowed with all their might. Orpheus beat out the time with his lyre and the ship cut through the waves like an arrow. One after the other the heroes grew tired and pulled in their oars. Only Heracles and Jason were left rowing, each trying to outlast the other. Jason finally fainted, but just as he slumped forward, Heracles's huge oar broke in two, so equal glory was won by them both.

The Argonauts landed at a wooded coast so Heracles could cut himself a new oar. While Heracles searched for a suitable tree, his young friend Hylas went to a pool to fill his jar with fresh water. When the nymph of the pool saw the handsome boy bending down, she fell in love with him. She pulled him down with her to the bottom of the pool and Hylas vanished forever without leaving a trace.

Heracles went out of his mind with grief when he could not find his friend. He ran through the woods, calling for Hylas, beating down whatever was in his way. The Argonauts, brave as they were, all feared Heracles when he was struck with **folly.**[5] They hastily boarded the ship and sailed away without him.

On toward the east the Argonauts sailed until they came to a country ruled by a king who was known for his knowledge and wisdom. They went ashore to ask the way to Colchis, but the king was so weak that he could barely answer their questions. He was so thin that only his skin held his bones together. Whenever food was set before him, three disgusting Harpies, fat birds with women's heads, swooped down and devoured it. What they did not eat they left so foul and filthy that it was not fit to be eaten. No one in his kingdom could keep the Harpies away.

The Argonauts felt sorry for the starving king. They told him to have his table set, and when the Harpies swooped down again, Zetes and Calaïs, the sons of the North Wind, took to their wings. They could fly faster than the Harpies, and when they caught them, they whipped the evil pests so hard that they barely escaped with their lives. The Harpies flew to the south, never to be seen again. At last the famished king could

eat in peace. He could not thank the Argonauts enough and told them how to set their course and what dangers they would encounter. No ship had yet been able to reach the shores of Colchis, he said, for the passage to the Black Sea was blocked by two moving rocks. The rocks rolled apart and clashed together, crushing whatever came between them. But if a ship could move as fast as a bird in flight, it might get through. He gave Jason a dove and told him to send the bird ahead of the ship. If the dove came through alive, they had a chance, he said. If not, they had better give up and turn back.

The Argonauts took leave of the king and sailed toward the clashing rocks. From afar they could hear the din and the heroes trembled, but as the rocks rolled apart, Jason released the dove and the bird flew between them like a dart. Only the very tips of its tail feathers were clipped off when the rocks clashed together.

"All men to the oars!" Jason shouted. Orpheus grasped his lyre and played and his music inspired the heroes to row as never before. The *Argo*

---

[5] **folly**—a lack of good sense.

shot ahead like an arrow when the rocks rolled apart, and only the very end of its stern was crushed as they clashed together. Again the rocks rolled apart and stood firmly anchored. The spell was broken, and from then on ships could safely sail in and out of the Black Sea.

The Black Sea was a dangerous sea to sail upon, and Hera had her hands full, guiding the Argonauts through **perils.**[6] But with her help Jason brought his ship safely through raging storms, past pirate shores and cannibal island, and the Argonauts finally arrived in Colchis.

Aeëtes, King of Colchis, a son of Helios, the sun, was a very inhospitable king. In fact he was so inhospitable that he killed all foreigners who came to his country. When he saw the *Argo* landing he was furious, and when Jason led his men to his palace and said that they were all great heroes and had come to offer the king their services in return for the Golden Fleece, he fumed with rage. "Very well," he said to Jason. "Tomorrow, between sunrise and sunset, you must harness my fire-breathing bulls, plow up a field, and sow it with dragon's teeth as Cadmus did at Thebes. If you succeed, the Golden Fleece is yours. But if you fail, I shall cut out the tongues and lop off the hands of you and all your great heroes." King Aeëtes knew well that no man could withstand the searing heat that blew from the bulls' nostrils. What he did not know was that Hera was helping Jason.

Hera knew that the king's daughter, Medea, who stood at her father's side with modestly downcast eyes, was the only one who could save Jason. She was a lovely young **sorceress,**[7] a priestess of the witch-goddess Hecate, and must be made to fall in love with Jason. So Hera asked Aphrodite to send her little son Eros to shoot one of his arrows of love into Medea's heart.

Aphrodite promised Eros a beautiful enamel ball, and he shot an arrow into Medea's heart just as she lifted up her eyes and saw Jason. Her golden eyes gleamed; never had she seen anyone so handsome. She just had to use her magic and save him from her cruel father; there was nothing she would not do to save Jason's life. She went to Hecate's temple and implored the

---

[6] **perils**—dangerous situations.

[7] **sorceress**—a woman who practices witchcraft.

witch-goddess to help her and, guided by the witch-goddess, she concocted a magic salve[8] so powerful that for one day neither iron nor fire could harm the one who was covered with it.

In the dark of the night, Medea sent for Jason. When he came to the temple, she blushingly told him that she loved him so much she would betray her own father to save him. She gave him the magic salve and told him to go up to the fire-breathing bulls without fear. Jason took the young sorceress in his arms and swore by all the gods of Olympus to make her his queen and love her to his dying day. Hera heard him and nodded, very pleased.

When the sun rose in the morning, Jason went straight up to the fire-breathing bulls. They bellowed and belched flames at him, but with Medea's salve he was invulnerable and so strong that he harnessed the bulls and drove them back and forth till the whole field was plowed. Then he seeded the dragon's teeth, and right away a host of warriors sprang up from the furrows. As Cadmus had done, he threw a rock among them and watched from afar as they killed one another. Before the sun had set, they all lay dead.

Jason had fulfilled his task, but King Aeëtes had no intention of keeping his part of the bargain. He called his men together and ordered them to seize the *Argo* and kill the foreigners at daybreak. In secrecy, Medea went to Jason and told him that he must take the Golden Fleece, now rightfully his, and flee from Colchis before dawn. Under cover of night she led him to the dark grove where the Golden Fleece, shining like the sun, hung on a branch of a tree. Around the trunk of the tree lay coiled the never-sleeping dragon. But Medea chanted incantations[9] and bewitched the dragon. She stared at it with her golden eyes and it fell into a deep magic sleep. Quickly Jason took the Golden Fleece and ran with Medea to the waiting *Argo*, and quietly they slipped out to sea.

At daybreak, when the king's men were to attack the ship, they found it was gone. So were the Golden Fleece and the king's daughter, Medea. Red-faced with fury, Aeëtes set off in pursuit with his great fleet of Colchian warships. He wanted the Golden Fleece

---

[8] salve—ointment.

[9] incantations—charms or spells to produce a magic effect.

back and he wanted to punish his daughter. The fastest of his ships, steered by one of his sons, soon overtook the *Argo*.

The Argonauts thought themselves lost, but again Medea saved them.

She called to her brother, who stood at the helm of his ship, and pretended to be sorry for what she had done. She said she would go home with him if he would meet her alone on a nearby island. At the same time, she whispered to Jason to lie in wait and kill her brother when he came. She knew that her father would have to stop the pursuit to give his son a funeral.

Hera and all the gods looked in horror at Medea, stained with her brother's blood. No mortal could commit a worse crime than to cause the death of his own kin. Zeus in anger threw thunderbolts. Lightning flashed, thunder roared, and the sea foamed. Then the sacred piece of oak in the bow of the *Argo* spoke. "Woe," it said, "woe to you all. Not a one among you will reach Greece unless the great sorceress Circe consents to **purify**[10] Medea and Jason of their sin."

Tossed about by howling winds and towering waves, the Argonauts sailed in search of Circe's dwelling.

At long last, off the coast of Italy, they found her palace. Medea warned the Argonauts not to leave the ship, for Circe was a dangerous sorceress who amused herself by changing men who came to her island into the animal nearest the nature of each man. Some became lions, some rabbits, but most of them were changed into pigs and asses. Medea took Jason by the hand so no harm would befall him and went ashore.

Circe was Medea's aunt. Like all the descendants of Helios, the sun, she had a golden glint in her eyes, and the moment she saw Medea, she recognized her as her kin. But she was not happy to see her niece, for through her magic she knew what Medea had done. Still she consented to sacrifice to Zeus and ask him to forgive Medea and Jason for their crime. The scented smoke of her burnt offering of sweetmeats and cakes reached Zeus and put him in a good humor. He listened to Circe's words and again smiled down upon Medea and Jason.

They thanked Circe and rushed back to the ship. The Argonauts rejoiced. Now they could set sail for

---

[10] **purify**—cleanse.

Greece. But still they had to pass through dangerous and bewitched waters. Soon they came to the island of the Sirens. The Sirens were half birds, half women, not **loathsome**[11] like the Harpies, but enchanting creatures. They sat on a cliff, half hidden by sea spray, and sang so beautifully that all sailors who heard them dived into the sea and tried to swim to them, only to drown or pine to death at the Sirens' feet. When the alluring voices of the Sirens reached the ears of the Argonauts, Orpheus grasped his lyre and sang so loudly and sweetly that all other sounds were drowned out, and not one of the Argonauts jumped overboard.

After a while the *Argo* had to sail through a narrow strait that was guarded by two monsters. On one side lurked the monster Scylla. From her waist up she looked like a woman, but instead of legs, six furious, snarling dogs grew out from her hips, and they tore to pieces whatever came close to them. The monster Charybdis lived on the other side of the strait. She was forever hungry and sucked into her gullet all ships that ventured within her reach.

Helplessly, the *Argo* drifted between the two monsters, and the Argonauts again gave themselves up for lost, when up from the bottom of the sea rose the playful Nereids.[12] They had come at Hera's bidding and they lifted up the *Argo* and threw it from hand to hand over the dangerous waters until it reached the open sea beyond. Poseidon called for the West Wind and the *Argo* sped homeward under full sail.

A loud cheer rang out from the valiant crew when they sighted the shore of Greece. They had been away for many long years and were homesick. But as the *Argo* neared the port of Iolcus, the ship was hailed by a fisherman who warned Jason that King Pelias had heard of his safe return and had made plans to kill him. Jason was downcast at his uncle's treachery, but Medea, her eyes flashing, asked to be set ashore alone. Once again she wanted to save his life.

Disguised as an old witch, she entered Iolcus, saying that she had magic herbs to sell that would make old creatures young again. The people crowded around her, wondering from where the witch had come. King Pelias himself came out from his palace

---

[11] **loathsome**—abhorrent; disgusting.

[12] Nereids—sea nymphs.

and asked her to prove that what she said was true, for he felt he was growing old.

"Bring me the oldest ram in your flock and I will show you the magic of my herbs," said Medea.

An old ram was brought to her and she put it into a caldron[13] full of water. On top she sprinkled some of her magic herbs, and lo! the water in the caldron boiled and out of the steam and bubbles sprang a frisky young lamb.

Now King Pelias asked Medea to make him young too. She answered that only his daughters could do that, but she would gladly sell them her magic herbs. But the herbs she gave them had no magic at all, and so King Pelias found his death in the boiling caldron at his own daughters' hands.

Now the throne of Iolcus was Jason's, but again Medea had committed a terrible crime. She had tricked innocent daughters into killing their own father. The gods turned from her and she changed from a lovely young sorceress into an evil witch. The people of Iolcus refused to accept her for their queen and took another king in

Jason's stead.[14] With the loss of his throne, Jason also lost his love for Medea. He forgot that he had sworn to love her till his dying day and that she had committed her crimes for his sake. He asked her to leave so he could marry the Princess of Corinth and inherit her father's kingdom.

Medea, scorned[15] and furious, turned more and more to evil sorcery. To revenge herself on Jason, she sent a magic robe to his new bride. It was a beautiful gown, but the moment the bride put it on she went up in flames and so did the whole palace. Then Medea disappeared into a dark cloud, riding in a carriage drawn by two dragons.

Jason found no more happiness, for when he broke his sacred oath to Medea, he lost Hera's good will. His good looks left him and so did his luck and his friends. Lonesome and forgotten, he sat one day in the shade of his once glorious ship, the *Argo*, now rotting on the beach of Corinth. Suddenly the sacred piece of oak in the prow broke off, fell on him, and killed him.

---

[13] caldron—a kettle or vat, used for boiling.

[14] **stead**—place or position.

[15] **scorned**—rejected.

The Golden Fleece was hung in Apollo's temple in Delphi, a wonder for all Greeks to behold and a reminder of the great deeds of Jason and the Argonauts.

QUESTIONS TO CONSIDER

1. Why did Pelias want to do away with Jason?

2. What was special about the crew of the *Argo*?

3. Why were the gods so offended by Medea's plan to kill her brother?

4. What causes Jason's downfall?

5. Would you say that he deserved the punishment he received? Explain.

Ulysses and the Sirens

BY BERNARD EVSLIN

You might recall that Ulysses (or Odysseus, as the Greeks called him), was the mastermind behind the Trojan Horse during the war between Greece and Troy. Thanks to Ulysses, the Greeks won the war and the lovely Helen was returned to Sparta (see pages 239–241). As soon as the Trojan War ended, Ulysses made preparations to return to Ithaca and his wife, Penelope. Homer's Odyssey tells the story of the hero's return voyage, which takes ten long years to complete. Along the way, Ulysses meets with witches, monsters, giants, and all sorts of beings, including two sisters, called Sirens, who sing melodies so beautiful that sailors passing their rocky island are lured to shipwreck. These are the same Sirens that cause so much trouble for Jason and his band of Argonauts (see pages 264–273).

In the first light of morning Ulysses awoke and called his crew about him.

"Men," he said. "Listen well, for your lives today hang upon what I am about to tell you. That large island to the west is Thrinacia, where we must make a landfall, for our provisions[1] run low. But to get to the island we must pass through a narrow strait. And at the head of this strait is a rocky **islet**[2] where dwell two sisters called Sirens, whose voices you must not hear. Now I shall guard you against their singing, which would lure you to shipwreck, but first you must bind me to the mast.[3] Tie me tightly, as though I were a dangerous captive. And no matter how I struggle, no matter what signals I make to you, do not release me, lest I follow their voices to destruction, taking you with me."

Thereupon Ulysses took a large lump of the beeswax that was used by the sail mender to slick his heavy thread and kneaded it in his powerful

---

[1] provisions—supplies of food and water.

[2] **islet**—a very small island.

[3] mast—a tall vertical pole, sometimes sectioned, that rises from the keel or deck of a sailing vessel to support the sails.

hands until it became soft. Then he went to each man of the crew and plugged his ears with soft wax; he caulked their ears so tightly that they could hear nothing but the thin pulsing of their own blood.

Then he stood himself against the mast, and the men bound him about with rawhide, winding it tightly around his body, lashing him to the thick mast.

They had lowered the sail because ships cannot sail through a narrow strait unless there is a following wind, and now each man of the crew took his place at the great oars. The polished blades whipped the sea into a froth of white water and the ship nosed toward the strait.

Ulysses had left his own ears unplugged because he had to remain in command of the ship and had need of his hearing. Every sound means something upon the sea. But when they drew near the rocky islet and he heard the first faint strains of the Sirens' singing, then he wished he, too, had stopped his own ears with wax. All his strength suddenly surged toward the sound of those magical voices. The very hair of his head seemed to be tugging at his scalp, trying to fly away. His eyeballs started out of his head.

For in those voices were the sounds that men love:

Happy sounds like bird railing, sleet hailing, milk pailing. . . .

Sad sounds like rain leaking, tree creaking, wind seeking. . . .

Autumn sounds like leaf tapping, fire snapping, river lapping. . . .

Quiet sounds like snow flaking, spider waking, heart breaking. . . .

It seemed to him then that the sun was burning him to a cinder as he stood. And the voices of the Sirens purled[4] in a cool crystal pool upon their rock past the blue-hot flatness of the sea and its lacings of white-hot spume.[5] It seemed to him he could actually see their voices deepening into a silvery, cool pool and must plunge into that pool or die a flaming death.

He was filled with such a fury of desire that he swelled his mighty muscles, burst the rawhide bonds like thread, and dashed for the rail.

But he had warned two of his strongest men—Perimedes and Eurylochus—to guard him close. They seized him before he could plunge into the water. He swept them aside

---

[4] purled—made a murmuring sound, like the sound of rippling water.

[5] spume—foam or froth on a liquid, as on the sea.

as if they had been children. But they had held him long enough to give the crew time to swarm about him. He was overpowered—crushed by their numbers—and dragged back to the mast. This time he was bound with the mighty hawser[6] that held the anchor.

The men returned to their rowing seats, unable to hear the voices because of the wax corking their ears. The ship swung about and headed for the strait again.

Louder now, and clearer, the tormenting voices came to Ulysses. Again he was aflame with a fury of desire. But try as he might he could not break the thick anchor line. He strained against it until he bled, but the line held.

The men bent to their oars and rowed more swiftly, for they saw the mast bending like a tall tree in a heavy wind, and they feared that Ulysses, in his fury, might snap it off short and dive, mast and all, into the water to get at the Sirens.

Now they were passing the rock, and Ulysses could see the singers. There were two of them. They sat on a heap of white bones—the bones of shipwrecked sailors—and sang more beautifully than senses could bear. But their appearance did not match their voices, for they were shaped like birds, huge birds, larger than eagles. They had feathers instead of hair, and their hands and feet were claws. But their faces were the faces of young girls.

When Ulysses saw them he was able to forget the sweetness of their voices because their look was so fearsome. He closed his eyes against the terrible sight of these bird-women perched on their heap of bones. But when he closed his eyes and could not see their ugliness, then their voices maddened him once again, and he felt himself straining against the bloody ropes. He forced himself to open his eyes and look upon the monsters, so that the terror of their bodies would blot the beauty of their voices.

But the men, who could only see, not hear the Sirens, were so appalled by their **aspect**[7] that they swept their oars faster and faster, and the black ship scuttled past the rock. The Sirens' voices sounded fainter and fainter and finally died away.

---

[6] hawser—cable or rope.

[7] **aspect**—appearance.

When Perimedes and Eurylochus saw their captain's face lose its madness, they unbound him, and he signaled to the men to unstop their ears.

QUESTIONS TO CONSIDER

1. Why doesn't Ulysses plug his own ears with beeswax?

2. What makes the music of the Sirens so appealing?

3. What is unexpected about the Sirens?

4. In your opinion, is Ulysses a good leader for the men on his ship?

Perseus Slays the Gorgon

BY SALLY BENSON

In Greek mythology, Perseus was a great adventurer, similar in strength and ability to Jason and Odysseus. Because his father was a god, he had some magical powers; because his mother was a mortal, however, he could be injured or killed. To some, Perseus's journey to capture the head of Medusa is the most exciting journey in all of mythology. Medusa was one of three horrifying sisters known as the Gorgons. The three Gorgon sisters (Medusa, Euryale, and Stheno) all had serpents for hair, long, snake-like tongues, bodies covered with scales, and claws made of brass. Of the three, only Medusa could be killed. Euryale and Stheno were both immortal.

Perseus was the son of Jupiter[1] and Danae. When he was born, his grandfather, Acrisius, consulted an oracle and prayed to know what the infant's fate would be. To his horror, the oracle answered that the child would one day slay him. Acrisius was terrified over this prophecy. He wanted to murder Perseus, but he was too tender-hearted to do the deed himself. He finally decided to shut up Danae and her baby in a chest and set them adrift on the sea. He secretly hoped they would be dashed to pieces on the rocks. Clinging to her baby in the dark, hot chest, Danae huddled in terror while the box whirled and dipped in the waves. It seemed days before they were washed upon the shores of Seriphus, where they were found by a fisherman. He took the mother and her baby to Polydectes, the king of the country, who took them into his own home and treated them with kindness. Here Perseus grew to manhood.

Not far from Seriphus, there lived a horrible monster named Medusa the Gorgon. She had once been a beautiful

---

[1] Jupiter—the Roman name for Zeus.

maiden whose hair was her chief glory, but, like Psyche who was also punished for her charms, Medusa had dared to **vie**[2] in beauty with Minerva.[3] Minerva in a rage turned her into a horrible figure, and changed her beautiful ringlets into hissing serpents. She became cruel and of so frightful an **aspect**[4] that no living thing could behold her without being turned to stone. She dwelt in a foul, **dank**[5] cavern and all around lay the stony figures of men and animals that had unfortunately chanced to catch a glimpse of her and had been petrified with the sight.

When Perseus became of age, Polydectes told him the story of the monster and begged him to attempt her conquest. Although Minerva had been the cause of Medusa's downfall, she favored Perseus and lent him her shield to take on his journey, while Mercury[6] gave him his winged shoes so that he might travel with the speed of the wind.

As he neared the mouth of the cave where the dreadful maiden lived, Perseus turned his back lest he see Medusa and share the fate of others who had tried to kill her. Slowly and **stealthily,**[7] he walked backwards, holding his shield before his eyes and guiding himself by the reflections in it. He entered the cave and beholding

Medusa's head mirrored in the shining metal, he stopped in horror. Medusa lay asleep. Fastened securely to her scalp by the tips of their tails, **noisome**[8] snakes writhed and twisted about her face and neck. Their breaths were **fetid**[9] and their eyes winked evilly. Water dropped from the roof of the cave and the air was dank. In the half-light, Perseus saw hundreds of lizards and giant toads crawling over her body. The sight was so dreadful that he almost ran from it in terror, but remembering his vow to Polydectes who had raised him, he advanced slowly, keeping Medusa's image reflected in the shield. Closer and closer he crept until he stood within reach of the **pestilential**[10] serpents of her hair. And then he struck. Her head fell to the ground.

After the slaughter of Medusa, Perseus, bearing with him the head of the Gorgon, flew far and wide, over land and sea. As night came on, he

---

[2] **vie**—compete.

[3] Minerva—the Roman name for Athena.

[4] **aspect**—appearance.

[5] **dank**—unpleasantly moist.

[6] Mercury—the Roman name for Hermes.

[7] **stealthily**—secretly.

[8] **noisome**—very harmful.

[9] **fetid**—smelly.

[10] **pestilential**—deadly.

reached the western limit of the earth, where the sun goes down. He was tired and would have gladly rested here until morning. It was the **realm**[11] of King Atlas, brother of Prometheus, who was more tremendous than any man on earth. Atlas was rich and had no neighbor or rival to dispute his supremacy of the land. His gardens were his chief pride. Here golden fruit hung from golden branches, half hid with golden leaves. Perseus presented himself to Atlas and said, "I come as a guest. If you honor illustrious descent, I claim Jupiter for my father. If you honor mighty deeds, I plead the conquest of the Gorgon. I seek rest and food."

Atlas was about to welcome him to his castle when he remembered an ancient prophecy which had warned him that a son of Jupiter would one day rob him of his golden apples. So, turning away, he answered, "Begone! Neither your false claims of glory nor parentage shall protect you!"

When Perseus did not move, Atlas turned on him and attempted to thrust him from the door. Perseus, finding the giant too strong for him, said, "Since you value my friendship so little, deign to accept a present!"

And, turning his own face away, he held up the Gorgon's head. Atlas changed into stone. His beard and hair became forests, his arms and shoulders became cliffs; his head became a summit and his bones turned into rocks. Each part increased in bulk until he became a mountain and the gods willed that heaven with all its stars should rest upon his shoulders.

Perseus continued his flight and eventually arrived at the country of the Aethiopians, of which Cepheus was king. His queen, Cassiopea, had been so proud of her beauty that she had dared to compare herself to the sea-nymphs, which roused their **indignation**[12] to such a degree that they sent a prodigious sea-monster to ravage the coast. Fishermen and ships were destroyed by the dreadful monster, and Cepheus in dismay consulted the oracle who directed him to sacrifice his daughter, Andromeda, to appease the deities. Weeping and sad, Cepheus ordered his beautiful daughter to be chained to a rock where the monster could find her and devour her. He kissed her tenderly and hastened away, fearing to look back.

---

[11] **realm**—domain; ruled territory.

[12] **indignation**—anger, caused by something unworthy.

At this moment, Perseus, flying far overhead, glanced down and saw the maiden. She was so pale and motionless, that if it had not been for her flowing tears and her hair that moved in the breeze, he would have taken her for a marble statue. He was startled at the sight and almost forgot to wave his wings. As he hovered over her, he said, "O maiden, undeserving of those chains, tell me, I **beseech**[13] you, your name and the name of your country. Tell me why you are thus bound."

At first she was silent, half-frightened at the sight of the hero who floated in the wind above her. But seeing that he was not going to harm her, she told him her name and that of her country, and the punishment that had fallen on the land because of her mother's pride of beauty. Before she had finished speaking, a sound was heard far off on the water, and the sea-monster appeared with his head raised above the surface, cleaving the waves with his broad breast. Andromeda shrieked in terror, and her father and mother who were hiding not far away, rushed back to the rock. They stood near, wretched and helpless.

Perseus flew close to them and said, "There will be time enough for tears. This hour is all we have for rescue. My rank as the son of Jupiter and my renown as the slayer of Medusa might make me acceptable as a suitor. I will try to win her, if the gods will only favor me. If she be rescued by my valor, I demand that she be my reward."

The parents eagerly consented.

The monster was now within a stone's throw of Andromeda, when, with a sudden bound, Perseus soared high into the air. As an eagle in flight sees a serpent basking in the sun and pounces on him, so the youth darted down upon the back of the monster and plunged his sword into its shoulder. Irritated by the wound, the monster raised himself up and then plunged into the depths. Like a wild **boar**[14] surrounded by a pack of barking dogs, it turned swiftly from side to side. Perseus stuck to its back and stuck it time and again with his sword, piercing its sides, its flanks and its tail. The brute spouted water and blood from its nostrils, and the wings of the hero were wet with them. He no longer dared trust them to carry his weight and he alighted on a rock which rose above the waves. As the

---

[13] **beseech**—ask.

[14] **boar**—male swine.

monster floated near, he gave it a death stroke.

The people who had gathered on the shore shouted so that the hills re-echoed the sound. The parents, wild with joy, embraced their future son-in-law, and Andromeda was unchained and descended from the rock.

At the palace a banquet was spread for them, and joy and festivity ruled the land. But, suddenly, a noise was heard and Phineus, the **betrothed**[15] of Andromeda, burst in and demanded the maiden as his own. It was in vain that Cepheus reasoned, "You should have claimed her when she lay bound to the rock, the monster's victim. The sentence of the gods dooming her to such a fate dissolved the engagement, as death itself would have done."

Phineus made no reply and hurled his javelin[16] at Perseus. It missed its mark and fell to the floor. Perseus would have thrown his in turn, but the cowardly **assailant**[17] ran and took shelter behind the altar. His act was a signal to his band who set upon the guests of Cepheus. They defended themselves and a general conflict ensued. The old king retreated from the scene after fruitless arguments and called the gods to witness that he was

guiltless of this outrage on the rights of hospitality.

Perseus and his friends fought on, but the numbers of their assailants were too great for them. Then Perseus thought once more of the Gorgon's head. "I will make my enemy defend me," he said to himself. He called out, "If I have any friend here, let him turn away his eyes!"

He held Medusa's head high. "Seek not to frighten us with your tricks," a man cried, and raised his javelin to throw it. He was instantly turned to stone. Another was about to plunge his sword into the **prostrate**[18] body of his foe when his arm stiffened and he could neither thrust it forward nor withdraw it. Men were petrified with their mouths open as they shouted in anger, and the swords of those still alive hit against the bodies of their enemies and broke.

Phineus, behind the altar, beheld the dreadful result of his injustice. He called aloud to his friends, but got no answer. He touched them and found

---

[15] **betrothed**—person engaged to be married.

[16] javelin—light spear.

[17] **assailant**—attacker.

[18] **prostrate**—stretched out with face to the ground.

them stone. Falling on his knees, he stretched out his hands to Perseus. "Take all," he begged. "Give me but my life!"

"**Base**[19] coward," Perseus cried, "this much I will grant you. No weapon shall touch you. You shall be preserved in my house as a memorial of these events."

So saying, he held the Gorgon's head in front of Phineus, and in the very form in which he knelt with his hands outstretched and face half **averted**,[20] he became fixed, a mass of stone!

---

[19] **Base**—lowly.

[20] **averted**—turned away.

QUESTIONS TO CONSIDER

1. Why did Atlas tell Perseus to leave?

2. How do the gods punish those with too much pride?

3. In what ways was Perseus a hero?

4. Do you feel sorry for Phineus when Perseus turns him to stone? Explain your opinion.

5. What, in your opinion, are Perseus's chief virtues, and what are his chief flaws?

The Taming of the Sun

(Hawaiian myth)

BY DONNA ROSENBERG

Storytelling is an important part of the Polynesian culture of Hawaii. Because Hawaii is rich in vegetation, and fish are plentiful, the Polynesian people have always had enough leisure time to cultivate their love of song, dance, and oral tales. "The Taming of the Sun" is one of the more popular Hawaiian myths. It tells the story of what happens when the demigod Maui decides to lighten his mother's workload. (A demigod is the male offspring of a god and a mortal, who has some but not all of the powers of a god.) In this myth and in others, Maui is both hero and trickster. Some of his exploits cause trouble, although his intent is always good.

Life was easier for those on earth after Maui had raised and fastened the sky high above. However, life was still very difficult because the sun god now traveled quickly across the sky and made each day much too short.

In fact, it was impossible for trees and plants to produce enough food for the human family because it took them so long to grow. And it was impossible for men and women to finish any one task within the few hours of available light. Farmers did not have time to plant or to harvest a crop. Hunters did not have time to set their traps or to empty them. Fishermen did not have time to reach their fishing grounds or to return from them. And women did not have time both to prepare and to cook the day's food, or to make the bark cloth that they used. Even prayers to the gods were completed after the sun had returned to his home. For most of each day, the world was damp, dreary, and dark.

From the time that he could remember, Maui would watch his mother, Hina-of-the-Fire, as she tried to make the bark cloth, called kapa, during the brief time that the sun was traveling across the sky. It was a long and complex task at best.

First, Hina-of-the-Fire had to take branches from the mulberry trees and soak them in seawater until their bark was soft enough for her to remove it. Once she had removed the bark, she had to separate the inner layer from the outer layer, since she would only be able to use the inner bark to make kapa. She would stack the wet pieces of inner bark in bundles and lay them upon the kapa board where, beginning at one end of the board and moving to the other end, she would pound them with a four-sided wooden beater until the bark had become soft, thin sheets of pulp. Finally, she would paste these thin sheets together into large cloths that would make fine clothes to wear and mats on which to sleep.

Since the sun traveled so quickly across the sky, the process of collecting the bark took one month. The process of soaking it took a second month. The process of separating it took a third month. And the process of pounding it into thin sheets took six more months. In the early stages of this process, it was difficult to keep the bark wet. After the sheets had been pasted together, it was difficult for the

kapa to dry. The entire process could take as long as a year, and making kapa was only one of a woman's daily tasks!

Maui watched his mother hard at work day after day, rushing to prepare her materials for one task, working faster at another task, sighing in despair as the sun entered his home before she had completed anything, and his heart ached for her. And the more Maui's heart ached for his mother, the more his heart filled with anger at the sun. So it came to pass that Maui turned his attention away from his mother and toward the sun. In order to observe the sun more carefully, he climbed the extinct volcano that can be found on the northwest side of the island. From there, he noticed that each morning as the sun began his journey, the sun would travel up and over the eastern side of the great mountain called Haleakala (the House of the Sun).

Then one day Maui asked his mother, "Why does the sun have to travel so quickly? Why doesn't he care about those who live on the earth? Is there a way to stop him from behaving so selfishly? I am going to tame him! What if I cut off his legs? That should keep him from running so fast!"

"The sun does what he has always done and what he will always do," his mother replied. "No ordinary person can confront him and live to tell about it. If you are going to try to change his behavior, you have set yourself a great task, and you will need to prepare yourself well. The sun is very large and powerful, and his rays are fiery hot. Once you come face to face with him, your courage will dry up in his heat as if you were no more than a dead plant!

"I think that you had better visit your grandmother and ask her to help you," Hina-of-the-Fire suggested. "She can give you good advice, and she has just the weapon that might bring you success.

"Your grandmother lives on the side of Mount Haleakala, not far from where the sun always begins his morning journey. You will know that you have found the place when you come upon a large wiliwili tree. Your grandmother prepares breakfast for the sun every morning, and he stops there to eat before he begins his journey.

"Your grandmother cooks bananas for the sun to eat," Hina-of-the-Fire explained. "You must be at the wili-wili tree as the sun makes the sky rosy-red with his first rays. A rooster stands watch by the tree, and he announces the sun's arrival by crowing three times. It is then that your grandmother will come out with a bunch of bananas and put them on the ground while she makes a fire in order to cook them for the sun to eat. You must take these bananas.

"Your grandmother will then come out with a second bunch of bananas and put them on the ground in order to cook them for the sun to eat. You must take these bananas as well."

Maui's mother concluded, "Your grandmother will then come out with a third bunch of bananas and put them on the ground in order to cook them for the sun to eat. She will notice that someone has taken the first two bunches of bananas and will begin searching for the thief. It is then that you must present yourself to her. You must tell her that you are Maui, and that you are the son of Hina-of-the-Fire."

So it came to pass that, while the sun was asleep, Maui set out to climb Mount Haleakala. Just as the sun made the sky rosy-red with his first rays,

Maui saw the great wiliwili tree painted in black against the pale-colored sky. The rest happened just as his mother had told him it would. The rooster crowed three times. The old woman, who was his grandmother, appeared two times with a bunch of bananas that Maui took. When she discovered that these two bunches were missing, she cried, "Where are the sun's bananas?" and began to search for the thief.

Maui's grandmother was so old that she was almost totally blind. As she searched for the thief, she came close enough to Maui to smell the scent of a man. She then approached him, peered into his face with her clouded eyes, and asked, "Who are you? And what do you want with the sun's bananas?"

"I am Maui, the son of Hina-of-the-Fire," Maui replied, "and I have come for your help. I want to tame the sun! I need to find a way to stop him from behaving so selfishly. He travels much too quickly! He makes each day so short that even my mother cannot finish any of her tasks. It can take her a full year to make kapa! Those who are not gods must have an even more difficult time!"

Maui's grandmother listened carefully to his words. And as she listened, the things of the earth and sky praised Maui. In his honor, thunder roared and the rainbow bridge appeared. In his honor, pebbles chattered and ants sang. In his honor, dogs without fur walked the land. Surely, Maui was born to be a hero among men!

So it came to pass that Maui's grandmother decided to help him. "Listen carefully to my words, my grandson," she said, "and I will help you tame the sun. First, you must make sixteen ropes that you must twist from the strongest coconut fiber. Then, you must ask your sister, Hina-of-the-Sea, to give you enough of her hair to enable you to make a noose for the end of each of them.

"When these are ready," she concluded, "return to me, and I will tell you how to arrange the ropes so as to catch the sun. I will also give you a magic axe of stone so that you will have a great weapon to use against the sun."

Given the short days, it took many months for Maui to make the ropes and nooses, but finally he was ready to return to his grandmother's home. While the sun slept, she showed him how to set the nooses as traps and how to tie the ropes to the great wili-wili tree. Then Maui dug a hole for himself by the roots of the great tree and hid inside the hole so that the sun would not be able to see him when he began his morning journey.

When the sun made the sky rosy-red with his first rays, Maui was ready for him. Soon, the sun's first ray appeared over the top of Mount Haleakala and became caught in one of Maui's nooses. Then the sun's second ray appeared over the top of Mount Haleakala and became caught in one of Maui's nooses. One by one, the fourteen other rays of the sun came over the top of Mount Haleakala, and, one by one, each ray became caught in one of Maui's nooses. Finally, the sun, dressed in his bright crimson robe, stood on top of Mount Haleakala. He was ready to begin his morning journey, but he was unable to move even one of his rays.

At first, the sun violently thrashed this way and that, desperately trying to pull his rays out of the nooses and to retreat down the back of Mount Haleakala into the sea-home from which he had come. But he could not pull the ropes off the wiliwili tree,

and the roots of that great tree held the tree fast.

"Who has trapped me in these snares? And what do you hope to gain by it?" the sun roared.

"I am Maui, the son of Hina-of-the-Fire," Maui replied, "and I have come for your help. You must stop behaving so selfishly. You travel much too quickly! You make each day so short that my mother cannot finish any of her tasks. It can take her a full year to make kapa! Those who are not gods must have an even more difficult time!"

"I don't care about your mother and her kapa!" the sun exclaimed. "And I certainly don't care about those who are not gods! The faster I travel each day, the longer I can sleep each night. This is what I have always done, and this is what I will always do! As for you, if you don't release me from these snares right now, you will not live to see your mother again!"

Maui immediately bent down, but he did not intend to release the sun's rays. Instead, he picked up his grand-mother's magic axe and waved it threateningly at the sun.

The sun responded by turning his blazing face upon Maui. He seared Maui with his fiery breath, hoping to burn him quickly to ashes.

Maui retaliated by attacking the sun. Despite the intensity of the sun's heat, Maui mercilessly struck the sun, again and again, with the stone axe.

Finally, the sun screamed, "Stop it! I can't stand the pain any longer! If you keep beating me like this, you're going to kill me! And if I die, you and everything that lives will die as well! As it is, I'm going to hobble all the way home!"

"I will stop," Maui replied, "if you promise me that you will travel slowly across the sky each day."

"Do I have to travel slowly every day from this day forth and forever?" the sun wailed.

"No," Maui replied, relenting. "It will be good enough if you travel slowly for just half of the year. Your light and your heat will enable plants to grow faster and produce more fruit, and they will permit men and women to get their work done faster and more easily. Then, for the other half of the year, you can travel as fast as you wish."

The sun was quick to agree to this compromise. So it came to pass that Maui released the sun's sixteen rays from the nooses. However, as a daily reminder of their agreement, he left the ropes and nooses next to the great wiliwili tree on the side of Mount Haleakala, where the sun would be sure to see them as he climbed over the top of the mountain.

So it came to pass that, because of Maui's efforts, life became much easier for human beings. Each day during the long season that came to be known as summer, the sun traveled across the sky so slowly that the days were very long.

Now it was possible for trees and plants to produce enough food for the human family because they grew fast and well. And now it was possible for men and women to finish a difficult task within the long hours of available light. Farmers now had time to plant or to harvest a crop. Hunters now had time to set their traps or to empty them. Fishermen now had time to reach their fishing grounds or to return from them. And women now had time to prepare their food and to cook it, or to make the bark cloth that they used.

In honor of Maui's taming of the sun, the people celebrated and sang, "How good it is that the sun's journey is long and that he now gives us the light we need for our daily work!"

QUESTIONS TO CONSIDER

1. What is the problem with the sun that Maui feels he needs to solve?

2. How is Maui's grandmother responsible for the rising of the sun each morning?

3. Why does Maui take the sun's bananas?

4. What steps does Maui take to tame the sun?

The Dream Journey

(Maori myth)

BY GERALDINE MCCAUGHREAN

The Maori are people of New Zealand who speak a language that is part Tahitian and part Hawaiian. Many anthropologists believe that the Maori are descended from groups of Polynesian canoe travelers who reached New Zealand around A.D. 900. From A.D. 900 to around 1800, the Maori lived on fish from the sea and sweet-potato crops that they grew in nearby fields. In their free time, the Maori indulged in their love of wood-carving, poetry, chants, dances, and songs. "The Dream Journey" may well have been one of the myths the Maori men and women told during their long evenings of storytelling.

There once was a great chieftain named Kahakura whose mind was as wide as the plain and whose dreams were as bright as sunshine. One night, a dream shone on his sleep that was almost too dazzling to comprehend, but it filled him with feelings of great hope and excitement. "Go north," said the voice in his dream. "Go north and I will show you the shape of happiness.

> "Go alone, without a sound
> Like the shadow of a bird
> Passing over broken ground,
> Or flies' flicker. Be not heard
> More than time passing."

Kahakura was so thrilled by his dream that he got up at once and ran down to the beach to tell his people. The young men of his tribe stood about, balanced precariously[1] on the seaside rocks, aiming spears at the fish in the water. They would throw, jump in, retrieve their spears, and

---

[1] precariously—dangerously.

begin again. Their catch lay on the shore—a couple of bass and a flatfish.

"I must go away! I've dreamed a dream," announced Kahakura. "I've seen a vision. I've been made a promise by the gods! Stay here and wait: I'm going north to fetch the gift the gods have promised us!"

The young men stood on one leg and stared at him open-mouthed. Go away? Leave them without a chief and go north into hostile country? Not if they could help it.

"We'll come with you!" they said, jumping down into the surf. "We'll all go!" They wanted neither to miss out on the adventure nor to see their chief disappear over the horizon without knowing when or if he would return. So, although Kahakura insisted he must go alone, they dogged his footsteps around the settlement and stuck as fast to him as his own shadow. Kahakura began to think he might not be able to do as his dream instructed: his own people would stop him from making whatever marvelous discovery awaited him in the north.

One evening, when the whole village was dancing, the music loud, and the singing **cacophonous,**[2] Kahakura backed away into the surrounding darkness. He cast a last fond look at his people dancing in a pool of firelight, then turned and began to run—northward.

For many days, he trekked through the provinces of tribes whose warriors would have speared him as eagerly as fishermen spearing a fish. But Kahakura wove his way through the gray tassels[3] at either end of day, when the ground is carpeted neither with light nor dark. At long last, he came to a country called Rangiaowhia, fluffy with white flax and fringed with yellow sand. He first glimpsed the sea in the early morning. It seemed to Kahakura that the moon, in leaving the sky, must have fallen and smashed. For the sea was silver with sparkling lozenges[4] of metallic light. Then the water began to rattle and leap, to explode with fish, such crowds of them that they shouldered each other out of the water to somersault in the surf. A feast of fish! Kahakura's first instinct was to race into the surf and gather them up in armfuls—but instead, he hid himself. He was not first on the scene. Someone was already busy catching the fish.

---

[2] **cacophonous**—jarring, discordant; dissonant.

[3] tassels—something like a hanging bunch of threads.

[4] lozenges—diamond shapes.

The fishermen were the frail, slender, tiny Sea People—a tribe who lived among the ocean waves and came ashore only as often as the Land People put out to sea. Kahakura had heard tell of them, and now here they were—in front of his very eyes—fishing. And not with spears!

Looking once more at the multitude of fish in the bay, Kahakura saw that they were being hauled in and harvested in a giant bag—a spider's web of woven thread, delicate as hair yet strong as sinew. When the mouth of the bag was closed, inside it were trapped not one fish or two, but one or two thousand!

Kahakura stared. "This is what I was sent here to see," he thought. "A way of catching fish that will feed my tribe for all time! As long as the sea runs and fish run in the sea, we'll never be hungry again! I must take that bag home with me, to copy how it is made."

From his hiding place, Kahakura watched the Sea People struggle. Though they were pretty, with their yellow hair and pale, smooth skins, they were a puny race, narrow-chested, thin-shanked,[5] with pinched moonish faces. It took twenty men to land the catch, whereas Kahakura could have done it with a couple of friends.

The work done, the young men lay about exhausted among their canoes, while their blond women gutted and cleaned the fish. A flock of gulls gathered to eat the offal,[6] and frightened the Sea People's tiny children.

Apart from the other women sat a girl quite different from the rest. She had the task of mending the net. Children sat about her feet, laughing at the stories and jokes she told them, but the other women sat with their backs turned, and threw her not so much as a civil word. Perhaps it was her beauty that made them resent her. Perhaps it was her **formidable**[7] size that made the men equally unkind. Taller than the tallest fishermen, she had hips like the curving bole[8] of a tree, and arms strong enough to carry a family of children. Her clever hands wove and knotted flaxen thread into the holes where the net had torn. Kahakura was so entranced by the sight of her and her quick, darting fingers that he almost forgot why the gods had sent him to Rangiaowhia.

---

[5] thin-shanked—having slender legs between the knee and the ankle.

[6] offal—waste parts, especially of a butchered animal.

[7] formidable—arousing fear, dread, or alarm.

[8] bole—stem or trunk.

The net!

He jumped up from his hiding place, and as his head rose above the bushes, he realized he had not even thought what to say, or how to come by the precious net that now lay stretched at the girl's feet. He had nothing to trade for it, no weapon to fight with for it, and the language of the Sea People was strange to him. So when they caught sight of him, he spoke with a great loud voice—as people do to make foreigners understand them.

"I am Kahakura of the Maori People! I dreamed a dream and I saw a vision . . . Wait, don't go!"

The Sea People took one look at his towering frame, huge shoulders, broad chest. Then mothers snatched up their children and threw them into the canoes, jumping in after them. The men plunged into the surf and dragged the canoes out to sea.

The big yellow-haired girl took two steps from her seat and fell, her feet tangled in the net she had been mending. Her basket of threads and tools was spilled on the ground. For a moment, Kahakura thought to bundle her up in the net like a giant tuna and sling her over his back. He had to have her for his wife, to stroke that golden hair, and watch her bounce his children on her knee.

But the thought came to him—as clearly as the dream had come to him in sleeping—that a man does not take a wife in the same way as a fisherman takes a tuna. So he stood just where he was, and allowed her to untangle her feet and get up.

She ran a few steps toward the sea, saw her tribe and family paddling away, abandoning her, but she did not cry out. She looked back to where Kahakura stood wearing a crooked, uncertain smile. He gathered up the spilled tools and thread and handed the basket back to her. "It is as the gods wish, or my eyes would not have seen you," he said. And she seemed to understand.

So Kahakura took home to his tribe the amazing secret of fishing nets— how they are used and how they are made. And he took home, too, a wife with golden hair and hips curved like the bole of a flourishing tree, and strong arms destined to hold a family of children. As long as the sea runs and the fish run in the sea, the Maori People will never go hungry for fish, nor empty of love. It is as the gods wish.

QUESTIONS TO CONSIDER

1. What is the purpose of Kahakura's journey?

2. Why does Kahakura stop himself from grabbing the yellow-haired girl and running?

3. What type of leader was Kahakura?

4. What do you suppose was the purpose of this myth?

Part Eight

Friend and Foe

"The goddess Athena had caught and tarried the horse. It was she who brought him to the field. But no one was allowed to come near him. He had never been ridden by a mortal."

◀ **Pegasus and the Hydra** *by Odilon Redon*

Pegasus was the fabulous winged horse that sprang from the blood of Medusa. With the goddess Athena's help, the great Greek warrior Bellerophon managed to ride Pegasus, but ultimately died as a result of his attempt to tame the special horse.

The Calydonian Boar Hunt

BY INGRI AND EDGAR PARIN D'AULAIRE

How can a wild boar possibly destroy an entire kingdom? In the D'Aulaire version of this story, a pig runs around in a murderous rage, while Greece's finest warriors gather to try to kill him.

Meleager of Calydonia was one of the heroes who had sailed with Jason on the *Argo*. No one could throw a spear with greater skill than he. Still he was powerless to stop a fearful boar[1] that was ravaging[2] his father's kingdom. The king, one day, had forgotten to include Artemis when he sacrificed to the gods, and in revenge the angry goddess sent the biggest boar ever seen. The boar had tusks as big as an elephant's and bristles as sharp as steel. Meleager sent for the Argonauts and all the great athletes of Greece and asked them to come to Calydonia and hunt down the monstrous beast. Great glory awaited the one who could destroy the Calydonian Boar.

Many heroes came to the hunt, and also a girl whose name was Atalanta.

She was the fastest runner in Greece and a great huntress as well. When some of the men grumbled at hunting with a girl, Meleager ruled that a girl who could outrun them all would certainly be welcome to join the chase. Still grumbling, the men had to give in.

For days the heroes feasted at the Calydonian court. Then they offered rich sacrifices to the gods and went off to the hunt. They drove the boar out of its lair,[3] and as it charged, spears and arrows flew wild. When the dust settled, seven men lay dead, some killed by the boar, some by the arrows of their excited companions. Atalanta alone kept a cool head. She ran swiftly

---

[1] boar—a male pig.

[2] ravaging—laying waste; destroying.

[3] lair—the den or dwelling of a wild animal.

hither and thither till she could take good aim, and then she let an arrow fly. The arrow stopped the boar just in time to save the life of a hero who had stumbled in front of the onrushing beast. Quickly Meleager leaped forward and hurled his spear with all his might. The beast rolled over and lay dead.

Meleager offered the hide and the tusks to Atalanta. These trophies were hers, he said, for it was she who stopped the boar. Again the men protested, for it hurt their pride to see a girl walk off with all the glory. Meleager's two uncles teased him and said that he must be in love with the girl. "Just wait till your wife finds out about this!" they said, smiling **maliciously.**[4]

In a rage Meleager hurled his spear at his taunting uncles, killing them both. When Meleager's mother heard that her son had slain her two brothers, she, too, flew into a rage. She ran to her treasure chest and took out a half-charred log. It was a magic log that held Meleager's life.

This log had been burning in the hearth when Meleager was born. The three Fates[5] had come to see the infant, and the mother had overheard them say it was a pity that the handsome child would die as soon as the log had burned up. Quickly the mother had seized the log, beaten out the flames, and had hidden it among her dearest treasures. Thus Meleager had lived to become a great hero.

Now in her fury, the queen flung the old dry log into the fire. As it burst into flames and was consumed, Meleager felt a searing pain shoot through his body and fell dead.

The Calydonian Boar Hunt, which had begun with a feast, ended with a funeral. Only Atalanta was happy. She had won her trophies in competition with the greatest heroes of Greece.

---

[4] **maliciously**—with extreme ill will.

[5] three Fates—the three goddesses of destiny known to the Greeks as the Moerae and to the Romans as the Parcae.

QUESTIONS TO CONSIDER

1. Why does Artemis send a boar to Calydonia?

2. Who is Atalanta and what is her role in the boar hunt?

3. What is your opinion of Meleager? Do you feel sorry for him? Why or why not?

Pegasus

BY JANE YOLEN

Close your eyes and picture a mythical being. Whom or what do you see? It's possible that you can catch at least a glimpse of Pegasus, the famous winged horse. For most people, Pegasus represents everything that is wonderful about Greek mythology. Pegasus is a huge white horse with a tremendous wingspan and the strength of ten oxen. He can fly faster than any bird in the sky and run faster than any mammal on the ground. Here is his story.

In the city of Corinth,[1] many years ago—the beggar said—there lived a young man named Bellerophon. His hair was the blue-black of the deep ocean, his eyes the lighter blue-green of waves. Some said he was the son of King Glaucus, but more said he was Poseidon's own son—Poseidon, god of the sea.

The women of Corinth whispered and sighed whenever Bellerophon walked by, for he was very handsome. But he did not desire any of them. Nor did he desire gold or power. All he wanted was to ride the great winged horse, Pegasus, who it was said was to be found in a field outside of the city and guarded by the gods. Bellerophon had never seen the horse except in dreams. Still, the flying horse was all he desired.

Now Pegasus was clearly no ordinary horse. Above his broad white shoulders grew great wings, with **alabaster**[2] feathers and vanes[3] of gold.

And he had not been born in any ordinary way either. When the hero Perseus had slain the snake-haired gorgon, Medusa, her blood had rained down upon the ground. There earth

---

[1] Corinth—one of the wealthiest and most powerful cities of ancient Greece.

[2] **alabaster**—a pale yellowish pink to yellowish gray.

[3] vanes—the flattened, web-like parts of a feather, consisting of a series of barbs on either side of the shaft.

and blood had combined to create the flying horse Pegasus.

The goddess Athena herself had caught and tarried[4] the horse. It was she who brought him to the field. But no one was allowed to come near him. He had never been ridden by a mortal.

All the young men in Corinth desired Pegasus, but none wanted him as much as Bellerophon. Bellerophon found he could not stop thinking about the winged horse. He could not sleep or eat for the wanting. He paced back and forth talking about the horse, forgetting his friends, ignoring his studies, dreaming only of Pegasus. It was as if he were possessed.

His mother watched him grow thin, watched him grow pale, watched the rings form under his sea-colored eyes. Fearing he would die of such a longing, she sent him to consult the wise man Polyidus for advice.

"Go to the temple of Athena," said Polyidus, "she who caught and tamed the horse. Put aside all thoughts, all desires. Go to the temple and sleep. Surely the goddess will speak to you in your dreams."

Bellerophon bade his mother good-bye, took a thin wool blanket that she had woven, and went to Athena's temple. It was a large building, with great white pillars and a floor of colored tiles.

When dusk came and all the other worshippers went home, Bellerophon alone stayed on. He spread his blanket near the goddess's altar, sat down, and closed his eyes. As night trembled around him, he fell asleep. He did not know he dreamed, but he dreamed.

He dreamed that Athena stood before him, something gold and shimmering in her hands, saying, "You are my brother Poseidon's true son. I will let you alone ride the winged horse. You will need my magic bridle.[5] Take it." And then she was gone.

Bellerophon awoke and it was still night, yet the temple was lit by a strange light. There, on the temple floor, not far from the altar, was a golden bridle. When he touched it, his hand tingled; when he picked it up, the light vanished.

"Thank you, Athena," he whispered. Then he lay down on the blanket and fell asleep, the bridle clutched in his arms.

He had no more dreams.

In the morning, Bellerophon went to the field where Pegasus was

---

[4] tarried—delayed.

[5] bridle—a harness used to restrain or guide an animal.

pastured. Slowly he walked toward the horse, who seemed to be waiting for him. When at last he reached Pegausus, he touched the great white shoulder with a tentative hand. The horse did not even twitch.

"I am Bellerophon, son of Poseidon," he said, whispering his boast. "Will you let me bridle you?"

Pegasus shook his head, but only to rid himself of flies, and Bellerophon slipped the golden bridle over the horse's muzzle, up over his eyes, over the crown of his head.

"Now will you let me ride?" whispered Bellerophon. Without waiting for an answer, he leaped lightly onto the horse's back.

Startled, Pegasus pumped his mighty wings once, and flew up into the air. If Bellerophon had not been holding tight to the reins, had his legs not been wrapped tight around the horse's great barreled body, he would surely have fallen off.

Another great cleaving of the white wings, and they were above the field and the sea beyond, above trees, above the hills, above the far mountains, just under the plump clouds.

Cautiously, Bellerophon peered down. He saw how the land stretched out, now green fields, now gold. He saw how the waves in the water made runnels[6] in the sea. He felt the cold wind on his arms, the rush of air making streamers of his dark hair. He knew he could never be happier.

---

[6] runnels—narrow channels.

QUESTIONS TO CONSIDER

1. How was Pegasus born and what does he look like?

2. Why do you think all the men want to ride Pegasus?

3. Why does Athena choose Bellerophon for the honor?

Typhon, The Hydra, and The Empusae

BY ANNE ROCKWELL

In her introduction to these myths, Anne Rockwell explains: "Everywhere in the world, people have imagined monsters, made up stories about them, and tried—in art—to show us what they looked like." Some of the most terrifying monsters in literature belong to the Greeks and Romans, of course, who encouraged their storytellers to tell one grisly tale after another. In many Greek and Roman myths, a heroic man, woman, or child battles a monster in a heroic attempt to save the world. In other myths, monsters roam free, while humans and gods alike flee in terror.

Typhon

Of all the monsters that ever were, Typhon was the biggest. His head, which nearly touched the stars, was that of an enormous mule. He could imitate the sound of any beast. The spread of his wings darkened the earth. His arms stretched farther than the eye can see, and his hundreds of fingers were the heads of serpents. Where his legs should have been were great coiled serpents. Fire and burning rocks poured out of his mouth whenever he roared. He was married to the terrible snake-woman, Echidna, who ate men raw. The two of them were the proud parents of a hundred terrible monsters.

Typhon was afraid of no one, not even the gods. One day he decided to go to war with the immortal ones who lived on Mount Olympus. The gods and goddesses were so terrified at the sight of him that they all ran away and disguised themselves as animals. But Typhon pursued them until he finally captured almighty Zeus himself and imprisoned him in a cave. Here the ruler of the gods remained until his messenger, crafty Hermes, finally set him free.

Zeus regained his courage. He hurled thunderbolts at Typhon until one wounded the monster. Then Zeus picked up a mountain and threw it at him with all his godly force.

Typhon roared out in pain. Zeus had finally won. The mountain was even larger than Typhon. It covered every bit of him.

The gods and goddesses returned home in peace, but Typhon continued to bellow from beneath the mountain until fire and rocks from his mouth spurted up and made a volcano called Etna.

The Hydra

One particularly horrible child of Typhon and Echidna was the Hydra, a huge monster with many serpent heads. He lived in a swamp, where his venom poisoned the water all around. No one could kill him, for whenever anyone chopped off one of his heads, another immediately grew in its place.

Heracles, a powerful hero and the strongest mortal who ever lived, decided to do battle with the monster. The Hydra summoned his friend, a gigantic crab, to help him fight Heracles. But Heracles, too, had brought a helper named Iolaus.

As fast as Heracles cut off one of the Hydra's heads, Iolaus **seared**[1] the stump with his red-hot sword, so it could never grow back. At last all the Hydra's heads were gone. And Heracles tossed the giant crab out of the swamp, high up into the sky, where we can see it still as the constellation known as Cancer.

The Empusae

The Empusae were the three repulsive daughters of Hecate, the witch goddess. Their only companions were the dead, and they themselves looked like ghosts. They were also very dirty and stank horribly.

Whenever dogs howled late on moonless nights, it meant the Empusae were roaming about. These monsters liked to hide near dark and lonely crossroads, where they moaned and wailed to frighten nighttime travelers. Those who journeyed frequently along such roads knew they could chase the dreaded spooks away simply by insulting them and calling them names, but most travelers didn't know that.

---

[1] **seared**—charred, scorched, or burned.

In order to bribe the Empusae to stay away from crossroads, people often left plates of rotten fish and the flesh of dogs. It was disgusting food, but the Empusae loved such treats. And after they had eaten, they usually behaved themselves—until they were hungry again.

QUESTIONS TO CONSIDER

1. How does Zeus destroy Typhon?

2. What remains of Typhon now, and how does that help us understand the way myths were used to explain things?

3. Why were people frightened of the Empusae?

4. Which of the monsters—the Typhon, the Hydra, or the Empusae—would you have wanted to avoid at all costs?

5. Why do you think Greek storytellers invented myths about such horrible monsters?

The Two Hunchbacks

(Italian folk tale)

BY ITALO CALVINO

An important theme in the mythology and folklore of many cultures is punishment. Since most myths and tales have at least one evil or naughty character, the question of how to punish the character for his or her misdeeds almost always comes up. In most cases, the storyteller would try to invent a punishment that fitted the crime. For example, in a well-known Greek myth, a weaver who is overly proud of her tapestries is changed into a spider by the goddess Athena. In "The Two Hunchbacks," a group of little old women must find a way to punish an intruder. Does their punishment seem appropriate?

There were two hunchbacks who were brothers. The younger hunchback said, "I'm going out and make a fortune." He set out on foot. After walking for miles and miles he lost his way in the woods.

"What will I do now? What if **assassins**[1] appeared . . . I'd better climb this tree." Once he was up the tree he heard a noise. "There they are! Help!"

Instead of assassins, out of a hole in the ground climbed a little old woman, then another and another, followed by a whole line of little old women, one right behind the other, who all danced around the tree singing:

Saturday and Sunday!
Saturday and Sunday!

Round and round they went, singing over and over:

Saturday and Sunday!

---

[1] **assassins**—murderers.

From his perch in the treetop, the hunchback sang:

And Monday!

The little women became dead silent, looked up, and one of them said, "Oh, the good soul that has given us the lovely line! We never would have thought of it by ourselves!" Overjoyed, they resumed their dance around the tree, singing all the while:

Saturday, Sunday,
And Monday!
Saturday, Sunday,
And Monday!

After a few rounds they spied the hunchback up in the tree. He trembled for his life. "For goodness' sakes, little old souls, don't kill me. That line just slipped out. I meant no harm, I swear."

"Well, come down and let us reward you. Ask any favor at all, and we will grant it."

The hunchback came down the tree.

"Go on, ask!"

"I'm a poor man. What do you expect me to ask? What I'd really like would be for this hump to come off my back, since the boys all tease me about it."

"All right, the hump will be removed."

The old women took a butter saw, sawed off the hump, and rubbed his back with salve, so that it was now **sound**[2] and scarless. The hump they hung on the tree.

The hunchback who was no longer a hunchback went home, and nobody recognized him. "It can't be you!" said his brother.

"It most certainly is me. See how handsome I've become?"

"How did you do it?"

"Just listen." He told him about the tree, the little old women, and their song.

"I'm going to them, too," announced the brother.

So he set out, entered the same woods, and climbed the same tree. At the same time as last, here came the little old women out of their hole singing:

Saturday, Sunday,
And Monday!
Saturday, Sunday,
And Monday!

From the tree the hunchback sang:
And Tuesday!

---

[2] **sound**—in good condition.

The old women began singing:

Saturday, Sunday,
And Monday!
And Tuesday!

But the song no longer suited them, its rhythm had been **marred.**[3]

They looked up, furious. "Who is this criminal, this assassin? We were singing so well and he had to come along and ruin everything! Now we've lost our song!" They finally saw him up in the tree. "Come down, come down!"

"I will not!" said the hunchback, scared to death. "You will kill me! "

"No, we won't. Come on down!"

The hunchback came down, and the little old women grabbed his brother's hump hanging on a tree limb and stuck it on his chest. "That's the punishment you deserve!"

So the poor hunchback went home with two humps instead of one.

---

[3] **marred**—damaged.

QUESTIONS TO CONSIDER

1. What is funny about this tale?

2. For what reason, if any, does the second man deserve to be punished?

3. Would you call the little old women friends or foes?

4. How does the punishment fit the crime in this case?

Image Gallery

Gods, Mortals, and Monsters

Pan
engraving from a statue, artist unknown
In this line engraving, Pan, the god of shepherds, forests, wildlife, and fertility, directs his attention toward what was probably a part of a syrinx, or panpipe. ▶

▲

Centaur

artist unknown, 19th century

The centaurs lived mostly in the mountains of Greece. Occasionally a centaur would
come down from his mountain cave in order to steal a nymph or young woman to have
as a wife. For this reason, and because they had a reputation for being cruel and vicious,
the centaurs were disliked by mortals and immortals alike.

▲

Theseus Battling the Centaur
artist unknown, 1495

The centaurs were always on the lookout for females to kidnap. On one memorable occasion, Theseus was forced to battle a whole group of centaurs who were trying to carry off the bride and all the women guests at a wedding.

 The Minotaur
**by George Frederic Watts,
19th century**
The Minotaur was a Greek mythological monster that
was half-man and half-bull. He was the son of Queen
Pasiphaë and a beautiful white bull that Pasiphaë had fallen
in love with. The Minotaur, who was kept in a labyrinth
designed by Daedalus, demanded that 14 Greek children
be sacrificed to him each year. In this oil painting, the
Minotaur does not appear ferocious; instead, he seems
almost melancholy as he ponders the view before him.

Medusa
**by Michelangelo Merisi
da Caravaggio, c. 1597?**
Of all the Greek monsters, Medusa was perhaps the most
terrifying. In addition to having serpents for hair and long,
sharp teeth, Medusa had a body that was covered with
scales and a set of deadly claws that could shred an animal
or person in just one swipe. On this painted shield, Medusa
is shown beheaded.
▼

▲

Aladdin

by Anne Grahame-Johnstone, 1965

In most versions of the Aladdin story, Aladdin is an idle, good-for-nothing boy who finds a magic lamp with a genie inside. The genie—who is as smart as Aladdin is dull—is able to obtain for Aladdin all the wealth and power he desires.

Quetzalcoatl
artist unknown, c. 1500

The Aztec god-man Quetzalcoatl was the god of self-sacrifice, wisdom, and science. He was also a priest known for his good works among humans. In most paintings and sculptures of Quetzalcoatl, you can see godlike characteristics in addition to the human ones. ▶

Shiva

This is a detail of a carved exterior of the Shiva Meenakshi Temple in India. Shiva, who was known as the great destroyer, had many arms and hands in order to make his job of destroying and then creating life a little easier. Notice that in this carving, Shiva wears a friendly expression. In other pieces of art, Shiva looks quite ferocious.
▼

▲

Daedalus and Icarus
by Bernard Picart, 1731

Daedalus, a brilliant inventor, was imprisoned in the Labyrinth of Crete with his son,
Icarus. Unwilling to serve out his term, Daedalus fashioned two sets of wings from wax
and feathers and then taught himself and Icarus how to fly. Icarus, who had none of his
father's common sense, flew too close to the sun and melted his wings.

▲

Hercules and the Hydra
late-18th-century engraving, artist unknown,
For Hercules's second labor, he was directed to kill the Lernaean Hydra, a water snake that had a huge, doglike body and many snakelike heads. (Some storytellers say the Hydra had as many as 9,000 heads; others say there were only seven.) The Hydra was so dangerous a monster that even its breath was poisonous.

◀ *Atlas*
artist unknown, c. 1880
Atlas was a Titan who was forced to bear the weight of the sky on his shoulders as a punishment for battling Zeus. For the most part, Atlas is portrayed as a dimwitted giant, although later he was given the important job of helping to guard the golden apples of the Hesperides.

▲
The Building of the **Argo**
artist unknown

The *Argo* was the ship Jason had built in order to complete his quest for the Golden Fleece. The ship, which was larger and more magnificent than any other ship on the sea, was forever memorialized by its crew, who called themselves the Argonauts.

◄ *Odin*
artist unknown

In this portrait, the great Norse God Odin stands with his two crows, Hugin (who represented thought) and Munin (who represented memory). Odin relied on both crows to inspire him in his writing.

▲

Thor

artist unknown

In Norse mythology, Thor (the son of Odin) was the god
of war. At all times Thor kept with him his hammer (Mjolnir)
that boomeranged back to his hand after he hurled it at
his enemies. He also wore a belt that doubled his strength
whenever he put it on, and iron gloves that helped protect
him. Most of Thor's battles were waged against the Giants.
As such, he was a great friend of all humans.

King Arthur

The real King Arthur was probably a Celtic British king
or chieftain of the sixth century. The mythic King Arthur
that we read stories about today was first described in Sir
Thomas Malory's *Morte d'Arthur*. In Sir Malory's tale, a
young Arthur must first pull the sword Excalibur from a
rock before he can assume the throne of England. This
illustration depicts that scene. ▶

Cú Chulainn

Although he was not a god, Cú Chulainn was capable of superhuman feats that were similar to those of the Celtic hero Beowulf. When angry, Cú Chulainn could be a terrible sight: one eye bulged while the other shrank back in his head, his mouth fell open, his hair stood up, and a column of blood spurted from the top of his head.

▼

▲

Beowulf and the Dragon
by Rockwell Kent, 1932

Beowulf, Prince of the Geats, was a tremendously courageous mortal who was admired throughout Geatland. As a young man, Beowulf rescued the Danes by slaying the monster Grendel and Grendel's mother. Fifty years later he died saving his own people from a fire-breathing dragon.

Part Nine

Metamorphosis

"Then, just as Athena had changed from an old woman into her true shape, she transformed Arachne."

◀ Ariadne and Arachne by Andre Durand, 1980

In Greek and Roman mythology, the mortal Arachne is punished for her hubris, or excessive pride. The goddess Athena turns Arachne into a spider and announces that the girl will spend the rest of her life spinning webs that people will sweep away in disgust.

Zeus, Metis, and Athena

BY ROGER LANCELYN GREEN

Of all the Olympians, few were as well liked or respected as Athena, daughter of Metis and Zeus. Part of the reason for this was her mysterious and traumatic birth, which all of the Olympians were there to witness. Another reason Athena was held in awe was because she was such a paradox. She was the goddess of war, yet she hated to fight. She dressed in armor, yet she spent most of her time weaving, sewing, and sculpting. She was easy to please, yet she had a ferocious temper. It is no surprise that Athens, the Greek city built as a tribute to this goddess, was known the world over for both its blood-thirsty armies and its wonderful art.

When Zeus first began his campaign against Cronos and the Titans it was Metis, the daughter of Oceanus, whose wise counsel helped him most. It was she who showed him how to rescue his brothers and sisters whom the monstrous Cronos had swallowed; and she continued to assist him with her prudence[1] and good advice until the war was won and the Titans were imprisoned forever in Tartarus.

When the time came for Metis to receive her reward she demanded nothing less than to be the wife of Zeus. This was before he married his sister Hera and made her queen of Heaven, so he consented, though not very happily. For Metis was one of the Titan kind, and although in the reign of Cronos she had been the goddess of prudence and good counsel, she had also magical powers such as that of changing herself into any shape she chose.

Naturally, when she became the bride of Zeus she took on the form of a beautiful goddess, and for a little while Zeus was happy with her and his fears were laid at rest—but not for long. The wise Titan Prometheus, who had also helped Zeus to gain the

---

[1] prudence—careful management.

victory, and who was now busy creating mankind to people the earth, came to Zeus one day with words of warning. (For this was before Prometheus stole fire from the chariot of the Sun and suffered his terrible punishment on Caucasus.)

"Take care, great Zeus," said Prometheus. "I who have some power of seeing into the future, and who can hear and understand the words spoken by Mother Earth, have learned that if Metis bears children, the first will be a daughter—the wisest of all goddesses. But if she bears another child it will be a son who is fated to become the lord of Heaven."

Zeus was sorely troubled at this, and realized why he had felt so much hesitation over marrying Metis. He knew that he was in great danger not only from the son who might be born, but also from Metis herself, who would never agree to cease from being his wife and, being a Titaness, with such strong powers of magic, would probably wreak[2] some terrible vengeance on him if he tried to put her away.

Also he wanted his daughter to be born to inherit all the wisdom and wise counsel of Metis and to take her place among the new gods of Olympus.

At last he hit upon a strange scheme, which showed that he was still very much the son of Cronos the Titan. Whether or not it was Prometheus who told him how his daughter might still be born even after Metis was no more, and warned him of what he himself must suffer at her birth, Zeus proceeded with his plan.

As he and Metis sat together on mighty Olympus, looking out over the wide world, Zeus brought up the subject of her magic power of changing from one form to another.

"Is there no creature too vast and strong for you to take on its shape?" asked Zeus. "A lioness, for example?"

"That is easily done," smiled Metis. A moment later she was gone, and a huge golden lioness stood in her place, roaring until Olympus echoed.

When Metis was herself again Zeus remarked: "I should never have doubted that the queen of Olympus could take the form of the queen of beasts. But it seems to me harder for one so noble and mighty as you to become a small and worthless creature; a fly, for example."

Scarcely had he spoken when Metis vanished and an ordinary looking fly settled on his hand. In a moment Zeus had swallowed the fly—and that was the end of Metis.

---

[2] wreak—inflict.

But in swallowing her Zeus had swallowed all her wisdom, and her unborn daughter too—though her birthday was not yet. Indeed, before she was born, Zeus had married Hera and made her the queen of Heaven, instead of vanished Metis. Apart from Prometheus, neither gods nor mortals knew what had become of her, save only for Helios who drove the chariot of the Sun across the sky each day and saw everything that took place in Heaven or upon the earth.

About this time Zeus decided to divide the earth among the immortals, making one or another of them the special guardian of each district or island or site of a city that was to be. They cast lots on Olympus, parceling out the whole earth between them, and in doing so forgot Helios himself, the only god who was not present, since none but he could drive the Sun-chariot over the great arch of the sky.

When night came and Helios had stabled his horses in his palace with the silver doors which Eos the Dawn-goddess would open for him in the morning, he hastened to Olympus, crying:

"Father Zeus, what land has fallen to my lot? For surely one of you remembered me and wrote my name on a shell to be drawn out of the golden urn with the rest." The gods were filled with shame and sorrow; and Zeus was ready to command a new lottery so that this time none should be left out.

But Helios exclaimed:

"There is no need to cast lots again, for there is one land, the most beautiful of all islands, which has not been given to any immortal. It lies still beneath the sea between Crete and the tip of Asia; for you, Father Zeus, plunged it to its doom to stamp out those wicked goblins the Telchines who dwelt there when Cronos ruled. Fighting on the side of the Titans, they made rain, hail, and snow to vex the gods of Olympus, and had just invented a poisonous mist made of sulphur and the black water of Styx, the river of the dead, which would cause death to all living creatures and to the very trees and flowers, when their doom came upon them. Now, I beg you, raise up this island from beneath the sea and let me be its lord. If you do so, I will wed Rhode the daughter of golden Aphrodite, and make her the Nymph of the Island; and she, the Lady of the Roses, shall cover it with fair flowers and make of it the fairest isle in all the seas."

"Bright Helios, be it as you wish!" cried Zeus. "Now let the island of Rhodes rise out of the **azure**[3] sea to be forever the blessed kingdom of the Sun."

All came to pass as Helios had asked and Zeus commanded. Very soon Rhodes was the envy of all the immortals: trees and flowers covered its hills and valleys; winter did not come near it, and the butterflies made their home under the shelter of Mount Atabyrios.

Helios and Rhode had seven handsome sons who grew swiftly to manhood and became the rulers of the island. And to them alone Helios told the secret of what had happened to Metis, and of the wonderful daughter who would soon be born with no visible mother.

"The moment she comes into the world I will see and tell you," said Helios to his eldest son Cercaphus. "As soon as I do, climb in haste to the top of Mount Atabyrios and sacrifice an ox to her; then you will be the first men on earth to do so, and she who is to be the goddess of wisdom and skill will be so pleased with you that she will grant you the fairest gifts she has to give, and bring good fortune to Rhodes for evermore."

Cercaphus and his brothers had not long to wait. The day came when Zeus was troubled with a raging pain in his head. Knowing what this meant, he summoned all the immortals to Olympus, telling them that a new goddess was about to be born: "A glorious goddess, bright-eyed, inventive, unbending of heart, pure virgin, saviour of cities, and most valiant."

When all the gods and goddesses were assembled in Olympus, Prometheus came among them bearing a great axe. He went straight to the throne where Zeus sat, bowed low before the king of gods and men, and then, whirling up his axe, struck Zeus full upon the crown of the head with its sharp blade, for a moment splitting open his immortal skull.

There went up a great gasp from the gods and goddesses: and in that moment before the wound closed and was healed as if nothing had happened, there sprang a shining shape from the head of Zeus and stood before them all on the golden floor of Olympus. It was a tall and beautiful goddess, with flashing grey eyes, clad in shining armor and shaking a sharp spear. As Athena sprang from the immortal head and stood before Zeus all

---

[3] **azure**—sky blue.

Olympus rocked, the earth trembled and the sea was troubled; bright Helios himself stopped his swift horses, and the Sun stood still in Heaven for a while.

Then Athena put off her helmet and armor, and Zeus and the gods rejoiced at her coming, and made her welcome to her place among them in Olympus.

Helios continued on his way across the sky; but he contrived to send a swift message to his son Cercaphus that the time had come to offer the first sacrifice to the new goddess in the sight of all men to gladden the heart of Athena and of almighty Zeus her father and win her favor for Rhodes above all other lands.

Eagerly Cercaphus and his brothers set out for the top of high Mount Atabyrios, driving a fine ox for the sacrifice and carrying dry faggots[4] of wood. When they came to the summit they built a great altar, heaped the wood upon it, slew[5] and cut up the ox and prepared for the sacrifice. But a strange cloud of forgetfulness had lain over their minds; not one had thought to bring fire with them, nor the means of making fire. And so the sacrifice was incomplete, and no savor of burnt offering could rise to Olympus and

make Athena turn a kindly gaze towards Rhodes.

The honor of making the first sacrifice to the new goddess which the sons of Helios failed to gain was won by a little village called Cecropia, built upon a great rocky acropolis[6] which rose out of the plain of Attica a few miles from the sea, and thither in time Athena went to claim the site as the chief center of her worship.

Zeus, however, did not let the sacrifice attempted by Cercaphus and his brothers go unrewarded, nor did Athena herself. Zeus caused a yellow cloud to pass over the island from which fell a shower of gold; and Athena bestowed upon all who dwelt there the gift of surpassing all mortal men in their deftness[7] of hand. Soon the men of Rhodes were fashioning works of art—statues and pottery and gold shaped into cups of necklaces— more beautiful than those made anywhere else. And in days to come their descendants fashioned a statue of Helios, to stand beside the harbor, which for its size and beauty ranked

---

[4] faggots—bundles of twigs, sticks, or branches bound together.

[5] slew—past tense form of the verb to slay, which means "to kill."

[6] acropolis—high, fortified part of an ancient Greek city.

[7] deftness—skillfulness.

as a wonder of the world and was called the Colossus of Rhodes.[8]

Meanwhile Athena, though born fully grown and with so much of the wisdom of her mother Metis already hers, had certain things still to learn. For her upbringing she was entrusted to Triton, the son of Poseidon and his sea-bride Amphitrite. Triton was a merman[9] who lived most of the time in the sea, and might be seen riding on a dolphin and blowing a great curved shell, or conch, like a horn. But he sometimes dwelt by a river in north Africa whose nymph, Trito, was his wife. They had a daughter called Pallas,[10] and she became Athena's companion, and soon her close friend.

Together the two girls dwelt in the land of sunshine where the Lotus grew, where the river widened out into a lake called Tritonnis, and learned all those things that should be known by a goddess as well as by a mortal. They also learned to cast the spear and to wrestle. But one day they quarreled, and Pallas snatched up a spear and made as if to cast it at Athena. Zeus was watching and sent a flash of lightning which dazzled Pallas and made her miss her aim; but Athena cast her own spear true to the mark, and her beloved friend sank to the ground and died.

Bitterly sorry for what she had done, Athena cried out that her friend's name should be linked with her own ever afterwards, and that men should pray to her henceforth as Pallas Athena. She also made an image of Pallas and set it up in Olympus. But later Zeus cast it down to earth to show Dardanus, his hero son—whose mother was Electra the sister of Maia, one of the Pleiades— where to build his city. Dardanus set up the image, which was called the Palladion,[11] in the temple of Athena in his new city which was called Troy. There it became known as the Luck of Troy, and no one could conquer the city; until cunning Odysseus crept in during the siege and stole it, after which he made the famous Wooden Horse, by means of which the Greeks took Troy and destroyed it.

After the death of Pallas, Athena was ready to take her place among the Twelve Gods of Olympus and, like the rest of them, she demanded a city where she should receive special worship and honor.

---

[8] Colossus of Rhodes—the bronze statue of Helios at Rhodes; one of the Seven Wonders of the ancient world.

[9] merman—an imaginary creature of the sea, with the head and body of a man, and the tail of a fish.

[10] Pallas—in astronomy, one of the largest asteroids.

[11] Palladion—a statue of Pallas Athena, believed to have the power to preserve Troy. Also called the Palladium.

"There is a village in Attica called Cecropia after its ruler," she said. "Of all places upon earth it was the first to offer me a burnt sacrifice, and that village is my choice."

"It belongs to me!" cried Poseidon. "It stands on a great rock a little way from the sea; but I have only to strike the ground with my trident and Attica will be flooded, making Cecropia into an island."

Now it seemed likely that a great quarrel would break out between Poseidon and Athena; but to prevent it Zeus summoned a council of the rest of the Twelve Gods to decide between them.

They all met on the flat rocky top of Cecropia which rose out of the plain of Attica, with sheer cliffs on three sides and a steep slope at the narrowest end.

"Cecropia is mine!" cried Poseidon. "It already belongs to the sea!" So saying he struck the rock with his trident, and at once there was a round well of salt water from which came the sound of sea waves whenever the south wind blew.

"Salt water will be of little use to the people of my city," said Athena quietly. "Though in time they may rule the waves, and then pay due honor to great Poseidon the Shaker of the Earth. But see now the gift which I make to them, which shall bring them both comfort and wealth, and to all mankind also."

She touched the ground with her spear at a place where a hollow in the rock had become filled with earth, and at once the First Olive Tree pushed through the soil, grew to full size, and swelled until its trunk was thick and gnarled. Its branches put forth leaves of a beautiful greyish-green with undersides of silver, and then they began to bend and sag with thick clusters of ripe black olives.

"See!" cried Athena. "Here is fruit for my people; and, when they crush it, clear rich oil that may be put to many purposes: they may cook their food in it; at night their lamps will burn brightly when filled with olive oil; and with it they may cleanse and anoint their bodies and make them fresh and supple."

There was no doubt among the gods as to who had won the match. Poseidon went away in a whirlwind of fury, and raised a great tempest which flooded part of the land. But the result was only to give the people the wonderful natural harbors of Phaleron Bay, Piraeus, and the Bay of Eleusis.

Meanwhile Athena changed the name of her city to Athens and set about making it the most famous in all the Greek world, and the most skilled in literature and architecture and sculpture. Where the great contest with Poseidon had taken place the Athenians of later ages built a beautiful temple of marble, called the Erechtheum, to cover the salt well and protect the divine Olive Tree. But on the highest point of the Acropolis they built the Parthenon, the temple of Athena Parthenos: Athena the Maiden, to be the most beautiful building, even in ruins, that the world has ever seen.

Before the golden age of Athens dawned, however, the earliest Athenians had much to learn. When Athena became goddess of the city the first ruler, Cecrops, had no son to succeed him, but only three daughters called Herse, Aglauros, and Pandrosos. She made them her first priestesses, and they dwelt on the Acropolis in the earliest temple, the Royal House, which was built beside the well and the Olive Tree. Besides guarding and tending these, the three maidens learnt how to weave a beautiful robe by Athena's command to place on her statue when the time came for it to be set up.

One night Athena appeared to the maidens and told them to follow her. She touched the rock with her spear and a secret passage opened, leading down from the Acropolis by a steep stair. By this way she led them to the base of the rock and then on to the sacred garden of Aphrodite, where afterwards a temple stood. There she gave them a beautifully painted chest and told them to carry it back to the Acropolis by the way they had come, and guard it carefully in the Royal House.

"But do not open the chest," she cautioned them, "for what is inside it is not lawful for your eyes to look upon."

The three priestesses bore the chest back by the secret stair up to the Acropolis and into the Royal House, where they guarded it as Athena had told them. But Aglauros and Herse were filled with curiosity to know what was inside. For a long time their fear of Athena kept them from disobeying her command; but at last they could bear it no longer. They tried to persuade Pandrosos to join them in their disobedience, but she refused indignantly.[12] So they waited until one hot summer afternoon when Pandrosos was asleep, and then tiptoed to where the chest stood in the innermost shrine, and cautiously opened the lid.

Inside lay a baby boy, sleeping peacefully; and round him were curled

---

[12] indignantly—angrily.

two terrible serpents. At the sight of them and at the touch of the poisonous breath with which they hissed fiercely up at them, Herse and Aglauros went mad. Dropping back the lid they rushed screaming from the Royal House and flung themselves over the steep edge of the Acropolis and down on to the rocks far below at that very moment Athena was on her way to Athens, bringing a huge mass of rock to build up the one end of the Acropolis where there was a slope and not a sheer cliff. When she saw what had happened, she let fall the rock a mile away on the plain— where it stands to this day, and is called Mount Lycabettos.

But in spite of their disobedience Athena decided not to abandon Athens. So she herself, with the aid of Pandrosos, brought up the marvellous child, Erechtheus, who had been born out of the earth and reared by the two snakes. When he was a man, Athena made Erechtheus both her high priest and the first true king of Athens and the whole Attic plain. For Cecrops was dead, and he had ruled only over the little village which had now become the City of Athens. Erechtheus built a temple, the Erechtheum, on the site of the Royal House, and made the first and most sacred statue of Athena to stand in it. He also taught the

Athenians to hold the great festival each year called the Panathenaea in honor of Athena, when the great procession wound its way up on to the Acropolis to present her statue with a newly woven robe.

Pandrosos had completed the first robe which she and her foolish sisters began; and ever afterwards the maiden priestesses of Athena followed her example. For weaving had been invented by Athena, and she had taught it to the three daughters of Cecrops, the first of all mortals to practice the art.

But after the First Web had been woven in the Erechtheum on the Acropolis of Athens, the art of weaving became known to mankind and spread over the world. Athena herself instructed her priestesses in other cities besides Athens, and indeed saw to it everywhere that women excelled in this her special art.

QUESTIONS TO CONSIDER

1. How did Zeus trick his wife Metis, and why did he do it?

2. How was the goddess Athena born?

3. Why were Poseidon and Athena battling over Cecropia, and who won?

4. What happened to Cecrops's three daughters?

Arachne the Spinner

BY GERALDINE MCCAUGHREAN

"Arachne the Spinner" is all about arrogance. To a Greek god or goddess, the worst sin a mortal could commit was the sin of arrogance. The Greeks called it hubris, *which means "excessive pride." The immortals of Mount Olympus viewed hubris as a direct challenge to their own superiority. Unfortunately, almost all mortals committed the sin of hubris at one time or another. Each time this happened, one of the gods or goddesses stepped in and gleefully doled out the appropriate punishment.*

Once, when all cloths and clothes were woven by hand, there was a weaver called Arachne more skillful than all the rest. Her tapestries[1] were so lovely that people paid a fortune to buy them. Tailors and weavers came from miles around just to watch Arachne at work on her loom. Her shuttle[2] flew to and fro, and her fingers plucked the strands as if she were making music rather than cloth.

"The gods certainly gave you an amazing talent," said her friends.

"Gods? Bodkins! There's nothing the gods could teach me about weaving. I can weave better than any god or goddess."

Her friends turned rather pale. "Better not let the goddess Athena hear you say that."

"Don't care who hears it. I'm the best there is," said Arachne.

An old lady sitting behind her examined the yarns Arachne had spun that morning, feeling their delightful texture between finger and thumb. "So if there were a competition between you and the goddess Athena, you think you would win?" she said.

"She wouldn't stand a chance," said Arachne. "Not against me."

---

[1] tapestries—heavy cloths woven with rich, often vari-colored designs or scenes. Tapestries are usually hung on walls for decoration.

[2] shuttle—a device used in weaving to carry the woof thread back and forth between the warp threads.

All of a sudden the old lady's gray hair began to float like smoke about her head and turn to golden light. A swish of wind blew her old coat into shreds and revealed a robe of dazzling white. She grew taller and taller until she stood head and shoulders above the crowd. There was no mistaking the beautiful gray-eyed goddess, Athena.

"Let it be so!" declared Athena. "A contest between you and me."

Arachne's friends fell on their faces in awe. But Arachne simply threaded another shuttle. And although her face was rather pale and her hands did tremble a little, she smiled and said, "A contest then. To see who is the best weaver in the world."

To and fro went the shuttles, faster than birds building a nest.

Athena wove a picture of Mount Olympus. All the gods were there: heroic, handsome, generous, clever, and kind. She wove all the creatures of creation onto her loom.[3] And when she wove a kitten, the crowd sighed, "Aaaah!" When she wove a horse, they wanted to reach out and stroke it.

Alongside her sat Arachne, also weaving a picture of the gods.

But it was a comical picture. It showed all the silly things the gods had ever done: dressing up, squabbling, lazing about, and bragging. In fact she made them look just as foolish as ordinary folk.

But oh! when she pictured a butterfly sitting on a blade of grass, it looked as if it would fly away at any moment. When she wove a lion, the crowd shrieked and ran away in fright. Her sea shimmered and her corn waved, and her finished tapestry was more beautiful than nature itself.

Athena laid down her shuttle and came to look at Arachne's weaving. The crowd held its breath.

"You are the better weaver," said the goddess. "Your skill is matchless. Even I don't have your magic."

Arachne preened herself and grinned with smug satisfaction. "Didn't I tell you as much?"

"But your pride is even greater than your skill," said Athena. "And your irreverence is past all forgiving." She pointed at Arachne's tapestry.

"Make fun of the gods, would you? Well, for that I'll make such an example of you that no one will ever make the same mistake again!"

---

[3] loom—an apparatus for weaving thread or yarn into cloth.

She took the shuttle out of Arachne's hands and pushed it into her mouth. Then, just as Athena had changed from an old woman into her true shape, she transformed Arachne.

Arachne's arms stuck to her sides, and left only her long, clever fingers straining and scrabbling. Her body shrank down to a black blob no bigger than an ink blot: an end of thread still curled out of its mouth. Athena used the thread to hang Arachne up on a tree, and left her dangling there.

"Weave your tapestries forever!" said the goddess. "And however wonderful they are, people will only shudder at the sight of them and pull them to shreds."

It all came true. For Arachne had been turned into the first spider, doomed forever to spin webs in the corners of rooms, in bushes, in dark, unswept places. And though cobwebs are as lovely a piece of weaving as you'll ever see, just look how people hurry to sweep them away.

QUESTIONS TO CONSIDER

1. What is Arachne's greatest fault, and how does it contribute to her downfall?

2. Why do you think Athena first disguises herself as an old lady?

3. Would you say Athena's punishment fits the crime? Explain.

Syrinx

BY INGRI AND EDGAR PARIN D'AULAIRE

In Greek mythology, there is a group of beings who are neither gods nor humans. They are the creatures who live in the woods, mountains, rivers, and oceans of Greece. In most myths, they are called satyrs and nymphs. The satyrs are woodland spirits who are part man and part animal. The satyrs are free-spirited, naughty deities who love to dance, sing, and chase after the nymphs, their female counterparts. Of course, the nymphs want nothing to do with the satyrs. They are too busy pining away for the gods of Mt. Olympus. Nymphs live in the forests, mountains, and water of Greece. They are quite lovely and are often a source of frustration for the jealous goddesses.

Syrinx ran away from Pan; she thought he was so ugly. Pan chased after her, and, to escape from him, she changed herself into a reed.[1] She stood among hundreds of other reeds on the river-bank, and Pan couldn't find her. As he walked through the reed patch, sighing and looking for her in vain, the wind blew through the reeds. They swayed and bent and made a **plaintive**[2] whistling sound. Pan listened, enchanted. "Thus you and I shall always sing together," he said.

He cut ten reeds into unequal lengths, tied them together, and made the first panpipe. He called the new instrument his syrinx, for every time he played on it he thought he heard the melodious voice of his beloved nymph. Again Pan was lonesome and he retreated to his cool cave, deep in the woods, and scared away all passers-by with his unearthly screams.

Splendid Apollo himself fared no better than Pan when he fell in love with a nymph called Daphne. Daphne had a cold heart, she had vowed never to marry, and when Apollo wooed her, she would not listen to the sound

---

[1] reed—a tall, thick piece of grass.

[2] **plaintive**—sorrowful, mournful.

of his golden lyre and ran away. As she fled, she was lovelier still, with her golden hair streaming behind her, and Apollo could not bear to lose her. He set off in pursuit, **beseeching**[3] her to stop. Daphne ran toward the bank of a river that belonged to her father, the river-god Ladon, calling to him to save her from her pursuer. Ladon had no time to rise out of his river bed and come to his daughter's rescue, but the moment Daphne's toes touched the sand of the riverbank, he changed them into roots. Apollo, who was close at her heels, caught up with her, but the instant he threw his arms around her, her arms changed into branches, her lovely head into the crown of a tree, and she became a laurel.[4] Still, inside the hard bark, Apollo could hear the beating of Daphne's frightened heart.

Apollo carefully broke off some twigs and made a wreath[5] of the shining leaves.

"Fair nymph," he said, "you would not be my bride, but at least consent to be my tree and your leaves shall crown my brow."

Ever after, the greatest honor an artist or hero could be given was to be crowned with a wreath from Apollo's sacred tree, the laurel.

Daphne would rather be an unloving tree than the bride of the great god Apollo, but all the other nymphs loved to sit at his feet and listen to his enchanting music, and were very honored when he or any of the other great Olympian gods chose one of them as a bride.

---

[3] **beseeching**—begging.

[4] laurel—an evergreen tree with aromatic, simple leaves and small blackish berries.

[5] wreath—ring of leaves or flowers twisted together.

QUESTIONS TO CONSIDER

1. Why does Daphne run from Apollo?

2. What do Syrinx and Daphne have in common?

3. Which do you think would make a better companion: Pan, god of nature, or Apollo, god of light?

Freedom for Prometheus

BY GERALDINE MCCAUGHREAN

This myth is a continuation of the Prometheus story, which begins on page 197. Prometheus, champion of all humankind, is chained to a rock as punishment for stealing from Zeus. Although life on the rock is agony, Prometheus doesn't complain. He is very proud that he was able to get the best of Zeus. In some versions of the Prometheus story, Prometheus frees himself. In others, Hercules comes to the rescue of his old friend. In Geraldine McCaughrean's retelling of the myth, Prometheus is freed thanks to a surprising change of heart.

Even the gods grow wiser as they grow older. Almighty Zeus, king of the gods, looked down one day from Mount Olympus and saw Prometheus still chained to his rock, condemned forever to be tortured by eagles. Zeus felt a kind of shame, because it is shameful for the strong to bully the weak.

And he felt a kind of pity, because it is sad to see a father kept from his children, an artist kept from his handiwork.

And he felt a kind of admiration: not just for Prometheus for enduring his pain, but for the little men and women Prometheus had made out of water and mud. If he had not given them the gift of fire, how could there be fires burning now on a thousand altars throughout the world, raising up holy, sweet-scented smoke to heaven?

For all they were irreverent[1] and ugly and caught cold and grew old and stole and quarreled and made mistakes and died, there were heroes and heroines among those men and women.

---

[1] **irreverent**—disrespectful.

So Zeus broke Prometheus's chains with pliers[2] of lightning, and wrapped the eagles in whirlwinds and spun them away to the four corners of the world. And Prometheus was free once more to champion the little people of the world, whom he had made out of water and soil.

---

[2] pliers—small tool with pincers used for holding, bending, or cutting.

QUESTIONS TO CONSIDER

1. Why does Zeus break Prometheus's chains?

2. How does Zeus feel about humans?

3. What kind of metamorphosis does Zeus experience?

4. Does this myth change your opinion of Zeus? Explain.

The Orders of Cagn

(South African myth)

BY JOAN C. VERNIERO AND ROBIN FITZSIMMONS

"The Orders of Cagn" is a myth that originated in the San (or Bushmen) tribes of South Africa. The San traditionally have lived as hunter-gatherers in small groups of 20 to 100 people. The San speak various dialects of a click language. Religious practices vary from order to order (an order is a group), although the many different San orders are linked by a rich and complex mythology. In San mythology, the first being—called Cagn—is all-powerful and all-knowing. Most San myths concern Cagn or his descendants.

Cagn was the first being. He was an animal spirit. He ruled on earth as the great magician and organizer. His orders caused all things to be made, including the sun, moon, stars, wind, mountains, and animals. Cagn's wife was Coti. They had two sons. Cogaz was the elder and the chief. The younger son was Gewi.

When Cagn ordered all things and animals to be made, he made them fit for the use of humans. He ordered snares, or traps, and weapons. Next he made the partridge and the striped mouse. He ordered the wind so it could carry the smell of game. And so on.

Here are two of the many myths about Cagn.

One day Cagn's daughter grew angry with her father because he **scolded**[1] her. She ran away, intending to throw herself among the snakes, the qabu. In the world that Cagn made, snakes were also men and they ate snake's meat. The chief of the snakes married the daughter of Cagn. But the chief served his new wife the meat of eland, or African antelope. He did this because he knew no child of Cagn could eat an evil thing.

---

[1] **scolded**—yelled at or criticized harshly.

Cagn knew what was in the far distance. He enlisted his first-born Cogaz to go to the land of the snakes and to bring back his daughter. With his father's tooth to make him strong, Cogaz gathered an army of young men to accompany him on his mission.

Seeing the party of Cogaz approach, some of the snakes grew angry. They began to hide their heads.

"Do not be angry. They have come for Cagn's child," said the chief of the snakes.

The sister of Cogaz gave her brother and his army the meat of eland.

"Tell your husband we are here to take you home," said Cogaz.

After doing so, Cagn's daughter prepared food for their journey. The next morning Cogaz, his sister, and the army found some rushes[2] that grew in the nearby marshes and bound them around their limbs and bodies. They departed for home while three snakes followed closely behind them.

First the snakes tried to bite Cogaz and his party. But the rushes protected them. The snakes tried to beat them with reins, but the rushes served as a shield. When the snakes threw sand at the foreigners in an attempt to drive them into the water, they failed once

more. They did not know that Cogaz carried Cagn's tooth for strength.

Meanwhile, the snakes that were at home with their chief knew that when the three snakes returned, they would fill the country with water. Upon willow poles, they built a high stage. The wives of the three snakes took their husbands and threw them into the water. The water rose to the height of the mountains. But the high stage kept the chief and the other snakes dry.

Cagn bid Cogaz to return to the snakes with an invitation to come to him. Cagn ordered the snakes to lie upon the ground. With his stick he struck each one. Every time he struck, the body of a person emerged from the snake. The new people saw the ground littered with the skin of the snakes they had been. Cagn sprinkled the snakeskins with the oil of canna, a tropical herb. In this way the snakes turned from being snakes. They became Cagn's people.

Another myth about Cagn tells of the thorns, or dobbletjes. They were called Cagn-cagn, and they were dwarfs. One day Cagn came upon the thorns, and he saw them fighting

---

[2] rushes—marsh plants.

among themselves. When Cagn went to separate the thorns, they turned their anger upon him. And they killed him. The biting ants who witnessed the killing devoured Cagn.

Time passed, and the biting ants and the thorns collected Cagn's bones. They arranged the bones in order, and they attached Cagn's head with cord. Thus assembled, Cagn stumbled home. When Cogaz, his elder son, saw his father, he cured Cagn. Once Cagn was whole again, Cogaz asked what had happened. On this occasion it was Cogaz that gave Cagn advice and power.

"The best way to fight the dwarfs is to pretend to strike at their legs. When they move to protect themselves, hit them on their heads," said Cogaz to his father.

As Cogaz instructed, Cagn killed many of the evil thorns. And he drove them into the mountains.

QUESTIONS TO CONSIDER

1. Who is Cagn? How would you describe him?

2. What are some of his powers?

3. What sort of powers do Cagn's children have?

4. Which of the two myths about Cagn did you find more interesting? Why?

The Children of the Sun

(Inca myth)

BY DONNA ROSENBERG

"The Children of the Sun" is a fertility myth. This means that it is a myth about the cycles of life. In a fertility myth, there is usually one being who is responsible for "birthing," and then another who is responsible for overseeing the people, animals, plants, insects, and so on. For example, in Greek and Roman mythology, all things originated with Gaea. Gaea gave birth to twelve Titans who acted as overseers of the universe. In Chinese mythology, a giant being called P'an-ku created the world and then maintained it for another 18,000 years. Day after day, century after century, P'an-ku watched over the earth and sky.

The Incas were an ancient people of South America. In the Inca tradition, all of life originated with Father Sun. It was Father Sun who began the process of peopling the earth. Father Sun created the animals, plants, stars, and oceans. Then he created two beings, Manco Capac and Mama Ocllo Huaco, to help oversee all aspects of life.

In times of old, our land was one of shrubs and small trees and tall mountains. The people were unmannered and untaught. They lived as wild animals live, without clothes made from woven cloth, without houses, and without cultivated[1] food.

They lived apart from other human beings in small family groups, finding lodging as nature provided it, within mountain caves and in hollow places beneath the great rocks. They covered their bodies with animal skins, leaves, and the bark of trees, or they wore no clothes at all. They gathered whatever food they could find to eat, such as grass, wild berries, and the roots of plants, and sometimes they ate human flesh.

---

[1] **cultivated**—produced by improving land for raising crops.

Father Sun looked down from the heavens and pitied these humans who lived like wild creatures. He decided to send down one of his sons, Manco Capac, and one of his daughters, Mama Ocllo Huaco, down to earth at Lake Titicaca to teach them how to improve their lives.

When his children were ready to leave, the Sun said to them, "I devote myself to the well-being of the universe. Each day, I travel across the sky so that I can look down upon the earth and see what I can do for the human beings who live there. My heat provides them with the comfort of warmth. My light provides them with the knowledge that comes from sight. It is through my efforts that fields and forests provide food for them, for I bring sunshine and rain, each in its proper season.

"Yet all this, good as it is, is not enough. The people live like wild animals. They know nothing of living in houses, wearing clothing, or raising food. They have no villages, they use no tools or utensils, and they have no laws.

"Therefore," Father Sun continued, "I am making you the rulers of all the races in the region of Lake Titicaca; I want you to rule those peoples as a father rules his children. Treat them as I have treated you, with tenderness and affection, with devotion and justice. Teach them as I have taught you, for the races of human beings are my children also. I am their provider and their protector, and it is time they stopped living like animals.

"Take this golden rod with you," the Sun concluded. "It is only two fingers thick and shorter than the arm of a man, yet it will tell you how good the soil is for cultivating crops. As you travel, whenever you stop to eat or to sleep, see if you can bury it in the land. When you come to the place where the rod sinks into the earth with one thrust, establish my sacred city Cuzco,[2] city of the sun. Soft soil as deep as this golden rod will be fertile soil."

So Manco Capac and Mama Ocllo Huaco went down to Lake Titicaca and set out on foot to examine the land. Wherever they stopped they tried to bury the golden rod, but they could not do it. The soil was too rocky.

Finally they descended into a valley. The land was wild and without people, but the plant growth was lush

---

[2] Cuzco—the capital city of the Incas.

and green. They climbed to the **crest**[3] of a hill (the hill where Ayar Cachi and Ayar Ucho[4] had turned to stone) and pressed the golden rod into the soil. To their great pleasure, it sank into the earth and disappeared.

Manco Capac smiled at Mama Ocllo Huaco and said, "Our father, the Sun, intends us to rule this valley. Here we will build his sacred city, Cuzco. Let us now go separate ways, you to the south and I to the north. Let us gather together the peoples we find and bring them into this fertile valley. Here we will instruct them in the ways of human beings, and we will care for them as our father has commanded us."

Manco Capac and Mama Ocllo Huaco set out for the mountain plateaus to collect the peoples of the land. The men and women they found in the **barren**[5] regions were impressed with their clothing and pierced ears, their **regal**[6] **bearings,**[7] and their message. "Let us teach you how to lead a better life," the children of the Sun[8] announced. "Let us teach you how to build houses, make clothes, and raise cattle and crops. Right now you live like wild animals. Let us teach you how to live like human beings. Our father, the Sun, has taught us and has sent us here to teach you."

The peoples of the land placed their confidence in these children of the Sun and followed as they led the way toward a new and better way of living. When many people had gathered together, Manco Capac and Mama Ocllo Huaco divided the group into those who would be responsible for gathering food and those who would learn how to build houses. Their new life had begun.

Manco Capac taught the males which foods were nourishing so their diet would include both grains and vegetables, how to choose the best seeds, and how to plant and cultivate each kind of plant. In the process, he taught them how to make the tools and equipment necessary for farming and how to channel water from the streams in the valley for irrigation. He even taught them how to make shoes. Meanwhile, Mama Ocllo Huaco taught the women how to weave wool and cotton into cloth and how to sew that cloth into clothing.

---

[3] **crest**—the top, as of a hill or wave.

[4] Ayar Cachi and Ayar Ucho—Ayar Cachi was a strange and powerful child of the sun who was able to divide hills and valleys with a slingshot. Ayar Ucho was his brother. Because he was not nearly as powerful, Ayar Ucho was jealous of Ayar Cachi.

[5] **barren**—lacking vegetation, especially useful vegetation.

[6] **regal**—magnificent; splendid.

[7] **bearings**—manners in which people carry or conduct themselves.

[8] children of the Sun—the Incas.

So it came to pass that the Incas became an educated people. In honor of their great provider and protector, the Sun, the people built a temple on the crest of the hill where Manco Capac and Mama Ocllo Huaco had plunged the golden rod into the earth and from which they had set out to gather the Inca people together and teach them. Their prosperity drew other peoples to join them and learn their ways. Manco Capac finally taught the men how to make weapons such as bows and arrows, clubs, and lances so that they could defend themselves and extend their kingdom. The Incas were on their way to becoming a great people.

QUESTIONS TO CONSIDER

1. Who are the children of the Sun?

2. What do Manco Capac and Mama Ocllo Huaco teach the people?

3. How do Manco Capac and Mama Ocllo Huaco know where to build Cuzco, and what is special about this place?

4. What do you think was the meaning of this myth for the Inca people?

Cú Chulainn

(Celtic myth)

BY YVONNE CARROLL

Cú Chulainn (or Cuchulain) is the hero of the Ulster Cycle of Irish stories. The Ulster Cycle is a set of myths and legends about the northern kingdom of Ulster, in Ireland. Although not a god, Cú Chulainn was capable of superhuman feats similar to those of the Greek heroes Perseus and Hercules. According to Irish legend, Cú Chulainn spent his life fighting evil all over Ireland. He was known as a protector of all innocents—humans and animals alike.

Seven-year-old Setanta was determined to become a member of the famous Red Branch Knights of Ulster.
His father, the King of Dundalk, had told him about the special school in Armagh, called the Macra, for the young boys who would one day join the brave warriors.

Setanta pleaded with his parents to let him go there but they refused.

"You are much too young, Setanta. Wait a little longer and then we will allow you to go," they said.

Setanta decided he could not wait any longer and so one day he set off for Armagh. It was a long journey but Setanta had his hurley and sliotar[1] to play with. He hit the sliotar far ahead and ran forward to catch it on his hurley stick before it hit the ground.

When Setanta reached the castle of King Connor at Armagh he found the hundred and fifty boys of the Macra gathered on the great plain in front of the castle. Some of them were playing hurling[2] and as this was his favorite game he hurried over to join in. Almost immediately he scored a brilliant goal.

---

[1] hurley and sliotar—equipment used in the game of hurling.

[2] hurling—a traditional Irish game similar to lacrosse.

The other boys were furious that this young boy had joined their game uninvited and they attacked him.

Setanta fought bravely. The noise disturbed the king who was playing chess. He sent a servant outside to see what was happening. Setanta was brought before the king.

"I am Setanta, son of the King of Dundalk, your brother. I have come all this way to join the Macra because I want to become one of the Red Branch Knights as soon as I am old enough."

The king liked Setanta's brave words and welcomed him to the Macra.

Time passed quickly for Setanta. He loved his new life at the Macra.

One day, Culann, the blacksmith who made spears and swords for Connor, invited the king, his knights, and Setanta to a feast.

When it was time to set off for the feast, Setanta was playing a game of hurling. He told the king that he would follow as soon as the game was finished. The feast began and Connor forgot to mention that Setanta would be joining the party later. Thinking all his guests had arrived, the blacksmith unchained his wolfhound[3] which guarded his house each night.

As soon as the game was over Setanta set out. When he arrived at Culann's house he heard the deep growls of the wolfhound. Suddenly the hound leaped forward out of the dark to attack. Setanta saw the sharp teeth bared.[4] With all his strength Setanta hurled his sliotar down the hound's throat. Then he caught the animal by its hind legs and dashed it against a rock. With a loud groan the wolfhound fell down, dead.

Inside, the feast had heard the dog growling. "My nephew Setanta," Connor cried. "I forgot about him." He and the Red Branch Knights rushed out expecting to find the young boy torn to pieces.

Connor was amazed and delighted to find his nephew alive and he was proud of his great strength.

Culann was relieved that the boy was safe but he was sad that he had lost the wolfhound he loved which had faithfully guarded his house every night. "Let me take the place of your hound until I have trained one of its puppies," said Setanta.

---

[3] wolfhound—any of various large dogs trained to hunt wolves or other large game.

[4] bared—exposed.

Culann agreed. From that day on
Setanta was called Cú Chulainn,
which means the Hound of Chulainn.

QUESTIONS TO CONSIDER

1. What three words would you use to
   describe Setanta?

2. How does Setanta change as a result of
   his fight with the wolfhound?

3. Why is Setanta called Cú Chulainn?

Part Ten

Search for Immortality

"The pair crossed the Styx safely and began the long climb up to the passage to the surface of the earth. Orpheus never looked back, though he was greatly tempted. . . ."

◄ **Orpheus and Eurydice** by Sir Edward John Poynter, 1862

The Greeks called Orpheus, son of Apollo, the greatest musician of all time. When Orpheus's wife, Eurydice, dies unexpectedly, Orpheus travels to the Underworld in order to bring her back to life. Hades agrees to let Eurydice go on one condition: that Orpheus refrain from looking at Eurydice's face until they are back on earth again.

Aeneas Visits the Lower World

BY WILLIAM F. RUSSELL

Much of Virgil's writing concerns Aeneas's conquering of Italy. According to William Russell, the following myth, which first appeared in the Aeneid, *"provides a colorful and imaginative point of departure. Virgil's vision of how earthly lives are punished or rewarded after death was intended to encourage his readers toward moral behavior. Whether it had that result is unknown, but the images that he created in this vision have been re-created by other writers for centuries, and are the basis for many references and* **allusions**[1] *today.*

The storm that Aeneas and the Trojans encountered after leaving Carthage[2] raged for several days, **buffeting**[3] the ships about and washing huge waves across the decks. In the darkest hours of the **tempest**,[4] Aeneas's agèd father, Anchises, died in his sleep, and Aeneas, overcome with grief, embraced his father's lifeless body and wept uncontrollably for many hours.

When, at last, the storm **abated**,[5] Aeneas ordered the ships to depart from their original course and to put in at the nearby island of Sicily, so that Anchises could be given a proper burial. Once on the shore, Aeneas called his people together and said, "This is a day that I shall always keep in sorrow and in reverence, and it is fitting that we celebrate it with proper rites." And so they built a tomb for

---

[1] **allusions**—references to historical events, persons, or places. Allusions are used to heighten the significance of a prose or poetic passage. For example, if you make an allusion to Athena in describing a woman, you can convey that the woman is beautiful, without ever saying so, because Athena was famous for her beauty.

[2] Carthage—a city on the Tunisian coast of North Africa. Carthage was a major Mediterranean power in ancient times.

[3] **buffeting**—battering.

[4] **tempest**—a violent windstorm, frequently accompanied by rain, snow, or hail.

[5] **abated**—reduced in amount, degree, or intensity; lessened.

Anchises and then proceeded to honor him in the manner that befitted great men of the time: They all crowned their heads with myrtle[6] wreaths and held a great feast, and then they joined in athletic contests featuring ship races and tests of running, boxing, and archery skill. Swords and garments and jewels were given as prizes to the winners, and these funeral games went on for nine days.

On the last night of the celebration, as Aeneas slept soundly in his tent, he was visited by the ghost of his father in a dream. Aeneas heard his father say to him: "My son, the great Jove wishes me to tell you many things about your journey to Italy, but first you must visit me where I dwell—in Pluto's[7] dark **domains.**[8] Fear not that I am tortured with the evildoers, for I am at peace in Elysium in the company of the blessed. The Sibyl[9] will show you how to find me, and then you shall learn of your glorious future and of the city you are to build. Till then, my son, farewell." The vision in the dream vanished like smoke into the air, and Aeneas awoke with a start.

He called to him his friends and captains, and he told them about what Jove had commanded him to do. Straightaway they set sail for the land of Cumae, where the Sibyl, who had the power to disclose the future, lived in a dark and hidden cave near the temple of Apollo. And when their boats were anchored at last along the shore, several of the Trojans went into the forest to cut firewood and to find fresh water; others hunted for whatever game the countryside might provide; Aeneas, though, went alone to find the cave of the Sibyl.

He located Apollo's temple easily enough, and as he stared at it wondering which direction to go next, he heard a strange voice, or voices perhaps, nearby, and he walked on to see from what source they were coming. All of a sudden he was at the mouth of a cave that was cut out of solid rock, and as he stepped just inside, he could see that it was very deep and spacious, with a hundred doors, out of which rushed the many voices of the Sibyl. Though his knees trembled and cold shudders ran through his bones, Aeneas offered a prayer to the

---

[6] myrtle—an evergreen shrub, tree, or plant.

[7] Pluto's—Pluto is the Roman name for Hades, god of the underworld.

[8] **domains**—territories.

[9] Sibyl—a priestess of Mother Earth at Delphi.

prophetess, saying, "O great Sibyl, grant me the power to descend to the Lower Regions[10] and to hear the message that is intended for my ears, and my people will honor thee forever."

The hundred doors flew open with a blast, and a voice from each **bellowed**[11] a reply: "Son of Anchises, it is easy to go down to the Land of the Shades, but to retrace one's steps and reach the upper air again—this is not so light a task. Only a few have done it, but if you are still of a mind to try, listen to my words. There lies hidden in the forest a **bough**[12] of gold which is sacred to Proserpine,[13] the queen of the dead. No one can go upon this journey unless he brings with him this bough as a gift for the queen." All the doors suddenly slammed shut, and an eerie silence was all that filled the deep, dark cave.

Aeneas searched the forest high and low but could find nothing like a bough of gold. Then a pair of doves swooped down from the sky and settled on some grassy turf near where Aeneas was walking. Almost in despair he called to them, "If only you could be my guides, for with your lofty view you must know where this golden bough is hidden." Then the birds rose

into the air and circled Aeneas's head several times before flying, very slowly, ahead of him. He followed their lead and within minutes they alighted upon the tree that bore the golden bough. Aeneas gave thanks to the gods for sending these guiding doves, then he quickly broke off the glittering branch and returned to the Sibyl's cave, glad of heart that he now had the means to gain the favor of the queen of the dead.

When Aeneas arrived back at the Sibyl's **abode**,[14] she appeared to him in her own womanly form, and she asked again whether he was certain that he wanted to go on. Aeneas replied that he was duty-bound to hear his father's message, and so the Sibyl led him into the deepest reaches of the cave, past a gloomy lake from which deadly vapors arose. They continued on deeper and deeper into the cave and into the earth. The path was steep and rocky and the footing uncertain. All about them there was gloom and silence. In the dim light of the single torch the Sibyl carried, shadows

---

[10] Lower Regions—the Underworld.

[11] **bellowed**—roared.

[12] **bough**—branch.

[13] Prosperine—the Roman name for Persephone.

[14] **abode**—home.

looked like **contorted**[15] faces, and the rocks protruding from the walls of the passageway seemed like arms jutting out to snatch at Aeneas as he passed.

After a great while, they came to the gates of Hades, where the figures of Grief and Remorse lay sleeping on their beds. There also Aeneas could see the shapes of Fear and Hunger, forms so horrible that he had to turn his eyes away. Gorgons[16] and Harpies[17] and all manner of monsters roamed about the entrance, breathing fire and screeching and gnashing their teeth. Aeneas drew his sword and would have rushed at them had the Sibyl not assured him that they were but airy **apparitions,**[18] ferocious but without substance.

Passing through the gates, they reached a wide stream where a ferryman, Charon by name, stood on the deck of his rusty boat, leaning on a pole. Upon the bank were throngs of souls—wives and mothers, men of war, boys and girls—as thick as leaves that fall to the earth at the first frost of autumn, and all stood stretching out their hands and calling to the ferryman to take them across to the other side.

Aeneas was moved by this sight, and he turned to the Sibyl, saying, "O lady, tell me who are these spirits and what do they seek?" And the Sibyl replied, "This is the River Styx, and those you see are souls whose bodies have been left unburied on earth. It is not permitted for spirits to be delivered to their rightful place in the Underworld until their bones have been laid to rest, and so they wander to and fro along the shores for a hundred years before they are allowed to cross."

Aeneas's heart was touched with pity at their sad fortune as he and the Sibyl pressed on through the crowd toward the ferryboat. When Charon saw them coming, he roared out in an angry voice, "Stay back, whoever you are, for this is the abode of ghosts, and no living soul can cross in my boat." But the Sibyl held up the golden bough for the ferryman to see, and he was amazed to behold this marvelous gift, and he laid his anger aside. Without a word more he brought his boat near the bank, and driving out the ghosts

---

[15] **contorted**—twisted or wrenched severely out of shape.

[16] Gorgons—three frightful sisters who spent much of their time on an island far out at sea.

[17] Harpies—birds with women's heads.

[18] **apparitions**—ghostly figures; specters.

that sat in crowds upon its benches, he took on board Aeneas and the Sibyl. The boat, accustomed only to the light freight of bodiless spirits, groaned under the weight of these living souls, but soon it reached the opposite shore.

Here Aeneas beheld another gate, and stretching in front of it lay three-headed Cerberus, the watchdog of Hades. The air resounded with the fierce barking from his triple throats, and the Sibyl, to quiet him, flung him a cake of honey and poppy seeds, which would drug him into a sound sleep. Mad with hunger, Cerberus tore at the morsel with his three mouths, and soon his limbs relaxed, and he stretched himself out before the gate, wrapped in the arms of Morpheus,[19] the god of dreams. Aeneas bounded from the ferryboat out upon the shore, from which no one could hope to return.

As he pressed on through the gate, he could hear the crying of the ghosts of young children, who had died before their lives had scarcely begun. Here, too, were the souls of those who, being tired of life, had sought death by their own hands, and now were wishing they might return to earth again.

Nearby, amid groves of myrtle, were the souls of those who had died of love, and among these was Dido, whom Aeneas could see faintly through the shadows. Tears came rushing to his eyes, and he called to her, "Dido, can it be you, O beautiful queen? And can it be, then, that it was I who sent you here? As the gods are my witness, I beg you to believe that I did not wish to leave you, but my duty gave me no other course." But she, standing for a moment with her eyes cast to the ground, set her heart against him and abruptly walked away.

The Sibyl took him by the hand and led him to a place where the path parted into two roads. "The one on the right," she said, "leads to Pluto's palace and to the Elysian Fields, but on the left lies the path to Tartarus, where the wicked of the world are punished for their crimes." Aeneas peered down the road on the left and saw in the distance a high wall, with a river of flames licking at it from below. He could hear a din of deep groans and cracking whips and dragging chains coming from behind the wall, and he asked the Sibyl to tell

---

[19] Morpheus—the son of Hypnos, god of sleep.

him their meaning. She answered him, saying, "The feet of the **righteous**[20] may not pass down that road, but Proserpine has told me of the terrors that are contained within those walls." And the prophetess described to Aeneas the many torments that there afflict those who had done the deepest wrongs to their fellowmen on earth. Among the tortures was that of Sisyphus, the cruel king of Corinth, whose task was to roll a huge stone up a hill, but when the top was nearly reached, the rock would rush headlong down to the plain again, and so he toiled and toiled, while the sweat bathed his weary limbs, but all to no effect. There, too, was Tantalus,[21] another wicked king, who was condemned for all time to stand in a pool, his chin level with the water, yet he was parched with thirst, for when he bowed his head to drink, the water **receded.**[22] Tall trees laden with luscious fruit stooped their branches to him, but just when he reached for their treasures, a sudden wind would raise the branch just above his grasp.

There were other torments, too, even harsher, but all had in common that they would endure for ever and ever without pause, nor was there any hope for those who suffered.

The Sibyl then advised Aeneas that it was time for him to turn his attention toward the abodes of the blessed, and she led him down the path on the right until they reached the fields of Elysium. Here the air is pure, the skies are bright, and the green of springtime abounds. Some of the happy souls could be seen exercising on the grassy lawn, while others joined in dance and song. Here Aeneas could see kings of old, who had died for their country, and priests, and those who had improved the world with their inventions, and those whose worthy deeds had lessened the suffering on earth.

Across a shining plain, he beheld Anchises, who stretched his arms out toward his son, tears of joy streaming down his cheeks. Aeneas wrapped his own arms around his father in a loving embrace, but found that he was embracing a phantom—there was no substance within his encircling grasp. Anchises then, with a knowing look,

---

[20] **righteous**—morally upright; without guilt or sin.

[21] Tantalus—the English form of this word (*tantalize*) means "teasing or tormenting with hopes that remain out of reach."

[22] **receded**—moved back or away from a limit, point, or mark.

comforted his son and assured him that his happiness was not diminished just because his mortal body had been left on earth. They walked along together, and Aeneas asked Anchises to identify the souls they met and to explain why so many were gathered on the bank of the peaceful river that flowed gently across the plain. "These souls," Anchises answered, "all seek to live again in a mortal body. They drink from the River Lethe,[23] whose waters bring about forgetfulness, and thus they lose all memory of the past and may return to the world above in another human form."

Anchises then went on to tell Aeneas and the Sibyl all the events that the future held for his son and the race that would be founded by the people of Troy. He showed them visions of how Aeneas would land in Italy and conquer the tribes who dwelt there, and give them laws and order. The great nation Aeneas would found there would have many heroes and in time would rule the world with imperial sway.[24] He told them of Romulus,

the founder of the city on the seven hills; of Brutus, the avenger of his country's wrongs; and of the line of Caesars, who would plant the Roman way in every foreign land. "All this, my son, will come to your children's children. Other civilizations may create great works of art, and some may devote themselves to science," he said, "but the work of the nation you shall found is to conquer the world, to set the rule of peace, to spare the **humble,**[25] and to subdue the proud."

And so it came to pass, just as Anchises had said. Aeneas conquered the tribes of Italy and brought them under the rule of law. Ascanius ruled the land after him, and his children after him. And Romulus founded the greatest city of all on the banks of the Tiber,[26] and its armies conquered the world and brought about a peace that would know no end. Thus did the seeds of Troy take root and flower in the Roman Empire.

---

[23] River Lethe—From the name of this river comes the English word *lethargic*, which means apathetic and listless.

[24] imperial sway—supreme power.

[25] **humble**—low in rank, quality, or station; unpretentious or lowly.

[26] Tiber—river flowing through Rome.

QUESTIONS TO CONSIDER

1. What were the funeral games, and what was their purpose?

2. What was on the other side of the River Styx, and why were some souls prevented from crossing?

3. Who was Sisyphus and what was his task?

4. Which kind of souls went to Tartarus and which kind went to the Elysian Fields?

5. What did Aeneas learn from his trip to the Underworld?

Orpheus, Eurydice, and Arion

BY MICHAEL GIBSON

One thing that Greek immortals and mortals had in common was their fear of the Underworld. They didn't want to see it, hear it, or know about it. The only real exception to this universal dislike of Hades's realm was Orpheus, a gentle poet and lyrist from Thrace. When Orpheus's beautiful bride, Eurydice, dies unexpectedly, he is overwhelmed with grief. Without hesitating, Orpheus sets out on a journey to the Underworld. His plan is simple. No matter what the cost, he will bring Eurydice back to earth again.

If Apollo was the greatest musician of the gods, Orpheus was supreme among the mortals. It was music from Orpheus's lyre which lulled the dragon that guarded the golden fleece to sleep and saved all but one of the Argonauts from the temptation of the Sirens. As a result, his fame had spread far and wide over the land of Thrace, where his father was king.

Orpheus was also a poet, whose inspiration came from the nine Muses, and a singer. At court, the people would listen spellbound as he sang the great **sagas**[1] of his country, plucking the strings of his instrument in soft accompaniment. At times he would wander out into the countryside, playing as he went. The birds and wild beasts that roamed there would draw close to listen and to follow him. Even the trees swayed in time to the tunes he played.

It was while he was strolling alone through the woods that he met the beautiful dryad[2] Eurydice and brought her back to the palace, to be his wife.

---

[1] **sagas**—prose narratives.

[2] dryad—a nymph.

The dryads were nymphs of the trees and woods. Sometimes, when she was tired of her busy life at court, Eurydice would visit her former companions. They would sit on a grassy bank while she told them about her strange new city life, where there were hard, paved streets instead of the soft turf of the forest, and stone houses and temples instead of groves of trees. If Orpheus was with her, the nymphs would dance and sing as he played to them.

At other times, Eurydice used to walk by herself through the woods, enjoying the dappled light which came down through the leaves above her and listening to the songs of the birds. She would stoop to pick the pink and mauve cyclamen[3] and wood sorrel which grew beneath the trees and make garlands of their blossoms for her hair. Sometimes she would rest on the bank of a stream and watch butterflies dancing over the water. In the winter months she loved the rustle of the fallen leaves under her feet and would pause to run her hand over the rough bark of her beloved trees.

At times it snowed in that part of Greece. When this happened, Eurydice could see clearly the tracks of rabbits, hares, deer, and of the larger beasts which preyed on them. Everything about her would be white. The familiar woods looked strange yet somehow even more beautiful. All around was silent; even the birds would stop singing. If, in the silence, a small gust of wind sent snow slithering down from the bare branches, Eurydice would start nervously.

One bright, warm summer's day when the sun was shining, she was watching a deer feeding in a grassy clearing when suddenly its ears pricked up and it raised its head. For a moment it stood like this, and then like a shadow it slipped away. A tall man whom Eurydice had never seen before strode from the trees into the clearing. He was handsome, but there was a cruel **glint**[4] in his eyes which she did not like. He carried a bow and arrows across his back and stopped when he saw the girl standing there. "I have heard of the nymphs of the Thracian woods, but you are the first I have seen," he said. "Everything that people say of their beauty is true if you are one of them."

---

[3] cyclamen—plants with decorative leaves and pastel-colored flowers.

[4] **glint**—gleam.

Eurydice was not vain and did not like to hear such **flattery**[5] from a stranger. "I thank you sir," she said, "but I suggest that you go on your way, for I have no wish to be disturbed."

"You may be beautiful, but by the gods you have a sharp tongue!" the man answered. "If you want to be rid of me, tell me first in which direction the deer I was stalking has gone. You must have seen it, for it came through here."

Eurydice shook her head. "No, sir," she said. "That I cannot tell you. It was too pretty to die."

The man frowned. "A nymph you may be but, by thunder, even the fairest nymphs do not defy a god! Tell me, I say!"

Stubbornly Eurydice shook her head. "A god you may be," she said, "though I somehow doubt it, for if you were you would not behave so rudely. Take care how you speak to me, for my husband is the king's son and will not take kindly to someone who does not respect his wife."

The stranger threw back his head and laughed. "The wife of Orpheus, the poet and singer!" he exclaimed. "I have heard he loves music more than

battle. You threaten me with him? Clearly you do not know who I am."

"No, sir," Eurydice said, more calmly than she felt. "I do not, and I do not wish to."

"Nevertheless I will tell you," said the stranger. "Perhaps it will humble your proud spirit a little. I am Aristaeus, the god of hunters."

"Then you should be more gentle," answered Eurydice, "for was not your own mother the nymph Cyrene? I have heard the story of how she was carried off from her home by Apollo and bore his son."

"Gentle? Yes, my mother was gentle. But I learned from my father, the great Apollo, to take what I want when I want it." The stranger paused and then added, gesturing to her: "Come here! I will have a kiss from Orpheus's wife! Then we will see if he dares defy me!" He strode forward, and Eurydice, terrified, turned and fled.

Swiftly she ran through the trees, dodging first right then left. The low boughs[6] brushed her face as she ran and, where the trees grew less thickly,

---

[5] **flattery**—excessive compliments, some or all of which may be insincere.

[6] **boughs**—tree branches.

brambles tore at her tunic as if to hold her back. But his life as a hunter had made Aristaeus a fine athlete and he ran as fast as she, crashing through thickets like a wounded boar. Eurydice could hear him behind her. Once she stumbled and thought that she would fall, but she regained her balance and ran on. Her voice echoed through the woods as she cried out desperately for help, but there was no one near to hear. The only answer was a cruel laugh from behind her.

The chase continued through mossy clearings and over half-hidden streams of clear water where the fish swam unconcerned in the shadows under the banks. Eurydice's heart was pounding, but it seemed at last that she was drawing away from her pursuer. As the ground began to rise and the trees became fewer, Aristaeus's footsteps grew more faint.

Presently, she scrambled upwards into the sunlight over a rock-strewn slope. At last the footsteps had ceased. Eurydice could not be sure that she had escaped and she continued upwards until, at the summit of the higher ground, she threw herself down exhausted on a flat-topped rock. Below her and all around she could see the green tops of the trees. From here she would be able to see Aristaeus a long way away, so she decided to rest for a while.

Eurydice saw no more of Aristaeus, and after a while she dozed in the hot sun. The whole world seemed to be at peace and drowsing. Suddenly another sun-lover appeared—a deadly viper which lived on the stony ground surrounding the place where the girl lay. It moved slowly over the warm earth by the flat-topped rock, its forked tongue darting in and out. As it passed near her, Eurydice stirred and turned in her sleep. One of her slender legs now barred the viper's path. The snake hissed and coiled its body quickly, raising its head to strike. Its fangs sank deep, spreading their venom, but Eurydice did not wake. A bee droned lazily by and was gone, and then no more sound was heard. The poison had done its deadly work.

Night came, and still Eurydice had not returned to the palace. At first Orpheus was not seriously worried, for no harm had ever come to his wife on her lonely wanderings in the woods where she was so much at home. But when midnight came, search parties were sent out to scour the surrounding countryside. Their calls echoed through the trees as they searched.

Lights flickered here and there through the woods like phantoms. It was morning when they at last found her. Placing her body on a stretcher hastily made from saplings bound with creepers, the searchers carried her back to the palace with heavy hearts.

Orpheus was inconsolable.[7] His father tried to comfort him but it was no use. Orpheus sat alone, playing sad tunes on his lyre and thinking only of his lost love.

But Aristaeus had been wrong about Orpheus. He was a brave man, braver by far than most, and perhaps his desperation to win back Eurydice gave him a greater courage than he would normally have had. For he decided that he would enter Hades[8] itself and fetch her back to earth from there. Everyone tried to dissuade him. "Not even in your wildest dreams should you consider going there," King Oeagrus told his son. "The dead are the dead and the living the living. You are mad to think you can change the way of the gods. Those who go to the Underworld can never return."

Nevertheless, Orpheus set out, his lyre slung from his shoulder, his mind full only of Eurydice. He journeyed overland to Aornum in Thesprotis, which borders the Ionian Sea. He had heard that a narrow passageway led from here, far beneath the earth, to the River Styx. The river was the only barrier to Hades itself. He found the passage and descended out of the sunlight into the gloom. Water dripped from the **dank**[9] ceiling and rats scuttled away into the dark corners as he made his way bravely forward. At last the Styx was before him. Charon the ferryman sat there in his boat, waiting for his next cargo of the dead.

Orpheus knew it would not be easy to persuade Charon to take a living cargo but, trusting to the magical powers of his music, he struck a note on his lyre. A rare smile lit the stern face of the boatman. He leaned back in his seat and his eyes closed as the music enveloped him, its wonderful harmonies echoing back from the cavernous walls. Few could have resisted its appeal for long, and Charon succumbed to it completely. "I can deny nothing to one who can play as you can," he said to Orpheus. "I will take you over the river, though I may pay for it later when my master finds out

---

[7] inconsolable—brokenhearted.

[8] Hades—the home of the dead.

[9] **dank**—disagreeably damp or humid.

what I have done." Charon moved to one side to let Orpheus clamber into the boat.

On the other bank stood the guard dog Cerberus, but Orpheus's playing soothed even this fierce animal and Cerberus, like Charon, allowed him to pass.

In due course, Orpheus was brought before Persephone, the queen of the Underworld. Before he spoke he once more played his lyre, and the shades of the dead clustered near to hear his music. Persephone's heart was touched by his story and his music and she agreed to let Eurydice return to earth.

"But on one condition only," she told Orpheus. "She must follow behind you as you go. If you turn round to see her before she reaches the upper air, she must return here for ever."

So Eurydice was brought to them and the young couple embraced while Persephone looked on with a half-smile, as if she already doubted her decision. But she did not change her mind. The pair crossed the Styx safely and began the long climb up the passage to the surface of the earth. Orpheus never looked back, though he was greatly tempted to make sure that the footsteps he could hear behind him really were those of his beloved wife and not some trickery of the shades. Up and up they climbed, until presently daylight showed ahead of them.

A few minutes later, Orpheus was at the mouth of the cave, and the warmth of the sun was on his face. A great joy flooded through his whole being. What had been only a wild dream of happiness regained had actually come true. He turned to take Eurydice in his arms. However, less strong than he, she had lagged some way behind him in the climb. He saw her dimly coming towards him, still in the shadowy passage. But even as he looked she seemed to fade away and then was gone. He rushed forward but it was too late. She had returned to the shadowy world of the dead and was lost to him forever.

* * *

The story of Arion, another famous musician, has a happier ending. Arion was a son of Poseidon, but lived in Corinth at the court of King Periander. Like Orpheus he was a renowned lyre player and he traveled far and wide to play and sing at the feasts and festivals of Greece.

Most of these festivals were held on the mainland, at the largest and most important towns, such as Tiryns,

Mycenae, Athens and Thebes, and these did not involve Arion in more than a few days journey. However, there came a time when Arion received an invitation to compete in a festival in Sicily. It was to be an occasion of great importance, with the finest players from many lands gathering to take part. Arion decided that, though it meant a long sea voyage to reach the island, he could not miss it.

At the end of the festival, Arion was chosen as the victor. Long speeches were made in praise of his playing, and gifts were showered upon him—jewels, richly embroidered cloaks, gold ornaments, armlets and medallions of silver, and vases, bowls and drinking vessels painted and decorated by the finest artists of the day with colorful scenes from the lives of the gods.

Dressed in his new finery, Arion took his prizes packed in huge, metalbound chests, and boarded the ship for the return journey. The ship sailed westward for two days. On the third morning, while Arion was strolling on the deck, he was suddenly seized by the sailors and dragged, struggling, before the captain. The captain, a bearded ruffian,[10] smiled cruelly as he tore a silver medallion from about Arion's neck. "I think that we can find a better use for all your treasures than to carry them back to Greece for you to enjoy," he said, taking a dagger from the sash about his waist. Chuckling, he drew his thumb along the razor-sharp edge of the blade.

Arion saw that, surrounded by so many armed and ruthless men, he stood no chance of resisting. But he stood up straight to show that he did not really fear death. "If I am to die," he said, "let it be in my own way."

The captain shrugged. It did not really matter to him how this rich stranger met his end, so Arion was allowed to mount the prow of the ship, where he played a few last defiant notes on his lyre before plunging into the waves.

So anxious were the captain and the sailors to get at the iron-bound chests and to gloat over the treasure inside them that they spared Arion no second glance. Had they done so, they would have seen a school of dolphins leaping through the waves near the ship. One of these took Arion on his back and sped away with him over the water. Soon they were far ahead of the ship, making for Greece.

---

[10] ruffian—rough, cruel person; bully.

Some days later the ship sailed into the harbor of Corinth and the captain related with great conviction how the passenger from Sicily had been swept overboard in a gale with all he possessed. The captain had just finished his story when he looked across the quay and his face went white. For there, walking slowly towards him, was the man who should now have been lying on the shifting sands far beneath the waves.

Arion said nothing to him, but walked purposefully past and up the gangway to the ship. The captain and crew were seized and led away in chains and Arion's treasure was carried safely away to the palace. It is said that in gratitude for his safe return, Arion ordered a fine bronze sculpture of a man riding a dolphin's back to be placed on the shore, just in the place where the real dolphins had left him.

1. On what condition can Eurydice leave Hades and return to Earth?

2. Is Orpheus brave or cowardly? Support your opinion.

3. How is the myth about Arion similar to the myth about Orpheus and Eurydice?

The End of the Olympians

BY ROBERT GRAVES

Because all things must come to an end, so did the rule of the gods and goddesses of Mount Olympus. Storytellers have all sorts of interesting ideas about what might have happened to end the reign of Zeus and the other deities. Robert Graves offers his theory in "The End of the Olympians."

As soon as the Emperor Julian of Constantinople, the last of the Roman emperors to worship the Olympians, had been killed fighting the Persians in A.D. 363, Zeus was told by the Three Fates that his reign had ended— he and his friends must leave Olympus.

Zeus angrily destroyed the palace with a thunder bolt, and they all went off to live among humble country people, hoping for better times. But Christian missionaries chased them out with the sign of the Cross, and turned their temples into churches, which they divided among the leading saints. Mortals were now allowed to **reckon**[1] by weeks again, as Prometheus the Titan had once taught them. The Olympians were forced to hide in woods and caves, and have not been seen for centuries.

However, Echo remains; and so does the narcissus flower, which hangs its head sadly, looking at its reflection in mountain pools; and Iris's rainbow. Moreover, the stars were never given new names by the Christians. You can still see in the night sky the Scorpion that bit Heracles; and Heracles himself; and the Nemean Lion he killed; and Artemis's She-Bear that nursed

---

[1] **reckon**—to count or compute.

Atalanta; and Zeus's Eagle; and Perseus and Andromeda; and Cepheus and Cassiopeia, Andromeda's parents; and Ariadne's Crown; and the Heavenly Twins; and Cheiron the Centaur, now known as "The Archer"; and Phrixus's Ram; and the Bull that carried off Europa; and the winged horse Pegasus; and Leda's Swan; and Orpheus's Lyre; and the stern of the *Argo*; and Orion the Hunter, with his belt and sword; and many other memorials of the Olympians' ancient and savage reign.

QUESTIONS TO CONSIDER

1. According to Graves, what religion followed the worship of the Olympians?

2. Why did the rule of the gods and goddesses have to end?

3. What remains of the Olympiad today?

4. Which of the gods and goddesses of Mount Olympus did you enjoy reading about most?

The Journey of Gilgamesh

(Sumerian epic)

BY JOAN C. VERNIERO AND ROBIN FITZSIMMONS

The story of Gilgamesh is one of the oldest in the world. It was written on stone tablets almost 4,000 years ago. Gilgamesh was two-thirds deity and one-third mortal, which meant that he had godlike powers, but that he would have to die some day, just as humans do. Unable to accept his mortality, he goes in search of the secret of eternal life from the one man who was said to have achieved it. He finds the man, who bears a remarkable resemblance to someone you may already know about: Noah, from the biblical story of Noah and the Ark.

Gilgamesh was the proud and beautiful king of Uruk. He was ambitious and smart and loved to learn all there was to know about life. Gilgamesh's curiosity troubled his mother, Ninsunna.

"Why do you desire to know so much, my son?" she asked him.

"It is important to me," Gilgamesh replied, "to experience everything in the world—to taste every type of food, smell every fragrance, journey to every land, enjoy every dance. Can't you understand that?"

Ninsunna shook her head.

"Gilgamesh, although you come from the gods, part of you is still mortal. You cannot know and experience everything. One day you will die, as all mortals die."

When Gilgamesh heard what his mother had told him, he flew into a rage.

"I do not wish to die!" he exclaimed angrily. "My great friend Enkidu died. I miss him terribly, and I do not wish to follow him into the land of the dead. I will learn the secret of living forever."

Gilgamesh's mother tried to comfort her son.

"I only know of one person who has managed to escape death. His name is Uta-Napishtim, or Uta-Napishtim, the **Remote**.[1] He survived a mighty ordeal and was granted everlasting life. He lives beyond Mount Mashu, which is very far away."

Gilgamesh made up his mind to find Uta-Napishtim, the Remote. He traveled toward Mount Mashu. It was a long journey filled with many perils. He was pursued by the fierce lions of the forest. The Scorpion Men, who hid behind the boulders of the mountains, jumped out at him and tried to frighten him.

Gilgamesh continued on his way. Sometimes it was so dark he could barely see in front of himself. Finally, in the distance, Gilgamesh saw a great, glowing light. He had reached the home of Uta-Napishtim.

The old man greeted Gilgamesh and asked him why he had come so far from his home.

"Tell me how you have earned the right to live forever, Uta-Napishtim," Gilgamesh asked him. "This is what I wish to learn."

Uta-Napishtim invited Gilgamesh to sit beside him on the ground.

"Here is my story. I lived in Shurippak, the city of the sun. One day the god Ea came to me and told me that the gods were displeased with humans and wished to destroy the earth. They were going to send a great flood to cover the world.

"Ea instructed me to build a very large ship and to prepare for the **deluge**.[2] Then he told me to bring my family into the ship, as well as many animals, and to wait for the rains to fall. I did this. A great storm came and the skies were filled with black clouds. Thunder shook the ground and bolts of lightning raced through the heavens with hot, white light. For many days it rained and rained without stopping. We almost forgot what it was like to see the sun or to walk on dry land.

"We were very afraid, but I trusted that Ea had told me the truth, and that I would be saved. After a long while, the rains stopped falling and I sent a bird out from my ship to seek land.

---

[1] **Remote**—hidden away; secluded.
[2] **deluge**—a heavy downpour.

The bird returned to me, exhausted after failing to find a place to land. In time I sent another bird, a raven, to fly from the ship. I was overjoyed when the raven did not return to me, for it had found a dry patch of earth on which to live. This was a very good sign.

"Eventually the great flood waters receded and our ship rested upon a cliff. We left the ship with all of the creatures we had carried with us, and gave thanks to Ea and Ishtar, the goddess of heaven."

"But how did you come to be immortal?" Gilgamesh asked.

"The gods saw that I obeyed Ea, and as a reward they granted me immortality."

Gilgamesh jumped to his feet. "That does not help me, Uta-Napishtim, for I have not been tested as you have. Is there no way I can live forever?"

"Everything in this world lives and dies, Gilgamesh," Uta-Napishtim told him. "Yet, there may be a way for you to get your wish. Here is a special plant. Take this plant with you, back to your home. When you are there, you may eat it, and perhaps it will give you eternal youth."

Gilgamesh did as he was told and began the long journey home again. On the way he stopped to rest near a clear pool of water. He was so thirsty that he put the magic plant on the ground, and stepped into the pool to drink from it. Gilgamesh did not notice the snake that crawled in the grass, not far from the water. The snake saw the plant and ate it.

Gilgamesh had lost his chance for immortality. Finally he realized that even though he was a rich and powerful man, he could not escape death.

Legend tells us that the snake, after eating the plant intended for Gilgamesh, was able to shed his skin and regain his youth. Therefore, all snakes have kept this unique ability to this very day.

QUESTIONS TO CONSIDER

1. Why does Gilgamesh's curiosity trouble his mother?

2. Who is Uta-Napishtim, the Remote?

3. What does this myth seem to explain?

4. Why do you think Gilgamesh wants immortality?

Havamal

(Norse poem)

BY E.O.G. TURVILLE-PETRE

In almost all mythology, death and immortality are popular themes. Norse (or Scandinavian) mythology is no exception. "Havamal" tells the story of the great Norse god Odin and his "death" upon a tree. In this poem, Odin's death is more symbolic than anything else. His suffering on the tree allows him to be reborn as a god with the gift of words.

I know that I hung
on the windswept tree
for nine full nights,
wounded with a spear
and given to Odin,[1]
myself to myself;
on that tree
of which none know
from what roots it rises.

They did not comfort me with bread,
and not with the drinking horn;
I peered downward,
I grasped the "runes,"[2]
screeching I grasped them;
I fell back from there.

I learned nine mighty songs
from the famous son
of Bolthor, father of Bestla,
and I got a drink
of the precious **mead**,[3]
I was sprinkled with Odrerir.

Then I began to be fruitful
and to be fertile,
to grow and to prosper;
one word sought
another word from me;
one deed sought
another deed from me.

---

[1] Odin—the oldest, wisest, and most powerful of the Norse gods; he is also remembered as the god of battle.

[2] **runes**—poems or verses with magical significance.

[3] **mead**—an alcoholic beverage made from fermented honey and water.

QUESTIONS TO CONSIDER

1. What does Odin mean when he says, "Then I began to be fruitful"?

2. How is the Odin of the final stanza different from the Odin of the first stanza?

Glossary of Classical and World Mythology

Achilles (uh KILL eez) Greatest warrior of the Trojan War; son of Peleus and Thetis.

Actaeon (ack TEE un) Greek hunter who was turned into a stag and killed by his own dogs after seeing Artemis bathing.

Adad (uh DAD) Sumerian god responsible for giving Gilgamesh courage.

Adonis (uh DON iss) Handsome son of Cinyras and his daughter Smyrna; worshipped by both Aphrodite and Persephone. Murdered by Ares who had taken the form of a wild boar.

Aegeus (EE jy oos; EE jee us) King of Athens and father or foster father of Theseus. Aegeus killed himself over the mistaken belief that Theseus had died in the Labyrinth of Crete.

Aeneas (i NEE us) Trojan prince who traveled to Italy and founded Rome.

Aeolus (EE oh luss) Keeper of the winds.

Aeolus (EE oh luss) King of Sisyphus; father of Sisyphus, Cretheus, Salmoneus, and Athamas.

Aeschylus (ESS kuh luss) Greek playwright of the fifth century B.C. who wrote tragedies.

Aesir (AY seer) The Norse deities were divided into two major groups, the Aesir and the Vanir. The most important of the Aesir were Odin and Thor. The Aesir were known for their magical powers and heroic deeds. The Vanir were more closely associated with nature.

Aethra (EE thruh) Mother of Theseus by either Aegeus or Poseidon.

Agamemnon (ag uh MEM non) King of Mycenae and Argos. He was the Greek commander-in-chief during the Trojan War. He was murdered after the war by his wife, Clytemnestra.

Ahura Mazda (AH hoor a MAZ da) Iranian god who represents truth and light.

Aioina (eye OY nah) Divine mortal sent to the floating world to teach the Ainu (the first inhabitants of Japan) how to hunt, cook, and build shelter.

Ajax of Locris (AY jacks of LO kris) Greek warrior during the Trojan War.

Ajax of Salamis (AY jacks of SAL uh mis) Greek warrior during the Trojan War. He went insane and killed himself after losing a contest with Odysseus for the armor of the fallen leader Achilles.

Alcimede (al SIM uh dee) Mother of Jason.

Amaltheia (am al THEE uh) Goat nymph who nursed the infant Zeus after his mother sent him to hide in a cave.

Amaterasu (AH mah tay RAH su) Shinto goddess of the sun.

Amazons (AM uh zons) A tribe of powerful women warriors.

Amphitrite (am fi TRY tee) Sea goddess; wife of Poseidon and mother of Triton, Rhode, and Benthesicyme.

An (AHN) Sumerian sky god.

Ananse See Kwaku-Ananse.

Anchises (an KIE seez) Father of Aeneas (by Aphrodite). Badly injured by Zeus after he revealed that Aphrodite was Aeneas's mother. Aeneas carried him on his back out of Troy once the city began to burn. He died on his way to Italy, although he appeared to Aeneas in the form of a ghost in order to give advice and directions to his son.

Andromache (an DROM uh kee) Wife of Hector and mother of Astyanax; she was enslaved by Neoptolemus after the Trojan War.

Andromeda (an DROM uh duh) An Ethiopian princess who was saved by Perseus from being eaten by a sea monster.

Anticleia (an ti KLEE uh) Mother (by either Sisyphus or Laertes) of Odysseus. She killed herself when she believed that Odysseus was killed in the Trojan War.

Antigone (an TIG uh nee) Daughter (by Jocasta) and sister of King Oedipus of Thebes. Antigone accompanied Oedipus into exile, wandering with him until his death.

Antiope (an TIE uh pee) Amazon queen carried away by Theseus. Mother (by Theseus) of Hippolytus. Killed in battle by either her Amazon sisters or Theseus himself.

Anu (AH noo) Sumerian creation god; father of Ea, the god of earth and air.

Apanugpak (ah pa NOOG pak) Central Yupik Eskimo warrior who encouraged the Eskimo to become a peaceful people.

Aphrodite (af roe DIE tee) Aphrodite was the beautiful and voluptuous Greek goddess of love. Said to be the daughter of Zeus and Dione, she was born from the foam of the sea. Although she was the wife of Hephaestus, she had many lovers, including Adonis and Ares. Known to the Romans as Venus.

Apollo (uh POL oh) Apollo and his twin sister, Artemis, were the children of Zeus and Leto. They were born on the island of Delos. Apollo was identified closely with Delphi, in central Greece, where he killed the serpent Python and founded the most renowned center for prophecy in the ancient world, the shrine of the Delphic Oracle. Apollo was also known as the god of prophecy, medicine, the fine arts, archery, beauty, flocks and herds, law, courage, and wisdom.

Apollonius Rhodius (ap uh LOE ni us ROE di us) A Greek poet of the second century B.C.

Apsu (AP soo) Sumerian god of all things. Great-grandfather of Ea.

Arachne (uh RACK nee) Mortal woman who infuriated Athena by bragging that her weaving was the most

◄ **Aphrodite**

beautiful in the universe. As punishment, Athena turned her into a spider.

Ares (AIR eez) Greek god of war; son of Zeus and Hera. Ares loved battle and bloodshed but was a terrible crybaby if he himself was injured.

Argonauts (AR guh nawts) The crew of the *Argo*, which was led by Jason.

Arion (uh RHY un) A remarkably swift and beautiful horse; son of Poseidon and Demeter, who mated after turning themselves into horses.

Aristophanes (a riss TOFF uh neez) Greek writer of comedies during the late fifth century B.C.

Artemis (AR tuh miss) Virgin goddess of hunting and the moon; daughter of Zeus and Leto. Known by the Romans as Diana.

Arthur (AR thur) Celtic king who presided over a court at Camelot. Married to Guinevere. In real life, Arthur may have been a Celtic chieftain who fought off the invading Saxons in southwestern England around 520 B.C.

Aruru (ah ROO roo) Sumerian sun goddess of creation. She created Enkidu so that Gilgamesh would have a friend and rival.

Astyanax (uh STIE uh naks) Infant son of Hector and Andromache; killed at the end of the Trojan War when either Odysseus or Neoptolemus heaved him off the side of a fort.

Atalanta (at uh LAN tuh) Greek huntress known for her speed and skill; heroine of the Calydonian boar hunt.

Athena (uh THEE nuh) Virgin goddess of wisdom, practical arts, and war. Athena sprang fully formed from Zeus's head. The Romans called her Minerva.

Atlas (AT luss) Titan brother of Prometheus. Because he was the leader of the Titans in their war against the Olympians, Zeus punished Atlas by forcing him to hold up the heavens on his shoulders.

Augeas (aw JEE us) King of Elis and owner of the Augean stables, which Hercules cleaned as his sixth labor.

Aurora (uh ROE ruh) Roman goddess of the dawn. Known as Eos by the Greeks.

Awonawilona (UH wahn UH will o nah) In Zuni mythology, the creator of the sun, sky, and all of earth. Also called the Maker.

Bacchants (BACK ents) Worshippers of Dionysus whose wild rituals shocked many Greeks.

Bacchus (BACK us) Roman god of wine, grapes, and revelry. See Dionysus.

Balder (BOL der) Norse god. He was the only son of Odin and Frigg and was accidentally killed by his blind brother, Hoder.

Bastet (ba STET) Egyptian cat goddess; daughter of Re. Goddess of love and fertility.

Bellerophon (buh LER uh fun) Hero who, with the aid of Pegasus, slew the Chimera.

Beowulf (BAY uh woolf) Anglo-Saxon prince of the Geats (a people who lived in what is now southern Sweden). He killed the monster Grendel and Grendel's mother and was killed by a fire-breathing dragon in a desperate attempt to free the people of Geatland.

Cadmus (CAD muss) Greek mortal who was sent by Apollo to found the city of Thebes.

Cagn (KAY ghn) South African First Being who was all-knowing and all-powerful.

Calchas (KAL kuss) Soothsayer who told Agamemnon that he would have to sacrifice his daughter Iphigenia to Artemis before Greek ships would be allowed to set sail for Troy.

Calypso (kuh LIP so) Daughter of Atlas who offered Odysseus immortality if he would remain with her on the island of Ogygia. He did so for seven years until Zeus insisted that she let him go.

Cassandra (kuh SAN druh) A seer who warned the Trojans not to bring the Wooden Horse within the walls of Troy. The Trojans refused to believe her.

Cassiopeia (kas ee o PEE uh) Queen of Ethiopia and mother of Andromeda. She was punished by Poseidon and sent to the heavens as a constellation.

Centaurs (SEN torz) A race of creatures, half men and half horses, who lived mostly in the mountains of Greece. They were driven out of their original homeland in Thessaly by Theseus. Later, Hercules forced them to retreat to Mount Melea.

Cepheus (SEE fee us) Powerful king of Ethiopia; husband of Cassiopeia and father of Andromeda.

Cerberus (SER buh rus) The three-headed watchdog who stood guard at the gate to the Underworld. Companion to Hades.

Ceres (SEER eez) Roman goddess of grain and agriculture.

Cerneian hind (ser i NEE an HIND) Magnificent deer with golden antlers and brass hoofs that was captured alive as Hercules's fourth labor.

Ceto (SEE toe) A sea monster; mother of the Graeae, the Gorgons, and Echidna.

Charon (KA ron) A Greek god of the Underworld. Worked for Hades ferrying souls across the River Styx.

Charybdis (kuh RIB diss) A monster that was actually a dangerous whirlpool in the Strait of Messina, located on the bank opposite Scylla.

Cheiron (KY ron) A wise and gentle Centaur, teacher of many heroes, including Hercules, Jason, and Achilles. Friend to Athena. After Hercules accidentally wounded him with an arrow, Cheiron lived in great pain until Prometheus assumed his immortality and allowed him to journey to the Underworld.

Chimera (kim EAR ah) A fire-breathing monster with the head of a lion, the tail of a serpent, and the body of a goat. Terrified the Greeks until the hero Bellerophon killed him.

Chrysaor (KRIS ay or) A giant warrior; son of Medusa (by Poseidon).

Circe (SER see) The terrifying sorceress who could transform people into lions, wolves, and swine. Circe turned half of Odysseus's crew into swine, although Odysseus (with the help of Hermes) forced her to change them back into humans again.

Clytemnestra (kly tem NESS truh) Daughter of Leda, sister of Helen, and wife of Agamemnon. Clytemnestra never forgave Agamemnon for sacrificing their daughter Iphigenia to Artemis. With her lover, Aegisthus, she plotted to murder Agamemnon. Later, their son, Orestes, killed her to avenge Agamemnon's murder.

Cocalus (KOK uh luss) King of Camicus on Sicily. After Daedalus fled from Crete, he took refuge in Cocalus's palace, where he became a beloved entertainer of the king's princesses. When King Minos demanded that Daedalus be surrendered to Crete, the princesses murdered Minos by pouring boiling water on his head.

Coyote (ky OH tee) The trickster figure in the mythology of numerous Native American peoples.

Creusa (kre OO zuh) First wife of Aeneas and daughter of Priam and Hecuba. When Troy fell, she became separated from Aeneas and was probably murdered by the Greeks. She appeared to Aeneas in a dream and predicted that he would marry again. Also known as Glauce (GLAU see).

Cronus (KRO nus) King of the Titans; son of Gaia and Uranus. Cronus castrated his father in order to set the Titans free. He was the father (by Rhea) of six Olympians: Hestia, Demeter, Hera, Hades, Poseidon, and Zeus. Eventually, Zeus wrested control from Cronus and sent his father to prison in Tartarus.

Cú Chulainn (or Cuchulain) (koo-KUL-in) The hero of the Ulster cycle of stories, which are full of heroic deeds and evil beings. He was known as the Hound of Ulster because he accidentally killed a watchdog, and to make up for the deed, took the dog's place.

Cupid (KYOO pid) Roman god of love. Called Eros by the Greeks.

Cyclopes (sie KLO peez) In Greek mythology, there are two traditions about the Cyclopes. According to Hesiod, they were the three sons of Uranus and Gaea who made thunderbolts for Zeus, the trident for Poseidon, and the cap of invisibility for Hades. According to Homer, the Cyclopes were savage, one-eyed giants who inhabited caves and rocky caverns. Their leader, Polyphemus, devoured several of Odysseus's crew before the survivors managed to escape death by blinding the monster.

Daedalus (DED uh luss) Brilliant inventor who was exiled after he killed his talented nephew, Talus. He moved to Crete where he created a Labyrinth for the Mintotaur. Eventually, he himself was imprisoned in the Labyrinth with his son Icarus. To escape, he created wings for himself and Icarus. When Icarus flew too close to the sun, his wings melted and he was killed. A heartbroken Daedalus took refuge in the palace of Cocalus on Sicily.

Damastes (duh MASS teez) Monstrous host who stretched or mutilated guests so that they would fit in his guest bed. Killed by Theseus.

Danaë (DAN ay ee) Mother of Perseus, daughter of King Acrisius of Argos. Fearing a prophecy that his grandson would kill him, Acrisius locked Danaë and Perseus in a chest and threw them into the sea. The chest reached safety; Perseus went on to devote much of his life to protecting his mother.

Daphne (DAPH nee) Mountain nymph who turned herself into a laurel bush in order to avoid being embraced by Apollo.

Deianira (dee un NIE ra) Wife of Hercules. According to some storytellers, she inadvertently killed Hercules when she gave him a shirt soaked in the poisonous blood of the Hydra.

Demeter (dee MEE ter) The Greek goddess of agriculture. She was the daughter of Cronus and Rhea and the mother of Persephone. When Persephone was kidnapped by Hades, Demeter purposefully neglected the Earth's crops. Finally, Zeus fashioned a compromise whereby Persephone would spend six months of the year with Hades (winter) and six months with her mother (summer).

Devi (DEH vee) The Hindu mother goddess and wife of Shiva. Also known as Parvati, Durga, and Kali.

Dido (DIE doe) Founder and queen of Carthage and lover of Aeneas. He lingered in Carthage for a year and then resumed his journey to Italy. Dido cursed the Trojans and killed herself as a result.

◀ **Demeter**

Diomedes (die oh MEE deez) King of Thrace and son of Ares who fed his mares human flesh. Hercules clubbed him to death and fed him to his own horses as his eighth labor.

Dionysus (die oh NIE suss) God of wine, grapes, and revelry; son of Zeus and Semele. Despised by many for his habits. Also called Bacchus.

Driads (DRY adz) Tree-dwelling wood nymphs.

Dryope (DRY uh pee) A nymph; mother of Pan.

Ea (AY ah) Sumerian god of earth, water, and wisdom. It was Ea who sent the Seven Sages to teach skills (such as hunting and planting) to humankind.

Earth-Maker Native American supreme god of the Maidu people.

Echidna (ee KID nuh) Considered the mother of all monsters. Offspring included the Lernean Hydra, the Sphinx, the Nemean lion, and the two-headed dog Orthus.

Echo (ECK oh) A nymph who chattered incessantly. Zeus used her to distract Hera's attention away from his infidelities. As punishment, Hera made Echo unable to speak except to repeat what another had said.

Eileithyia (eye lie THIGH uh) The Greek goddess of childbirth; daughter of Zeus and Hera.

Electra (e LEK truh) Daughter of Agamemnon and Clytemnestra.

Enkidu (en KEE doo) Loyal friend of Gilgamesh; murdered by Ishtar.

Enlil (en LIL) The Sumerian god of air. He separated the heavens from earth.

Epeius (e PEE us) Greek artisan who built the Trojan Horse.

Epimetheus (ep ih ME thee us) Titan brother of Prometheus; husband of Pandora; father of Pyrrha.

Erechtheus (ee REK thee us) Early king of Athens.

Erinyes (ee RIN i eez) The Furies (Alecto, Tisiphone, and Megara), who avenged perjury and crimes against one's family.

Eris (ER iss) Goddess of discord; great friend of Ares.

Erlik (air LEEK) A Siberian evil spirit that the creator god Ulgan made in order to be his helper. Later, Erlik became lord of the dead.

Eros (EE ros) Greek god of love; son of Aphrodite. Called Cupid by the Romans.

Erymanthian boar (er i MAN thi un BORE) Horrible wild boar that Hercules captured for his third labor.

Eteocles (i TEE uh kleez) King of Thebes; son of Oedipus; brother of Polyneices. When he refused to give up the throne to Polyneices, he set off the war of the Seven Against Thebes, in which the brothers killed each other.

Eumaeus (yoo MEE us) Swineherd who remained loyal to Odysseus during his twenty-year absence. Eumaeus was the first person Odysseus contacted when he finally returned home.

Europa (yoo ROE puh) Lovely young maiden who was abducted and ravished by Zeus, who had taken the form of an enchanting white bull. Mother (by Zeus) of Minos, Sarpedon, and Rhadamanthus.

Eurydice (u RID is see) The wife of Orpheus. Orpheus tried to fetch her from the Underworld, with disastrous results.

Fates (FAYTZ) Three ancient goddesses; daughters of Themis and Zeus. The Fates were able to decide the length of each mortal's life.

Father Sun Inca creator of all life.

First Creator Creation god worshipped by the Mandan Sioux.

Freya (FRAY uh) The beautiful Norse goddess of love and fertility who had the ability to turn herself into a cat. One of the Vanir.

Freyr (FRAYR) The Norse god of fertility and plenty; brother of Freya. When Freyr fell in love with a giant, he had his sword taken away in punishment.

Frigg (FRIGG) The Norse goddess of childbirth who had the ability to see into the future. Wife of Odin; mother of Balder and Hoder.

Frost Giants In Norse mythology, the frost giants are descended from Ymir, whom Odin killed near the beginning of time. They are enemies of the gods and fight against them at Ragnarok.

Furies (FUR eez) Three female creatures who drove those who killed their own relatives to their own deaths. Also called the Erinyes.

Gaia (GAY uh) The Earth; mother (by herself) of Uranus and Pontus; mother (by Uranus) of the Cyclopes and the Titans.

Geb (GEBB) The Egyptian earth god. Husband of Nut (the sky goddess) and father of Isis and Osiris.

Gilgamesh (GIL ga mesh) The Sumerian semi-divine king of Uruk who was desperate to find the secret of immortality.

Glauce (GLAU see) See Creusa.

Glooscap (GLOO skap) The Native American hero of the Alqonquin peoples.

Gorgons (GORE gonz) The serpent-haired monsters whose stare could turn a creature into stone.

Hades (HAY deez) The Greek god of the Underworld. Brother of Zeus, Poseidon, Hestia, Demeter, and Hera; husband of Persephone.

Harpies (HAR peez) Repulsive bird-women who doled out punishments at will.

Hebe (HEE bee) Daughter of Zeus and Hera; wife of Hercules after he ascended to Olympus.

Hecate (HECK uh tee) Terrifying goddess of sorcery; attendant to Persephone in the Underworld.

◀ **Hades**

Hector Commander of the Trojan forces during the Trojan War. Son of Priam and Hecuba; husband of Andromache. Hector was killed by Achilles, who then dragged the corpse behind his chariot.

Hecuba (HECK yoo buh) Wife of King Priam of Troy; mother of many children including Hector, Paris, Cassandra, Troilus, and Creusa. Enslaved by Odysseus at the end of the Trojan War.

Helen (HELL un) Considered the most beautiful woman in the world; daughter of Zeus and Leda; wife of King Menelaus. Abducted by or ran off with Paris, which set off the Trojan War.

Helenus (HELL uh nuss) Trojan seer who warned Paris away from Helen and later told the Greeks how they could win the Trojan War.

Helios (or Helius) (HEE li us) God of the Sun; father of Phaeton.

Hephaestus (hi FESS tuss) Lame god of smithery, metal-working, and craftsmanship. Son of Hera (by herself); married to Aphrodite. Known to the Romans as Vulcan.

Hera (HEE ruh) Goddess of marriage and childbirth; wife of Zeus; mother of Hephaestus, Ares, Hebe, and Eileithyia. Hera took great pleasure in torturing Zeus's many lovers and illegitimate children.

Hercules (HER kyoo leez) Greatest hero of classical Greek and Roman mythology. Famous for his courage and strength. Son of Alcymene (by Zeus). Mortal enemy of Hera, who was furious about Zeus's infidelity. She persecuted him mercilessly and caused him to kill his wife and children. To atone for the murders, he performed his 12 labors. When his mortal life ended, he rose to Olympus and married Hera's daughter, Hebe. The Greeks called him Heracles.

Hermes (HER meez) Greek messenger of the gods and the patron of all travelers, merchants, rogues, and thieves. Also responsible for leading dead souls to the Underworld. Son of Zeus and Maia. The Romans called him Mercury.

Hesiod (HE see ud; HESS i ud) Greek poet of the eighth century B.C. Wrote *Theogeny* and *Works and Days*.

Hesperides (hess PER i deez) A group of nymphs who watched over Hera's garden in which the Golden Apple Tree—Hera's most precious possession—grew.

Hestia (HESS ti uh) Virginal goddess of the hearth, home, and community.

Hippolyta (hi POL i tuh) The queen of the Amazons who was killed by Hercules in order to obtain her golden girdle (his ninth labor).

Homer (HOE mer) A Greek poet who lived around the eighth century B.C. Wrote the *Iliad* and the *Odyssey*.

Horace (HOR iss) A Roman poet and satirist who lived during the Augustan Age.

Horus (HORE us) The Egyptian sky god with the head of a falcon. Horus was the sworn enemy of Set, who murdered Osiris.

Humbaba (hum BAH buh) A Sumerian giant killed by Gilgamesh and Enkidu.

Hyperion (hie PEER i un) An ancient god of the sun; one of the original Titans.

Icarus (ICK uh russ) Son of Daedalus; fell to his death when the wings he was using to fly began to melt in the sun.

Ilmarinen (EEL mah ren en) The Finnish blacksmith of the heavens.

Iphigenia (if i juh NIE uh) Daughter of Agamemnon and Clytemnestra; sacrificed by her father so that Artemis would allow Greek ships to set sail for Troy.

Iris (EYE riss) Greek goddess of the rainbow and messenger of the gods, along with Hermes.

Ishtar (ISH tar) Sumerian goddess of love and war. When Gilgamesh rejected her, Ishtar asked the god Anu to send a bull to destroy Gilgamesh and his kingdom.

Isis (EYE sis) The Egyptian mother goddess; sister and wife of Osiris and the mother of Horus.

Izanagi (iz an NAH gee) The Shintu god who, with his wife Izanami, created the Japanese islands.

Izanami (iz an NAH mee) The Shintu goddess who helped create the Japanese islands. She died giving birth to the god of fire.

Jason (JAY sun) Greek leader of the *Argo* who led a quest to claim the Golden Fleece. Married the princess Medea after the quest, but was exiled to Colchis when he killed his uncle Pelias. Abandoned Medea in order to marry Creusa, which infuriated Medea to the point that she killed Creusa and their children. Jason died when a beam from the *Argo* fell on his head.

Jocasta (joe KASS tuh) Wife of Laius and mother of Oedipus. Agreed to have her son killed so that the prophecy that Oedipus would kill his father and marry his mother would not come true. By a twist of fate, the prophecy did come true; when Jocasta realized she had married her son, she killed herself.

Jove (JOHV) Roman ruler of the gods (also known as Jupiter). See Zeus.

Kahakura (KAH ah KYOOR ah) Maori chieftain who taught his people how to fish and hunt.

Ki (KEE) Sumerian earth goddess.

Kwaku-Ananse (KWA koo ah NAN say) The Ashanti spider-man trickster of West Africa.

Laertes (lay ER teez) King of Ithaca and father or foster father of Odysseus.

Laocoön (lay OCK oh on) Trojan priest who begged the Trojans not to accept the Wooden Horse as a gift from the Greeks. Killed by two sea-serpents sent by Athena to keep him quiet.

Leda (LEE duh) Queen of Sparta. When she was a young girl, Zeus took her to be his lover. Mother (by Zeus) of Helen and Polydeuces. Mother (by Tyndareus) of Castor and Clytemnestra.

Lernean Hydra (ler nee un HIE druh) Monster with the body of a dog and the head of a snake; killed by Hercules as his second labor.

Loki (LO kee) An immortal who was not accepted by the other Norse gods. He played tricks on the gods, including one that resulted in Balder's death.

Lotus-Eaters (LOE tuss EE terz) The Lotus-Eaters (or Lotophagi) were a people who lived on the coast of North Africa. They subsisted on the fruit of the lotus tree, which made them forget the past and live unambitious lives. When Odysseus landed on their coast, some of his crew tasted the lotus fruit, which made them forget their homes and families. They had to be forcibly carried back to the ships by the rest of the crew.

Mama Ocllo (MA ma OCK low) In Inca mythology, Mama Ocllo Huaco was the daughter of Father Sun. She and her brother, Manco Capac, were sent to help the Inca peoples learn to hunt, fish, build shelter, raise crops, and so on.

Manco Capac (MAHN ko kuh PACK) Son of Father Sun and brother to Mama Ocllo; sent to teach the Inca peoples how to fish, hunt, build shelters, raise crops, and so on.

Mars (MARZ) Roman god of war. See Ares.

Maui (MOW ee) The Polynesian god who pulled the islands of the South Pacific up from the bottom of the ocean. Also credited for the four seasons and giving fire to humans.

Medea (mee DEE uh) Sorceress and priestess of Hecate who helped Jason obtain the Golden Fleece. When Jason abandoned her, she took revenge by murdering his new wife and children.

Medusa (muh DOO suh) One of the three Gorgons. Unlike her sisters (Euryale and Stheno), Medusa was mortal. Once a beautiful woman, she was seduced by Poseidon at the temple of Athena. A furious Athena punished her by turning her into a hideous creature. Later, Athena helped Perseus kill her. Pegasus sprang from her blood at the moment of her death.

Megara (MEG uh ruh) First wife of Hercules. Killed along with her children when he mistook them for snakes.

Meleager (mel ee AY jer) Hero who eventually killed the boar in the Calydonian boar hunt. In some stories, he was assisted by Atalanta.

Menelaus (men uh LAY us) King of Sparta; husband of Helen. When Paris and Helen left for Troy, Menelaus called on Helen's former suitors to help bring her back. After the Trojan War was over, Menelaus forgave Helen and welcomed her back.

Mercury (MER kyoo ree) Roman messenger to the gods. See Hermes.

Metis (MEE tiss) An Oceanid who was Zeus's first lover. She gave him wise advice on how to overthrow his father, Cronus, and defeat the Titans.

Mictlantecuhtli (mek TLAHN huh coot lee) A god of the dead in the kingdom of the Mictlan.

Midas (MY duss) King of the Mygdonian peoples who was given by Dionysus the power to turn everything he touched into gold. When he found that he could not eat or drink, he begged Dionysus to take the power back.

Minerva (mi NER vuh) Roman goddess of wisdom and war. See Athena.

Minos (MY nos) King of Crete; son of Zeus and Europa. Married to Pasiphaë, who bore a son, the Minotaur, after coupling with a bull. Minos commissioned Daedalus to build a labyrinth to house the beast.

Minotaur (MIN uh tore; MY no tore) The monstrous offspring of Pasiphaë and a white bull that she fell madly in love with. King Minos, stepfather to the Minotaur, locked him up in a labyrinth built by Daedalus. The hero Theseus eventually killed him.

Moirai (MOY rye) The three Fates (Clotho, Lachesis, and Atropos), who were responsible for determining the length and quality of mortal lives.

Morpheus (MORE fee us) The god of dreams; son of Hypnos, the god of sleep.

Mulungu An African sky spirit who rescued a woman's baby after it was swallowed whole by a crocodile.

Muses (MYOO zez) Nine goddesses who inspired artists, musicians, writers, and so on.

Naiads (NY adz) Nymphs who lived only in water such as lakes, rivers, fountains, and so on.

Narcissus (nar SISS us) A beautiful young man who rejected all admirers, including the nymph Echo. As punishment for his vanity, Athena caused him to fall in love with his own reflection in a pool. Eventually he withered away and died and was transformed into the flower that bears his name. From his name comes the term *narcissism,* which means "exclusive love of self."

Nemean lion (ne MEE un LIE un) An enormous lion with skin so tough that no spear or arrow could pierce it. Hercules was sent to kill the Nemean lion as his first labor.

Neptune (NEP toon) Roman god of the sea. See Poseidon.

Nereids (NEE ri idz) Fifty sea nymphs, the daughters of Nereus and Doris.

Nessus (NESS us) A Centaur who attacked Deianira, wife of Hercules. Hercules shot a poison arrow at him, causing a mortal wound. Before he died, however, Nessus convinced Deianira to accept his blood-stained shirt which he said would ensure Hercules's faithfulness. Eventually the poison in this shirt killed Hercules.

Nike (NIE kee) Personification of victory; companion of Zeus.

Nintu (NIN too) Sumerian Mother Goddess responsible for creating the human race.

Niobe (NIE uh bee) The wife of King Amphion of Thebes and the mother of six sons and six daughters. Because she taunted Leto for having only two children—Artemis and Apollo—Leto's twins took revenge by killing all of Niobe's offspring. As a result, Niobe cried endless tears until Zeus took pity and turned her to stone.

Nyankonpon (ny ANG cong pon) The West African, Ashanti sky god whose tales were won by Kwaku-Ananse.

Nymphs (NIMFS) Female goddesses who were young and beautiful spirits of nature.

Oceanus (oh SEE uh nus) One of the thirteen original Titans.

Odin (OH din) In Norse mythology, the chief of the gods and the ruler of the universe. Odin was the son of the frost giant Bor and the giantess Bestla. Early in his career, together with his brothers Vili and Ve, Odin overthrew the frost giant Ymir and created the world from his remains.

Odysseus (oh DISS ee us) King of Ithaca who led the Greeks in their defeat of the Trojans during the Trojan War. The gods punished Odysseus for his brutality at the war's end by sentencing him to wander the oceans for ten long years before finding his way home again. When he finally made it home, he killed his wife Penelope's suitors who had been living off his wealth for years. He himself was killed by his son, Telegonus, who didn't recognize his own father. Ulysses is the Roman name for Odysseus.

Oedipus (ED i pus) King of Thebes, son of Laius and Jocasta. Oedipus unknowingly murdered his father and married his mother, thereby fulfilling a sacred prophecy. When he realized what he had done, he blinded himself and wandered the earth with Antigone, his daughter

Orestes (oh RESS teez) King of Argos and Sparta; son of Agamemnon and Clytemnestra; brother of Iphigenia and Electra. After Clytemnestra murdered his father, Orestes murdered her with the help of Apollo and Electra. As punishment, he was banished for a year. Furious at the leniency of his sentence, the Erinyes (Furies) drove him mad.

Orion (oh RYE on) A giant hunter killed by a scorpion sent by an angry Hera after he bragged one too many times about his skill with a bow and arrow.

Orpheus (OR fee uss) Son of Apollo and the muse Calliope. Orpheus, a talented musician, pursued his wife, Eurydice, into the Underworld in the hopes of bringing her back to life.

Osiris (o SIRE is) Egyptian god of the dead and the underworld.

Ovid (OV id) Roman poet during the Augustan Age.

Pallas (PAL as) There are several different Greek myths involving a being named Pallas. The two most memorable concern Pallas the giant who was slain by Athena during the war between the Olympians and the Giants, and Pallas the mortal who was the brother of Aegeus. Pallas the mortal tried several times to capture the throne of Athens but eventually was killed by Theseus.

Pan (PAN) A minor god of shepherds, forests, wildlife, and fertility. Pan was half-goat and half-god. His mother was Dryope and his father was Hermes.

Pandora (pan DOE ruh) Known as the first woman, Pandora was created by Zeus to punish mankind for encouraging Prometheus to steal the gift of fire. Zeus gave Pandora a box that contained all the troubles and diseases that the world now knows. When her curiosity overcame her, she opened the box, and out flew all sorts of trouble and unhappiness.

◀ **Pan**

P'an-Ku (pahn KOO) In Chinese mythology, P'an-Ku is the gigantic being who burst out of an egg and created the world and everything in it.

Parcae (par SEE) The Roman Fates. Called the Moirai by the Greeks.

Paris (PARE iss) The handsome Prince of Troy who fell madly in love with Helen and spirited her away, thereby setting off the Trojan War. Paris was the son of Priam and Hecuba. During the war, he killed Achilles and was later killed himself by Philoctetes.

Pasiphaë (pa SIF ay ee) The Queen of Crete and wife of Minos; Pasiphaë gave birth to the Minotaur after falling in love with a white bull.

Pegasus (PEG uh suss) Gorgeous winged horse who was, according to some storytellers, the offspring of Medusa and Poseidon. Pegasus was tamed by Bellerophon who made the mistake of riding him too close to heaven.

Penelope (puh NELL uh pee) Wife of Odysseus who waited twenty years for his return from the Trojan War. During this time, many suitors attempted to take Odysseus's place. She warded them off by saying she needed to finish weaving a shroud for Laertes, although each night she unraveled the day's work.

Persephone (per SEF uh nee) Queen of the Underworld; wife of Hades; beloved daughter of Demeter (by Zeus). Called Proserpine by the Romans.

Perseus (PER si us) Son of Zeus and Danaë. Shortly after Perseus was born, Danaë's father, fearing a prophecy that he would be murdered by his grandson, put Danaë and Perseus in a chest and threw them into the sea. The chest floated to safety, and Perseus grew up to become one of Greece's most impressive heroes.

Phaëthon (FAY uh thon) Son of Helios and Clymene; he borrowed the chariot of the sun and almost wrecked the earth. Killed by a thunderbolt from Zeus.

Pleiades (PLEE uh deez) Seven nymphs, daughters of Atlas and Pleione. While hunting with Artemis, they encountered Orion, who pursued them until Zeus turned them into a constellation. The Romans called them the Vergiliae.

Plutarch (PLOO tark) A Greek writer and biographer of the first and second century.

Pluto (PLOO toe) Roman god of the Underworld. See Hades.

Polydectes (pol i DECK teez) King of Seriphus who fell in love with Danaë after she and Perseus washed up on his shore. Sent Perseus to decapitate the Medusa so that he would be free to marry Danaë; Perseus returned and turned Polydectes to stone.

Polyneices (pol i NIE seez) Son of Oedipus. After his father's death, Polyneices and his brother Eteocles argued about who would rule Thebes. Their fighting led to the war of the Seven Against Thebes. Eventually, the brothers killed each other.

Polyphemus (pol i FEE muss) One of the man-eating Cyclopes; he was blinded by Odysseus.

Poseidon (puh SIE don) God of the sea and of earthquakes; son of Cronus and Rhea and brother of Zeus. A violent and powerful god who was involved in many battles. His chief weapon was the trident, a three-pronged spear. Although married to Amphitrite, Poseidon was renowned for his many love affairs. The Romans called him Neptune.

Priam (PRY am) King of Troy during the Trojan War; husband of Hecuba, father of 50 sons and 12 daughters, including Hector, Paris, Cassandra, Troilus, and Creusa. Dragged from the altar of Zeus and brutally slain at the end of the war, a deed that infuriated gods and goddesses alike.

Procrustes (pro CRUS teez) Monster slain by Perseus on his way to Athens. Also called Damastes and Polypemon. See Damastes.

Prometheus (pro MEE thee us) Prometheus, whose name means "forethought," was the Titan who stole fire from the gods and gave it to humans, along with all human arts and civilization. A furious Zeus chained Prometheus to a rock for all eternity. In some accounts, Zeus decided to let him go. In others, Prometheus's friend Hercules rescued him.

Proserpine (pro SER pi nee) Roman Queen of the Underworld. See Persephone.

Psyche (SIE kee) Mortal loved by Cupid and despised by Venus because her beauty overshadowed Venus's own. Eventually made immortal by Zeus.

Quetzalcoatl (KET sahl koh AH tuhl) The divine priest who, with his brother Xoltol, created the modern human race by grinding up the bones of the ancient dead and sprinkling them with his own blood.

Re (RAY) Re was the supreme god credited with creating ancient Egypt. Re, who had a man's body and a falcon's head, was believed to sail across the sky in a boat each day and under the world at night.

Remus (REE mus) In Roman mythology, the son of Rhea Silvia and Mars; twin brother of Romulus; killed by a group of Romulus's supporters.

Rhea (REE uh) An ancient earth goddess and one of the original six Titans; mother (by Cronus) of six Olympians: Hestia, Demeter, Hera, Poseidon, Hades, and Zeus. Helped Zeus overthrow his father during the war between the Titans and the Olympians.

Romulus (ROM yoo luss) In Roman mythology, the son of Rhea Silvia and Mars and twin brother of Remus. Romulus founded Rome after his brother was put to death by a group of Romulus's supporters.

Saoshyant (SOW shyunt) The Iranian savior in the Zoroastrian religion who will come at the end of the world to wash away evil and bring into being a new, perfect world.

Satyrs (SAY terz; SAT erz) Immortal creatures of the forest and hills and symbols of nature's wealth. Satyrs had the head, arms, and torso of a man and the horns, ears, and hind legs of a goat. Satyrs loved to dance, drink, chase nymphs, and play reed instruments. The Romans called them Fauns.

Scylla (SILL uh) A sea monster who lived on the Strait of Messina. She was originally a beautiful nymph who was adored by Glaucus, a minor sea god. When Glaucus asked Circe to give Scylla a love potion, the jealous sorceress chose instead to give her a poison that transformed her into a monster with 6 heads, 12 feet, and the loins of vicious dogs.

Sedna (SED nuh) The Inuit mother of the sea beasts and queen of the underworld. Sedna is the most important being in Inuit mythology, as she is the keeper of all fish and animals.

Selene (see LEE nee) Greek goddess of the moon.

Semele (SEM uh lee) Daughter of Cadmus and Harmonia; mother (by Zeus) of Dionysus.

Seneca (SEN uh kuh) Roman playwright of the first century.

Set (SET) The Egyptian lord of the desert and god of storms, confusion, and destruction. Brother to Osiris, whom he murdered by sealing him in a coffin.

Shamash (SHAH mahsh) Sumerian sun god.

Shiva (SHEE va) One of the two principal Hindu gods (the other being Vishnu). Shiva is thought of as the destroyer god, although anything he destroys is eventually reborn. In this way, he is both creator and destructor.

Sibyl (SIB ill) Prophetess who advised Aeneas and led him through the Underworld to find his father.

Sinis (SIE niss) Robber who killed his victims by bending two trees and tying their arms to one tree and their legs to the other. Killed by Theseus.

Sinon (SIE non) Greek spy who convinced the Trojans to take the Wooden Horse inside the walls of Troy.

Sirens (SIE renz) Frightening-looking women who sang melodies so beautiful that sailors passing their rocky island were lured to shipwreck and death. The Sirens were outsmarted twice—once by Odysseus and once by Jason. Odysseus ordered his men to plug their ears with beeswax so that they could not hear the Sirens' songs. Jason and the Argonauts were saved by Orpheus, who played music even more enchanting than the songs of the Sirens.

Sisyphus (SISS i fuss) Son of Aeolus and the king of Corinth; he was able to outsmart Death for a time. When Death came to fetch him, Sisyphus bound him in chains so that no one could die until Zeus freed him. Sisyphus then was sent to Hades, but since he had instructed his wife to give him an improper burial, he was allowed to return to earth to settle this matter. He then refused to return to Hades. As punishment, Sisyphus was condemned eternally to roll a heavy stone to the top of a hill, only to have it fall back each time.

Sita (SEE tah) Indian princess; wife of Rama. After she was kidnapped by Ravana the demon, she was rescued by Rama and a band of brave monkeys.

Sophocles (SOFF uh kleez) Greek playwright of the fifth century B.C.

Sphinx (SFINKS) A mythical creature that was frequently a subject of ancient Egyptian myths and sculpture. The Sphinx combined the body of an animal (usually a lion) with the head of a man. In Greek mythology, the Sphinx had the head of a woman, the body of a lion, the tail of a snake, and the wings of an eagle. Oedipus solved the riddle of the Sphinx, which caused her to jump to her death.

Spider Woman The all-powerful Earth goddess in the Hopi tradition. She also appears in the myths of other Native American peoples.

Stheno (STHEE noh) One of two immortal Gorgons; sister of Euryale and Medusa.

Stymphalian birds (stim FAY li an BURDZ) Crane-size, man-eating birds; driven away from Arcadia by Hercules as his fifth labor.

Styx (STIKS) Goddess of the main river, also called the Styx, of the Underworld; helped Zeus in his battle against the Titans.

Susanowo (soo sa NO woah) The angry storm god of the Japanese Shinto religion.

Sylvia (SILL vee uh) Mother of Romulus and Remus. Also called Rhea Sylvia and Ilia.

Syrinx (SIR ingks) Lovely nymph pursued by Pan. She turned herself into a reed in order to hide from him. He used that reed and others to create his first pan-pipe.

Taliesin (TAL i ay sin) A legendary Welsh storyteller.

Tantalus (TAN tuh luss) Son of Zeus and Pluto who tried to serve his son, Pelops, to the Olympians for dinner. Zeus punished him by hanging him from a branch in the Underworld that was tantalizingly close to food and drink.

Tawa (TAH wah) The Hopi god of the sun.

Telemachus (tuh LEM uh kiss) Loyal son of Odysseus and Penelope who helped Odysseus rid his father's palace of suitors after his return from the Trojan War.

Tezcatlipoca (tes KAHT lee POH ka) The Aztec warrior god known as "the smoking mirror." As the god of vengeance, he dedicated himself to destroying the divine priest Quetzalcoatl.

Theia (THEE uh) One of the twelve original Titans; mother by Zeus of Helios, god of the sun, and the three Moirai, or Fates.

Theseus (THEE see us) Son of either Aegeus, king of Athens, or Poseidon and Aethra; Theseus is said to be the hero who organized Athens into a city, became its first true king, and set it upon the path of civilization. As a young man, he performed many heroic feats, including killing the robbers Sinis, Sciron, and Procrustes. Later he killed the Minotaur and went to war against the Amazons. He was murdered by Lycomedes, king of Scyrus, who pushed him off a cliff.

Thor (THOR) The Norse god of war and thunder who used a magic hammer, belt, and gloves in battle. Although he was the son of the chief god Odin, Thor was noted for his ability to drink vast amounts of alcohol and is usually portrayed by storytellers as a crude, red-bearded, middle-aged warrior who relied on his immense strength rather than on his intelligence.

Tiamat (TEE ah maht) Babylonian mother of all things.

Toyotama (to yo TA ma) Japanese princess of the kingdom under the sea. Able to change herself into a dragon whenever she liked. Married a mortal named Hoori.

Triton (TRY ton) A minor sea god; son of Poseidon and Amphitrite.

Typhon (TIE fon) A monster who tried to overthrow Zeus; Zeus crushed it and threw it under Mount Aetna.

Ulgan (UL gan) The high god of the Siberian Tartars. Ulgan created the world from mud that his helper, Erlik, fetched from the bottom of the ocean.

Ulysses (YOO liss eez) Roman name for the warrior Odysseus. See Odysseus.

Uranus (YOO ruh nuss) Personification of the sky; son of Gaia; father of the Cyclopes and Titans. Uranus was overthrown and imprisoned in Tartarus by his son, Cronus.

Utnapishtim (oot na PISH tim) In Sumerian mythology, Utnapishtim and his wife were the only survivors of the great flood caused by the god Ea. Utnapishtim was Gilgamesh's ancestor.

Uzume (oo ZOO mee) The Japanese goddess associated with the dawn. Known as Ama-no-Uzume.

Valkyries (val KY reez) In Norse mythology, the Valkyries were nine semidivine virgins who rode armed on horseback to battlefields and decided which mortals would live and die.

Vanir (VAH neer) The Norse deities who were closely associated with nature. See Aesir.

Venus (VEE nus) Roman god of love. See Aphrodite.

Vesta (VES ta) Roman goddess of the hearth; see Hestia.

Virgil (VER jill) Roman poet of the first century B.C.

Vulcan (VULL ken) Roman god of fire and artisans. See Hephaestus.

Yhi (yuh HEE) Aborigine sun goddess responsible for the creation of several Australian animals.

Ymir (YUH meer) In Norse mythology, Ymir was the first giant. He was killed by Odin, Vili, and Ve, his grandsons, who made the heavens from his skull, the earth from his body, and the seas from his blood.

Zeus (ZYOOS) The principal god of the pantheon and the ultimate ruler of heaven and earth and of all gods and humankind. Son of Rhea and Cronus; husband of Hera; brother of five Olympians: Hestia, Demeter, Hera, Hades, and Poseidon. Father of Dionysus (by Semele), and five Olympians: Athena, Ares, Apollo, Artemis, and Hermes. Also father to many other children by various mistresses, including Perseus and Hercules.

Zeus ▶

Texts

2 From *Tales of the Greek Heroes* by Roger Lancelyn Green, (Puffin, 1958). Copyright © Roger Lancelyn Green, 1958. Reprinted by permission of Penguin Books Ltd. **6** "Zeus and His Family" from *D'Aulaire's Book of Greek Myths* by Ingri & Edgar Parin D'Aulaire. Copyright © 1962 by Ingri and Edgar Parin D'Aulaire. Used by permission of Random House Children's Books, a division of Random House, Inc. **10** "Hera" from *D'Aulaire's Book of Greek Myths* by Ingri & Edgar Parin D'Aulaire. Copyright © 1962 by Ingri and Edgar Parin D'Aulaire. Used by permission of Random House Children's Books, a division of Random House, Inc. **14** "Poseidon" from *D'Aulaire's Book of Greek Myths* by Ingri & Edgar Parin D'Aulaire. Copyright © 1962 by Ingri and Edgar Parin D'Aulaire. Used by permission of Random House Children's Books, a division of Random House, Inc. **16** "Demeter's Lost Daughter" from *Greek Gods and Heroes* by Robert Graves. Reprinted by permission of A.P. Watt Ltd on behalf of The Trustees of the Robert Graves Copyright Trust. **21** "Hephaestus" from *The Greek Gods* by Bernard Evslin et al. Copyright © 1966 by Scholastic Inc. Reprinted by permission. **22** "The Birth of Hermes" from *Greek Gods and Heroes* by Robert Graves. Reprinted by permission of A.P. Watt Ltd on behalf of The Trustees of the Robert Graves Copyright Trust. **25** "Aphrodite" from *The Greek Gods* by Bernard Evslin et al. Copyright © 1966 by Scholastic Inc. Reprinted by permission. **28** "Birth of the Twins" from *The Greek Gods* by Bernard Evslin et al. Copyright © 1966 by Scholastic Inc. Reprinted by permission. **34** "Ares, god of war" is reprinted from *Gods, Men & Monsters* by Michael Gibson © 1977. Used with permission of Eurobook Limited and Peter Bedrick Books. **40** "First Tale" from *Spider Woman Stories*, by G.M. Mullett. Copyright © 1979 The Arizona Board of Regents. Reprinted by permission of the University of Arizona Press. **45** "Izanagi and Izanami" from *Out of the Ark: Stories From The World's Religions*, copyright © 1996 by Anita Ganeri, reprinted by permission of Harcourt, Inc. **47** "Creation: The Nine Worlds" from *Favorite Norse Myths* retold by Mary Pope Osborne. Copyright © 1996 by Mary Pope Osborne. Reprinted by permission of Scholastic Inc. **64** "Lost At Sea" from *Favorite Greek Myths* retold by Mary Pope Osborne. Copyright © 1989 by Mary Pope Osborne. Reprinted by permission of Scholastic Inc. **67** Excerpt from "Cassiopeia" is reprinted with the permission of Simon & Schuster Books for Young Readers, an imprint of Simon & Schuster Children's Publishing Division from *The Macmillan Book of Greek Gods and Heroes* by Alice Low. Copyright © 1985 **68** Excerpt from "Castor and Pollux" is reprinted with the permission of Simon & Schuster Books for Young Readers, an imprint of Simon & Schuster Children's Publishing Division from *The Macmillan Book of Greek Gods and Heroes* by Alice Low. Copyright © 1985 Macmillan Publishing Company. **69** Excerpt from "Orion" is reprinted with the permission of Simon & Schuster Books for Young Readers, an imprint of Simon & Schuster Children's Publishing Division from *The Macmillan Book of Greek Gods and Heroes* by Alice Low. Copyright © 1985 Macmillan Publishing Company. **71** "The Great Flood" from *Greek Myths*. Copyright © 1949, renewed 1977 by Olivia E. Coolidge. Reprinted by permission of Houghton Mifflin Co. All rights reserved. **74** "How Shiva Got His Blue Throat" from *Out of the Ark: Stories From The World's Religions*, copyright © 1996 by Anita Ganeri, reprinted by permission of Harcourt, Inc. **76** "Quetzalcoatl" from *One-Hundred-And-One Read-Aloud Myths and Legends* by Joan C. Verniero and Robin Fitzsimmons. Copyright © 1999 Black Dog & Leventhal Publishers, Inc. Used by permission of Black Dog & Leventhal Publishers. **79** "The Creation of Humans" from *One-Hundred-And-One Read-Aloud Myths and Legends* by Joan C. Verniero and Robin Fitzsimmons, pp. 319-320. Copyright © 1999 Black Dog & Leventhal Publishers. Used by permission of Black Dog & Leventhal Publishers. **82** "The Man Who Married A Star" from *Tales From The Amazon* adapted by Martin Elbl and J.T. Winik. Copyright © 1986 by Hayes Publishing Ltd. Reprinted by permission. **98** *Demeter and Persephone* translated by Penelope Proddow. **112** "Oedipus" from *D'Aulaire's Book of Greek Myths* by Ingri & Edgar Parin D'Aulaire. Copyright © 1962 by Ingri and Edgar Parin D'Aulaire. Used by permission of Random House Children's Books, a division of Random House, Inc. **116** "The Ungrateful Daughter" from *Stories of the Gods and Heroes* by Sally Benson. Copyright 1940, renewed © 1968 by Sally Benson. Used by permission of Dial Books for Young Readers, a division of Penguin Putnam Inc. **119** "Phaeton and the Chariot of the Sun" is reprinted with the permission of Margaret K. McElderry Books, an imprint of Simon & Schuster Children's Publishing Division from *Greek Myths* retold by Geraldine McCaughrean. Text copyright © 1992 Geraldine McCaughrean. And is reprinted with permission from *The Orchard Book of Greek Myth* retold by

Geraldine McCaughrean first published in the UK by Orchard Books, a division of The Watts Publishing Group Limited, 96 Leonard Street, London EC2A 4XD. **123** "The Birth of Pan" from *Tales of Pan* by Mordicai Gerstein. Copyright © 1986 by Mordicai Gerstein. Reprinted by permission of the author and his agents, Raines & Raines. **125** "Glooscap and the Baby," from *American Indian Myths and Legends* by Richard Erdoes and Alfonso Ortiz. Copyright © 1984 by Richard Erdoes and Alfonso Ortiz. Reprinted by permission of Pantheon Books, a division of Random House, Inc. **127** "Aladdin: A Most Faithful Son" originally entitled "Aladdin, or the Wonderful Lamp" from *One-Hundred-And-One Read-Aloud Myths and Legends* by Joan C. Verniero and Robin Fitzsimmons. Copyright © 1999 Black Dog & Leventhal Publishers, Inc. Used by permission of Black Dog & Leventhal Publishers. **144** "The Four Tasks" from *Favorite Greek Myths* retold by Mary Pope Osborne. Copyright © 1989 by Mary Pope Osborne. Reprinted by permission of Scholastic Inc. **151** "The Lover of Beauty" from *Greek Myths*. Copyright © 1949, renewed 1977 by Olivia E. Coolidge. Reprinted by permission of Houghton Mifflin Co. All rights reserved. **154** "Pyramus and Thisbe" from *Stories of the Gods and Heroes* by Sally Benson. Copyright 1940, renewed © 1968 by Sally Benson. Used by permission of Dial Books for Young Readers, a division of Penguin Putnam Inc. **158** "Echo and Narcissus" from *Wisdom Tales From Around the World*. Compiled by Heather Forest. Copyright © 1996 by Heather Forest. Used by permission of August House Publishers, Inc. **160** "Atalanta's Race" is reprinted with the permission of Margaret K. McElderry Books, an imprint of Simon & Schuster Children's Publishing Division from *Greek Myths* retold by Geraldine McCaughrean. Text copyright © 1992 Geraldine McCaughrean. And is reprinted with permission from *The Orchard Book of Greek Myth* retold by Geraldine McCaughrean first published in the UK by Orchard Books, a division of The Watts Publishing Group Limited, 96 Leonard Street, London EC2A 4XD. **162** Reprinted with the permission of Atheneum Books for Young Readers, an imprint of Simon & Schuster Children's Publishing Division from Ashley Bryan's *African Tales, Uh-Huh* by Ashley Bryan. Copyright © 1971 by Ashley Bryan. Copyright © 1998 Atheneum Books for Young Readers. **165** "The Toad-Bridegroom" from *Folk Tales from Korea* by Zong InSob. Reprinted by permission of The University of Chicago Press. **169** "What Does Woman Want?" from *Myths and Modern Man* by Barbara Stanford with Gene Stanford, pp 79–83, Washington Square Press, 1972. **176** Excerpt from *Wings*, copyright © 1991 by Jane Yolen, reprinted by permission of Harcourt, Inc. **185** "Hercules and Prometheus" adapted from *Adventures of the Greek Heroes*. Copyright © 1961 by Mollie McLean and Ann M. Wiseman. Copyright © renewed 1989 by Ann Wiseman. Reprinted by permission of Houghton Mifflin Company. All rights reserved. **190** "Pandora" from *The Greek Gods* by Bernard Evslin et al. Copyright © 1966 by Scholastic Inc. Reprinted by permission. **194** "The Boatman" from *Wisdom Tales From Around the World* compiled by Heather Forest. Copyright © 1996 Heather Forest. Used by permission of August House Publishers, Inc. **195** "The Smuggler" from *Wisdom Tales From Around the World* compiled by Heather Forest. Copyright © 1996 Heather Forest. Used by permission of August House Publishers, Inc. **196** "Looking for the Key" from *Wisdom Tales From Around the World* compiled by Heather Forest. Copyright © 1996 Heather Forest. Used by permission of August House Publishers, Inc. **198** "A Wolf and Little Daughter" from *The People Could Fly* by Virginia Hamilton. Text Copyright © 1985 by Virginia Hamilton. Reprinted by permission of Alfred A. Knopf Children's Books, a division of Random House, Inc. **200** Reprinted with the permission of Atheneum Books for Young Readers, an imprint of Simon & Schuster Children's Publishing Division from *With a Whoop and a Holler* by Nancy Van Laan. Text copyright © 1998 Nancy Van Laan. **216** Reprinted from *Hercules: The Man, The Myth, The Legend* by Kathryn Lasky, illustrated by Mark Hess. Text copyright © 1997 by Kathryn Lasky. Published by Hyperion Books for Children. Reproduced with permission by Disney Publishing. **222** From "The Story of Theseus," in *Classic Myths to Read Aloud* by William Russell. Copyright © 1988 by William F. Russell. Reprinted by permission of Crown Publishers, Inc. **234** Extracts from *Dateline: Troy* Text © 1996 Paul Fleischman. Illustrated by Gwen Franfeldt & Glenn Morrow. Reprinted by permission of the publisher Candlewick Press Inc., Cambridge, MA. **239** Excerpt from "Odysseus" is reprinted with the permission of Simon & Schuster Books for Young Readers, an imprint of Simon & Schuster Children's Publishing Division from *The Macmillan Book of Greek Gods and Heroes* by Alice Low. Copyright © 1985 Macmillan Publishing Company. **242** From "The Wanderings of Aeneas" in *Classic Myths to Read Aloud* by William Russell. Copyright © 1988 by William F. Russell.

Reprinted by permission of Crown Publishers, Inc. **252** "Gassire's Lute" from Frobenius and Fox's *African Genesis*. Reproduced by permission of Stackpole Books. **260** "How War Was Ended" by Chuna McIntyre from *Wisdom Tales From Around the World*, retold by Heather Forest, August House Publishers, Inc, 1996. Reproduced by permission of Chuna McIntyre. **264** "The Golden Fleece" excerpt from *D'Aulaire's Book of Greek Myths* by Ingri & Edgar Parin D'Aulaire. Copyright © 1962 by Ingri and Edgar Parin D'Aulaire. Used by permission of Random House Children's Books, a division of Random House, Inc. **274** "The Sirens" excerpt from *The Adventures of Ulysses* by Bernard Evslin. Copyright © 1969 by Scholastic Inc. Reprinted by permission. **278** "Perseus Slays the Gorgon," from *Stories of the Gods and Heroes* by Sally Benson. Copyright 1940, renewed © 1968 by Sally Benson. Used by permission of Dial Books for Young Readers, a division of Penguin Putnam Inc. **284** "The Taming of the Sun," reprinted from *World Mythology* by Donna Rosenberg, © 1994. Used with permission of NTC/Contemporary Publishing Group, Inc. **291** "Dream Journey" is reprinted with the permission of Margaret K. McElderry Books, an imprint of Simon & Schuster Children's Publishing Division and The Orion Publishing Group Ltd., from *The Silver Treasure* by Geraldine McCaughrean. Text copyright © 1996 Geraldine McCaughrean. **298** "The Calydonian Boar Hunt" excerpt from *D'Aulaire's Book of Greek Myths* by Ingri & Edgar Parin D'Aulaire. Copyright © 1962 by Ingri and Edgar Parin D'Aulaire. Used by permission of Random House Children's Books, a division of Random House, Inc. **300** "Pegasus" from *Pegasus, the Flying Horse* by Jane Yolen, pp. 2, 4, 6, 8,10,12, and 14. Penguin Putnam Inc, 1998 (Dutton Children's Books). **303** "Typhon" from *The One-Eyed Giant and Other Monsters From the Greek Myths* by Anne Rockwell. New York: Greenwillow Books. **304** "The Hydra" from *The One-Eyed Giant and Other Monsters From the Greek Myths* by Anne Rockwell. New York: Greenwillow Books. **304** "The Empusae" from *The One-Eyed Giant and Other Monsters From the Greek Myths* by Anne Rockwell. New York: Greenwillow Books. **306** "The Two Hunchbacks" from *Italian Folktales: Selected and Retold* by Italo Calvino, copyright © 1956 by Guilio Einaudi editore, s.p.a., English translation by George Martin copyright © 1980 by Harcourt, Inc., reprinted by permission of Harcourt, Inc. **322** "Zeus, Metis and Athena" from *A Book of Myths*, retold by Roger Lancelyn Green, J. M. Dent & Sons Ltd, 1965. Reproduced with permission of The Orion Publishing Group Ltd. **331** "Arachne the Spinner" is reprinted with the permission of Margaret K. McElderry Books, an imprint of Simon & Schuster Children's Publishing Division from *Greek Myths* retold by Geraldine McCaughrean. Text copyright © 1992 Geraldine McCaughrean. And is reprinted with permission from *The Orchard Book of Greek Myth* retold by Geraldine McCaughrean first published in the UK by Orchard Books, a division of The Watts Publishing Group Limited, 96 Leonard Street, London EC2A 4XD. **334** "Syrinx" from *D'Aulaire's Book of Greek Myths* by Ingri & Edgar Parin D'Aulaire. Copyright © 1962 by Ingri and Edgar Parin D'Aulaire. Used by permission of Random House Children's Books, a division of Random House, Inc. **336** "Freedom for Prometheus" is reprinted with the permission of Margaret K. McElderry Books, an imprint of Simon & Schuster Children's Publishing Division from *Greek Myths* retold by Geraldine McCaughrean. Text copyright © 1992 Geraldine McCaughrean. And is reprinted with permission from *The Orchard Book of Greek Myth* retold by Geraldine McCaughrean first published in the UK by Orchard Books, a division of The Watts Publishing Group Limited, 96 Leonard Street, London EC2A 4XD. **338** "The Orders of Cagn" from *One-Hundred-And-One Read-Aloud Myths and Legends* by Joan C. Verniero and Robin Fitzsimmons, pp. 307-308. Copyright © 1999 Black Dog & Leventhal Publishers. Used by permission of Black Dog & Leventhal Publishers. **341** "The Children of the Sun" reprinted from *World Mythology* edited by Donna Rosenberg © 1994. Used with permission of NTC/Contemporary Publishing Group, Inc. **345** "Setanta" from *Irish Legends for Children*, by Yvonne Carroll, Derrydale Books. Reproduced with permission of Quadrillion Publishing. **350** "Aeneas Visits the Lower World" from *Classic Myths to Read Aloud* by William Russell. Copyright © 1988 by William F. Russell. Reprinted by permission of Crown Publishers, Inc. **358** "Orpheus and Eurydice" is reprinted from *Gods, Men & Monsters* by Michael Gibson © 1977. Used with permission of Eurobook Limited and Peter Bedrick Books. **366** From "The End of the Olympians" in *Greek Gods and Heroes* by Robert Graves. Copyright © 1960 by Robert Graves. Reproduced with the permission of A. P. Watt Ltd on behalf of The Trustees of the Robert Graves Copyright Trust. **368** "The Journey of Gilgamesh" from *One-Hundred-And-One Read-Aloud Myths and Legends* by Joan C. Verniero and Robin

Fitzsimmons, pp. 270-273. Copyright © 1999 Black Dog & Leventhal Publishers. Used by permission of Black Dog & Leventhal Publishers. **371** "Havamal" from *Myth and Religion of the North: The Religion of Ancient Scandinavia* by E.O.G. Turville-Petre. 1964.

Illustrations

Position of illustration on a page is indicated by these abbreviations: (T) top, (C) center, (B) bottom, (L) left, (R) right.

Every effort has been made to secure complete rights and permissions for each selection presented herein. Updated acknowledgments, if needed, will appear in subsequent printings.

Index of Authors and Titles